# Time and the Rose Garden

Encountering the Magical in the life
and works of J.B. Priestley

T0338984

# Time and the Rose Garden

## Encountering the Magical in the life and works of J.B. Priestley

Anthony Peake

BOOKS

Winchester, UK
Washington, USA

First published by O-Books, 2018
O-Books is an imprint of John Hunt Publishing Ltd., No. 3 East St., Alresford,
Hampshire SO24 9EE, UK
office1@jhpbooks.net
www.johnhuntpublishing.com

For distributor details and how to order please visit the 'Ordering' section on our website.

ISBN: 978 1 78279 457 8
978 1 78535 191 4 (ebook)
Library of Congress Control Number: 2017931110

A CIP catalogue record for this book is available from the British Library.

Design: Stuart Davies

The views expressed in this book are not necessarily endorsed by the Estate of J.B. Priestley.

Printed and bound by CPI Group (UK) Ltd, Croydon, CR0 4YY, UK

We operate a distinctive and ethical publishing philosophy in all
areas of our business, from our global network of authors to
production and worldwide distribution.

# CONTENTS

# Other Books by Anthony Peake

# Foreword

In my later childhood, I developed an imaginative but slightly anxious disposition, along with an interest in UFOs, ghosts, and cryptozoology. I would glimpse an oddly flashing light in the sky and take it as the scout craft of an invasion descending from above; I remembered odd dreams from my early childhood that seemed terrifyingly real; I had the vertiginous sensation of slipping into an alternate universe, almost identical but for some peculiar quality of the light. It was in the midst of one of these little paranoias, probably related to dreams, time, or déjà vu, that my mother recommended her grandfather J.B. Priestley's book, *Man and Time*, to assuage my anxiety. I flicked through the introduction and found a picture of J.B. dressed as Old Father Time, scythe in one hand and pipe in the other, white-robed and decked with timepieces, with a look on his face that was wry, yet benign. The significance of the picture never dawned on me until very recently: here we have my great-grandfather in the role of Chronos, the god of Time. As ancestor-spirits go, it's hard to get much better.

I was born 3 years after Jack died, but his presence was very strong in my household. His statue looks over my brother and I in a photo taken in Bradford in 1994, the year of the statue's unveiling; my brother looking sombre in his long dark coat, I looking less reverential, wearing a ridiculous asymmetrical smirk copied off my shamanic totem of that period, Sonic the Hedgehog (I was about 6 years old, my brother was around 11 or 12). Most of the J.B.-related events I remember were in Yorkshire, which caused a momentary crisis of geo-psychic orienteering at a plaque unveiling in Highgate, where it seemed to an eight-year-old me as though we'd hopped on a bus from East Finchley and got out in a disarmingly salubrious district of Bradford. I'm told that, from photos of the infant Jack, we looked rather similar as babies, but babies tend to look rather similar to each other anyway; what I have certainly inherited from my great-grand-father is the sort of face that seems to have its own will, and as a consequence, makes expressions that are constantly being misread. "Time and again," he writes in *Delight*, "my real feelings have been misinterpreted. I may not have been enjoying myself, but at least I have not been suffering as intensely as the rest of the company imagined." So, the conversation turns to King Charles spaniels, and I am surprised to hear that my face registers a tone of such disgust that my companions declare my dislike of these poor spaniels to be self-evident – to all except me, it seems, who has never once entertained a single negative thought towards any spaniel, whether in the singular or the collective. I have learned to accept these social hiccups with weary resignation, as too strenuous a denial would seem defensive, and nobody wants to be the lady that doth protesteth too much.

As I grew older, I developed the ungracious habit of name-dropping my esteemed ancestor on highly tenuous grounds (I hope I'm a little more discerning now). His time-contorting narratives fascinated me, and seemed to be echoed in some of my favourite works of film and literature; for instance, 2001's *Donnie Darko*, which profoundly affected me at the age of 15, or Kurt Vonnegut's wonderful novel *Slaughterhouse 5*. However, when it came to my university studies, J.B. almost seemed too close to be a topic of research interest; I would head for Borges, the Kabbalah, Slavonic science-fiction, Sufi poetry, the Modernists, or William Burroughs, but the idea of actually exploring my great-grandfather's work didn't really occur to me, until the October of 2015, when I attended an event at Queen Mary University in East London.

Anthony Peake and Dr Kitt Price (who writes the Introduction to this book) were giving talks on Priestley's interest in time and precognition. I had seen Anthony before, at the National Theatre in the summer of 2009. Anthony had been invited to speak to the audience before a performance of my great-grandfather's play, *Time and the Conways*, at the Lyttelton Theatre. After his presentation at Queen Mary, I went over to thank him for the talk, whereupon he seemed to recognise me from somewhere; it turned out he had seen my talk at Breaking Convention, an interdisciplinary conference on psychedelic studies, in the summer of 2015. It was an uncanny feeling, a bit like running into a friend from another continent in the tiny village of one's birth. It was this meeting that inspired me to shift the topic of my studies towards Priestley, and I am in the process of drafting a thesis proposal, under the guidance of Dr Price, on my great-grandfather's work.

Anthony is something of a polymath, whose work touches on quantum physics, psychology, parapsychology, philosophy, literature, and many other fields; his detailed and exhaustive approach to the topics of his research is very much present in *Time and the Rose Garden*, which uncovers work never before studied, such as the (at the time of writing) unpublished play *Time Was, Time Is*, and consolidates material from across Priestley's body of work relevant to his interest in the nature of time, the survival of consciousness after death, and related topics. Those attracted to Peake's 'Itladian' hypotheses, but unfamiliar with Priestley, will find much that resonates with them, while scholars and enthusiasts of J.B. will find a meticulous summary of Priestley's engagement with these subjects. A book like this is sorely needed, as Priestley has long been misunderstood as a dated writer of Edwardian manners and social comedy, especially from the post-war period up to the '80s and 90s; with a revival of interest and revaluation of Priestley in full swing, Peake has delivered a most timely piece of research.

Luke Goaman-Dodson

# Introduction

J.B. Priestley's book *Man and Time* features a full-page photograph of the author, left hand clasping the bowl of a pipe whose stem rests between his teeth, right hand leaning on a billiards table awash with hundreds of letters. Priestley gazes through his spectacles at this vast correspondence, sent in response to his appearance on the BBC Television programme *Monitor* on 17 March, 1963. Viewers had been invited to write in with three types of experience: "dreaming the future"; "the future affecting, or maybe effecting, the present"; and "any experience that leads one to a feeling about time which is different from the common sense or conventional one".[1] The BBC audience welcomed this opportunity to relay their anomalous temporal experiences, entrusting Priestley with their disorientation and appealing to him for explanations. A much-loved broadcaster and playwright, he represented hope that a new set of beliefs and values might emerge in the wide spaces still uncharted by scientific and religious authorities.

The lack of an adequate repository for precognitive experience was keenly felt throughout the twentieth century. The Society for Psychical Research and its sister society in America began the collecting of experiences from the public in the 1880s, but their focus was generally on telepathy, mediumship, hauntings and hallucinations. Dreams and prevision were harder to verify. The rise of Freudian psychoanalysis brought renewed attention to dreams, and while Freud's commitment to wish-fulfilment meant that he dismissed prophecy out of hand, the dream as a psychological research object gained a new status. Psychic researchers came under additional pressure to pay proper attention to dreams with the publication of *An Experiment with Time* by British aeronautical engineer J.W. Dunne in 1927. This book, which has remained almost continuously in print for the past ninety years in successive editions, and was translated into Spanish, Dutch, Italian, Swedish, Danish, and French, included simple instructions for checking one's own dreams for glimpses of the future. Thousands of people kept Dunne-style dream journals, and Priestley suspected that without this advice, "at least a third of the best precognitive dreams I have been sent would never have come my way."[2]

Yet until Priestley's *Monitor* appearance, no organized national endeavour to harvest the fruits of these journals was made. An attempted collaboration between Dunne and the SPR in 1932, using Oxford University students as subjects for a precognitive dream experiment, ended in dispute between Dunne and the SPR and the publication of a null result. Dunne himself was increasingly preoccupied with elaborating the physical and theological implications of his own time theory. In 1934 the SPR President, Dame Edith Lyttelton, appealed for cases of prevision on BBC radio, and the resulting book *Some Cases of Prediction* represents the height of the British SPR's accommodation of ordinary, everyday precognitive experience.[3] It is a modest volume, comprising sixteen good cases of precognition, preceded by sixteen cases of apparent prevision that are explainable as either coincidence or telepathy. Psychic research has never produced an equivalent for precognition of the 702 cases of telepathy presented in *Phantasms of the Living*,[4] though some notable collections of precognitive experience have been assembled by researchers outside the UK, including Charles Richet's study of dreams relating to World War I, and the extensive case reviews begun by Louisa Rhine and continued by Sally Rhine Feather in Durham, North Carolina.

Reviewing a total of 349 cases of precognition collected by the SPR during its first fifty years of operation, Herbert Saltmarsh set out the criteria for an ideal case in 1934: (1) a record of the precognition before its fulfilment; (2) sufficient matching detail between the precognition and its fulfilment to rule out chance coincidence;

(3) narrow limits of time or place for simple precognitions; (4) the precognition must be beyond the scope of an extended power of inference (to rule out hyperesthesia and subliminal knowledge); (5) auto-suggestion could not have brought about the fulfilment; (6) telepathy from another person could not have delivered the foreseen information; (7) a limited window of time between the precognition and its fulfilment.[5] "Needless to say," Saltmarsh reported, "I have not yet found one."[6] In order to fulfil these criteria, we would each have to have all our dreams notarized upon waking each morning, and would also need to scrupulously record all our waking activities, calling witnesses to affirm the details of any events matching our dreams, and producing further evidence against the telepathic and auto-suggestive explanations. This conjures up a dystopian mode of surveillance that might be comic if it were not so close to twenty-first century lived reality. As Jonathan Nolan, the creator of *Person of Interest*, has said in reference to the CBS show's fictive precognitive surveillance systems, this "started out science fiction, and then by season three was basically a documentary." Presumably life under such conditions is having a significant impact on the content of our dreams.

It is a sign of the SPR's generosity, and the value of its archives, that the larger part of the letters sent to Priestley in 1963 are held in the Society's historical collection at Cambridge University, for his approach to evidence was at odds with established SPR verification procedures. "I offer no careful analysis, no exact figures," Priestley stated in *Man and Time*, conceding that: "If without such treatment they cannot be accepted as evidence, then we shall have to do without evidence." (Page 192) Priestley's aims differed from those of the SPR, and this is vital to our assessment of the letters' value today. "I am not engaged in psychological or psychical research," he noted, "and it seems to me that for a personal essay of this kind, letters addressed to me while I am writing it are of more value than letters addressed to other people and then boiled down into evidence."[7] It matters, then, that viewers addressed their narratives to Priestley: a man who had broadcast regularly in the interests of British morale during the Second World War; who had brought Jung's ideas to the British public; and whose plays and fictions had determinedly explored the need for alternatives to feeling "absolutely clamped into this one way passing of time."[8]

For many, the invitation to submit their dreams and other experiences of being outside linear time was an opportunity to connect with a trusted interlocutor whose works and media presence were interwoven with their own biography. "I've always had a special feeling for your work," wrote one correspondent, "as if you were one of the family, like Gracie Fields or the Hallé orchestra, bless you all."[9] Few if any of the letters may fulfil the Saltmarsh criteria for an ideal case of precognition, but it is thanks to this sense of a familial relationship that we have such a rich store of evidence for the work that people did, in their daily lives, in struggling to make sense of anomalous temporal experiences.

On behalf of his "time-haunted" fellows, Priestley wrastled the endlessly proliferating dimensions of modern physical and transcendental theory into three practical aspects of our relationships with time. We are born, grow old, and die in the Time One of material history. In dreams we enter the more contemplative arena of Time Two, where multiple possible futures exist, waiting to be brought about by our actions in Time One. There need be nothing mystical nor mathematically obscure about Time Two: "It is this intellectually infuriating future, rather like an omelet just before it is ready to be lifted out, that we hold in our minds when we are actually planning our lives and not picking and choosing among Time theories," he reminds us in *Man and Time*. But beyond planning and dreaming, there was another, more elusive relationship to time that was seen at work in moments of creative imagination, when we are somehow involved in both contemplation and action. Priestley tentatively named this Time Three, while confessing that he could not explain how it worked. Somehow, he had managed to write "the technically complicated Act Two of *Time and the Conways* seemingly without effort and at a headlong pace."[10] The experience, rather than its precise relationship to any number of dimensions, was what mattered. Priestley placed the living of life before its theorization and also before any forms of escape.

Anthony Peake is ideally placed to set the experiences of Priestley's correspondents before us as we approach the half centenary of that *Monitor* broadcast, having for many years listened himself to the accounts of those who have had near death experiences, out of body experiences, and precognitive dreams. A repository, like Priestley himself, of the anomalous, the disturbing, the comforting and the inexplicable, Peake is a trustworthy guide to the patterns that emerge when such experiences are reviewed in the mass, as well as to the idiosyncrasies of individual cases, and their sometimes surprising affinities with broader cultural narratives.

Dr Kitt Price
Senior Lecturer in Modern and Contemporary Literature,
Queen Mary, University of London

# Preface: JB & ME

My relationship with Priestley is like one of his Time Plays.

It starts around 1959. I was a boarder at Clifton College. I was sixteen. Every Friday night there was a play reading group. One Friday we read an amazing play that fitted in with my intuitive feelings. It was called *Time and the Conways*, I had no idea who wrote it.

Jump about twelve years to the early seventies and André Previn, whose wife Mia Farrow I had just directed in another extraordinary time play, J.M. Barrie's *Mary Rose*, asked me to direct a musical of *The Good Companions* by J.B. Priestley that he wanted to compose with the legendary lyricist Johnny Mercer. I knew nothing of J.B. Priestley except that he was a solid Yorkshireman, who was the radio voice of Britain during the war and who wrote a famous comedy *When We Are Married*. I read *The Good Companions*. It is a wonderful picaresque journey that, while it entertains, has a profound undertow. It is a Jungian tale of individuation. I agreed to direct the musical.

Naturally I started to read Priestley extensively. In an extraordinary time jump I came across *Time and the Conways* again. I knew it was a masterpiece. I applied for the rights to direct it for the Royal Exchange Theatre only to be told that Priestley had refused to authorize a major production since the London premier in the 1930s.

Amazingly, the Gods were still with me, and a few weeks later the Agent phoned to say Priestley had phoned to change his mind.

I was invited to Kissing Tree House near Stratford where he lived with his wife, the redoubtable Jacquetta Hawkes. We became friends. He was, to me, one of the wisest and most stimulating people I have ever met.

In 1974 he gave me a new play called *Time Was, Time Is*. I

regarded it as the ultimate time play, as it moved between the years 1914 and 1974. I had two reservations. I didn't think the politics were especially relevant and the 'modern' 1974 dialogue didn't seem modern enough. It never went into production.

Jump another forty years and I am sent a play by the Canadian Playwright Brad Fraser, a play called *Time is Time*. I emailed him to say my hair stood on end when I saw the title because Priestley had written a play called *Time Was, Time Is* forty years ago. Brad replied that he had seen my (second) production of *Time and the Conways* and that had inspired his new play. I thought nothing further of it.

I had, very soon after, to wade through my pile of old papers to find my cut version of *Hamlet* that I had directed with Robert Lindsay many years before. After about an hour I found it. As I pulled it out, out came with it *Time Was, Time Is* by J.B. Priestley! I had no idea I had it. It felt that JB had said, "Here I am, read it!" I did and it was brilliant. The politics of a country on the brink of war was horribly relevant in 1974, and was now a period piece of its own. I hope that this remarkable play will be staged in 2017.

Finally, I was contacted by Anthony Peake who wanted to talk to me about the play as he was writing this biography about Priestley. We had a wonderful Skype conversation, which has resulted in us becoming friends. I am delighted that, with this reminiscence, I can make a small contribution to his important goal to make the public aware of just what a major artist and thinker J.B. Priestley was.

**Braham Murray OBE**

## Chapter One

# Priestley The Boy, The Soldier and The Student

*We might be close to one of the great revelations that suddenly enlarge and enrich our vision of life. We are, due one. And I believed that this revelation might explode once and for all the bewildering problem of Time.*
– J.B. Priestley

John (Jack) Boynton Priestley was born in Bradford, Yorkshire, in 1894. His father, Jonathan, was a schoolmaster who suggested that, on leaving school at sixteen, his ambitious son should pursue a career in the wool trade, an area of business for which Yorkshire was a world leader. In 1910 Jack, as he was known at the time and continued to be known throughout his life, started his working life at Messrs. Helm & Co based in the Swan Arcade, an imposing four-storey building of wrought iron and glass. But this was not the career Jack wished for himself. For him his future lay in words, not in worsted. He sent out various articles to local publications and was taken on in an unpaid position writing articles for a radical, left wing periodical, the *Bradford Pioneer*. This was in keeping with his own political beliefs, inherited from his father. His articles, actually short essays, were acutely obser-vational and written in a style suggesting far greater age and personal maturity.

This maturity was evidenced in his reading at that time. In his 1964 book *Man and Time*, Jack describes how one of the most influential discoveries of his life was his encounter with Indian metaphysics fifty years before. This takes us to the period of 1912 to 1914. He describes how the Vedantic concept of Atman fasci-nated him. This is the idea that at a much deeper level of consciousness we can discover the "essential self" and that this essential self, Atman, is simply part of a single unitary essence which is known as Brahman. Remember, Priestley was only in his late teens at this time and yet he was already fascinated by the idea that we are all simply emanations of a singular consciousness. In *Man and Time*, he reflected on this:

I can remember the exultation I felt, being in my late teens, when if we have any sympathy at all with speculative thought we long to encounter bold and gigantic metaphysical conclusions.[11]

It is important here to discuss exactly what Vedanta is. Vedanta is the esoteric aspect of Hinduism. But just as Gnosticism with regards to Christianity, Kabbalah in relation to Judaism and Sufism within Islam, each is an exclusive philosophy which presents a far deeper understanding of the universe than the 'religion' presented to the masses that follow the belief system as an accepted truth without thought or reflection. Vedanta is a non-dual philosophy. This means that within this system there is one, single 'essence' within the universe. This is in contrast with 'Dualism' which proposes that the universe consists of two very different essences: mind and matter. Of course, modern materialist-reductionist science argues that matter is all there is and that mind, or spirit, is non-quantifiable and non-measurable and therefore does not exist. Within Vedanta this non-dualism is known as *Advaita*. The unity consciousness that encompasses both matter and spirit is described by the term *Brahman*. It is this which intrigued the young Jack Priestley. As we shall discover, many times in his writings, novels and plays, he acknowledges that we are all one consciousness experiencing the physical universe subjectively. But what is the physical universe, the world of solid matter that presents itself to our senses? According to the teachings of Vedanta this seemingly tangible reality that exists outside of us is, in fact, a hallucination. Vedanta calls this *Maya*. The ego, the individual human consciousness, is also an illusion that exists within Maya. Vedanta suggests that we that are trapped within Maya sometimes have a brief glimpse of our collective consciousness. As we shall discover, Jack sensed Brahman many times during his life during periods of intense creativity or while being lost in music. We shall also discover that many of his plays attempted to place in a dramatic context these deeply esoteric ideas. Sadly, these were missed by the critics and the vast majority of the audiences.

That the young Jack Priestley was precociously intellectual is clearly evidenced by such interests. Remember this was the early years of the second decade of the 20th century. He was living in a provincial city without general access to the great flow of information found in London. He actively sought out these ideas. This gave him a particularly wide world-view. This was reflected in a particularly powerful article he wrote in 1913. With Europe obviously slipping towards a future conflict, only the source of ignition being unknown, the 18-year-old Jack Priestley argued that if he had his way "war would be abolished tomorrow."[12]

As we shall discover from his later fictional writings, the years 1912 to 1913 had a profound effect on Priestley. In one of his radio broadcasts, commemorating the outbreak of World War One twenty-six years before, during the dark days when England stood alone against the might of Nazi Germany, he asked his audience:

Do you ever look back on your life and see it as a road that wanders through wildly varying landscapes? I do. And now, as I look back, before August 1914 the road seemed to be a sunlit plain, coming out the mists of early childhood.[13]

This was a curious, linear way of looking at one's life and was probably influenced by his lifelong interest in Eastern Mysticism.

It is as if Priestley, looking down from a lofty position outside of normal time, could see his past life like a road winding out of the distant horizon that was his deep past. As we shall discover, for Priestley this was not an analogy but how he actually believed time worked.

It was on one of those sunlit plains, during the summer of 1914, that Jack had had his fortune told by a friend. Maybe this associate viewed life's path from slightly higher elevation and could see the road ahead. Priestley was informed that soon his whole way of living would change and that in the near future he would often find himself in great danger. The friend then stated quite categorically that Jack's life would never be the same again. This was the first of many encounters Priestley would have suggesting to him that the future is already out there to be experienced by those sensitive enough to perceive its call.

Sadly, the radical change foreseen that summer's day was soon to occur. After a series of diplomatic exchanges between the European powers war was declared on 4th August 1914. The day before had been a Bank Holiday Monday and Jack and his friends had attended the Manningham Tide, a popular annual fair. He was later to write that many of the faces he knew in the crowds that carefree afternoon would not survive to see 1918.

On the 7th of September 1914, just six days before his twentieth birthday, Jack Priestley, the young man who wished to abolish war, enlisted to fight for King and Country. It is of significance that Jack did not rush off with many of his friends and join the local battalions of the West Yorkshire Regiment, but for some reason made his way to Halifax and signed on with the Duke of Wellington's West Riding Regiment. Had he joined the local group, the 16th and 18th Battalions, which became known as the Bradford Pals, he would probably have died or been seriously wounded in the first hour of the first day of the Battle of the Somme on 16th July 1916. Of the 2,000 who enlisted in the Bradford Pals, 1,770 were killed in the first hour of the offensive.

It is highly likely that Jack would have been among them. He was later to write that this curious decision, made for no reason that he could understand, was a "signal from the unknown."[14]

It is clear from his plays that the events of this particular time were vivid in Priestley's later memories. For example, in his autobiographical essay *Margin Released* he describes how, on 4th August 1914, "the newsboys were running and shouting every day and all the day."[15] This image appears in his play *Johnson Over Jordan* in a stream-of-consciousness section and much later, in his unpublished and to-date unperformed last play, *Time Was, Time Is*, which is mostly set on the evening that news breaks that Archduke Franz Ferdinand has been shot in Sarajevo on the 28th of June. Indeed, we shall also discover soon that for Priestley, these evenings of high summer also have a particular magic.

Priestley experienced a much-reported First World War experience, one that he rarely wrote about but one that was to create in him an interest in the existence of a 'higher self'. During his time in the trenches he sensed that there was something watching over him, that this entity was both him and not-him. In his essay *Instead of the Trees* he describes how he was a casualty three times during the conflict. On each occasion he noticed that when terror was at its highest something inside him seemed to take over. This "something" was not frightened in any way. Priestley became intrigued as to the source of these sensations. If it was simply a psychological mechanism, then what was it that activated such a mechanism? He considered that this was something far more interesting than simply the ego. In *Rain Upon Godshill* he reconsidered these questions and wondered if some form of higher consciousness was active during these periods of creativity.

Later in his life he became more willing to discuss his experiences in the trenches. In 1964 he wrote a large 'tabletop' book entitled *Man and Time*. In the final chapter of this book, an essay entitled "One Man and Time", he discusses his own experiences of time perception. Without adding any further situational details, he describes how he and his fellow soldiers had:

> On some occasions (we) slipped out of passing time, became detached observers of our fortunes, with death approaching in slow motion, as if we were in some other time.[16]

In *Margin Released* Jack described the incident of his own wounding in June 1916:

> There I was then, deciding on each section's share, when I heard a rushing sound, and I knew what it meant and knew, though everything had gone into slow motion, I had no hope of getting away before the thing arrived. Just as on earlier and later occasions when I have thought all was up, the first shrinking in terror was followed, as I went into the new slow time, by a sense of detachment. I believe from what I learnt long afterwards that the Minenwerfer landed slap in the trench, two or three yards away. All I knew at the time was that the world blew up.[17]

From this it is clear that the sensation of time slowing down was something he experienced rather than simply him describing the experiences of others.

In his description of his wounding in June 1916 he refers to a "sense of detachment." This is also repeated in *Man and Time* where he comments how this feeling seemed to overcome soldiers who were about to die in the near future:

> Then again, there were those men, lively gossipers and wags, who became subdued and thoughtful some hours before the sniper's bullet found them or the shell tore their bodies to bleeding shreds – as if they had been watching, throughout a whole morning, death pointing a finger at them across No

Man's Land.[18]

Here we have his early encounters with both time perception and also his developing belief that under certain circumstances a person can be aware of events in their own future. In the essay he commented that under such extreme circumstances time refused to flow in the accepted way, "it did not adapt itself to the facts."[19]

Jack was buried alive by the German *minenwerfer* (a trench mortar) and was injured and deafened. In *Margin Released* he states that he had no recollection of how he was evacuated from the front lines and sent back to England and to a military hospital at North Evington, a suburb of Leicester. After fully regaining consciousness he ran a high temperature and was kept in bed for a few weeks. In the late summer he was then transferred to a convalescent home in Rutland. On his recovery he took a commission with the Devonshire Regiment and returned to the front in the summer of 1918. He was subsequently partly gassed when his gas mask malfunctioned allowing some of the poison to seep through. This was the official version but Jack felt that his actual condition may have been exacerbated by the large number of tots of rum he drank later that evening.[20] He found himself in a state of total confusion and suffering from breathing problems. Fortunately, he was found by a group of British stretcher-bearers who took him out of danger. This was the last military action he saw.

In 1918, after his return to Britain, Jack had a book of poems, *A Chapman of Rhymes*, self-published. He was later to describe this as being a "collection of dubious verse" written in a vainglorious attempt to "leave something behind". He goes on to add that on actually becoming famous he sought out every copy and had them destroyed. Sadly, as far as he was concerned at least, some of the copies escaped his personal Bonfire of the Vanities and were, in the mid-1970s, being sold at over £250 per copy.[21] Of significance was that Jack had dedicated this book to a young

woman called Pat Tempest who had been his Bradford 'sweetheart' throughout the war. On his return home Jack and Pat
rekindled their affection for each other.

In 1919 he was formally discharged from military service,
emerging from the army and the war as Lieutenant John
Priestley. He was keen to return to his hoped-for career as a
professional writer. He approached the *Yorkshire Observer*, a
popular local newspaper, and volunteered himself to write a
series of articles on walking in the Yorkshire Dales. Much to his
delight, and possible relief, they agreed. He spent the summer of
1919 out in the countryside and fresh air, a total contrast to his
experiences in the killing fields of Northern France. He published
the articles under the pseudonym "Peter of Pomfret" and was
paid a guinea (just over £1.00, a large sum in those days) per
article. But all summers come to an end and Jack had to think
about his future. As an ex-officer he was entitled to apply for a
small educational grant. He applied for one and was successful.
He was accepted by Cambridge University and offered a place at
Trinity Hall to read English and history. He was later to change
this to history and political science. However, he really did not
enjoy his time at Cambridge; he was older than most of his fellow
undergraduates and from a very different social class. However,
he found the environment extremely intellectually stimulating,
particularly the lectures of the eccentric philosopher, John
McTaggart Ellis McTaggart.

Although not part of his degree course Jack regularly attended
McTaggart's lectures. What fascinated him was McTaggart's
eccentric philosophy of time, something that may have helped
the ex-soldier understand some of his own extraordinary experiences in the trenches.

In simple terms (if it can be said that McTaggart's philosophy
can ever be simple) McTaggart argued that everything that exists
is real, and nothing can be real without existing. In this regard
anything made of matter, that is anything that has size, shape,

position, mobility and impenetrability, is, by definition, real. Can this definition of 'reality' be applied to something as ephemeral as time? McTaggart thought not. The only real quality that can be applied to time is that it has, in some difficult to define way, position and mobility. What it most definitely does not have is size, shape or impenetrability. In this regard McTaggart wrote:

> Positions in time, as time appears to us prima facie, are distinguished in two ways. Each position is earlier than some, and later than some, of the other positions. And each position is either past, present, or future. The distinctions of the former class are permanent, while those of the latter are not. If M is ever earlier than N, it is always earlier. But an event, which is now present, was future and will be past.[22]

From this McTaggart proposed that there must be two different types of time. He called these the "A Series" and the "B Series". The "A Series" can be described as containing specific moments in time that move through time in a sequence. By this he meant that the present must move along with the present moment. We have the concept of now and now moves through time. In the same way three hours ago similarly moves through time as does two weeks from now.

In his book *Representing Time* philosopher K.M. Jaszczolt gives two excellent analogies to facilitate understanding of these two complex concepts.[23] Jaszczolt compares the "A" series to a ski lift, specifically the designs that are in continual motion. He asks us to imagine that as the ski lift goes past skiers latch themselves on. Each event in time is similar to a skier in that only one skier at a time can latch on at any one point. For Jaszczolt the "B" series is likened to a long washing line in which a person can hang different articles of clothing in different positions. The line is static and it is the person who can move up and down.

The first metaphor is probably how most people understand

time, or more specifically, its motion. It flows from the future, becomes the present moment that then fades away into the past. This is 'internal time' whereas the washing line analogy is 'real time'. If we stand at a distance from the washing line then we will see it as an object that contains the past, the present and the future in a sequence-free 'now'. This is what McTaggart termed the "C Series". However, as McTaggart quite rightly observed, the "C Series" is not actually a form of time because no change is taking place. Indeed, what turns the static "C Series" into an 'in time' "B Series" is the addition of a conscious agent – an observer – who interprets the series in a before-and-after structure that imposes motion.

In his 1964 book *Man and Time* Priestley states that although he rarely agreed with anything McTaggart actually said, he could never find any flaws in his "lucid and highly ingenious arguments."[24] Although Priestley may have felt that McTaggart was "playing a wonderful game that has nothing to do with truth and reality" it was still an approach to time perception that delighted him and was probably a perfect primer for his later attraction to the work of J.W. Dunne. This idea that an "observer" was essential with regards to time perception and that time could exist in different aspects.

Jack's grant was never sufficient to cover his day to day living costs. He supplemented his income by continuing his career as a writer and doing the occasional lecture. While Jack was still at Cambridge he wrote his first proper book. This was published in 1922 under the title *Brief Diversions*; it was a collection of parodies, fables and epigrams and something of a continuation of the short articles he wrote in the pre-war years for the *Bradford Pioneer*. In this he made reference to one of his major influences as a writer, Lord Dunsany. This may be of significance as Dunsany was an author of the magical and the mythic rather than the prosaic and ordinary. This influence can be seen in such stories as *Appointment at Samara* and *The Uninvited Guest*. In both we have a personification of death. In the former it is in the guise of a beautiful woman and in the latter as a guest at a fancy-dress party.

Jack graduated on the 21$^{st}$ June 1921 and eight days later married Pat Tempest in a very low-key ceremony at the Westgate Baptist Chapel in Bradford. The young couple then left Cambridge for London where Jack hoped that he could earn a living as a freelance journalist and writer.

Later that same year a second volume of essays, *Papers from Lilliput,* was published. By this time Pat was pregnant and the fledgling writer needed money for his growing family. Through contacts he gained a job as a publisher's reader for The Bodley Head. As we shall later discover, Priestley developed a fascination with the idea that from a viewpoint outside of linear time we are a singular creature extending through the years from the point of our birth to the point of our death. This may have been subliminally stimulated by Jack being haunted by a popular advert of the time showing a series of male faces getting older and older. The advert was for a pension company and had no esoteric meaning. Was this image the one that brought about his subsequent attraction to the works of Peter Ouspensky and John William Dunne?[25] Indeed, it could be argued that it was this image that stimulated Jack's interest in the circularity of time, something that was to appear in his next collection of essays, *I for One,* which was published in 1923. This preoccupation was noted by his biographer, John Atkins.[26] The book opens with an essay, entitled *One Beginning,* which ends with a repeat of the first sentence. This was an intriguing and seemingly original plot twist that was to be used to great acclaim some years later by James Joyce in his 1939 novel *Finnegans Wake.* It may be of significance that Joyce began his writing of this work in the early 1920s, coincidental with the publication of *I for One.* So what was it that stimulated both men, from very different backgrounds and writing traditions, to focus in on the same theme?

*I for One* had been published by The Bodley Head, his part-time employer, and they were so impressed with both the book and the reviews it received that they quickly commissioned a second book from Priestley, *Figures in Modern Literature*.

His first daughter, Barbara, was born on the 4th of March 1923, followed by a second, Sylvia, in April 1924. Sylvia was born very premature and was, for a time, a cause for great concern. The baby did live but sadly the subsequent medical investigation had shown that Pat had advanced cancer of the bladder. In June 1924 Jack's father, Jonathan, died of stomach cancer. In 1925 Pat succumbed to her illness, leaving Jack, at twenty-nine, a widower with two small children. By this time Jack had also written a biography of George Meredith for Macmillan.

Meredith was an intriguing writer. His fantasy stories were very unusual for the Victorian period. He was heavily influenced by Arabian fiction and the stories of the Arabian Nights. A classic example of this is his 1856 novel *The Shaving of Shagpat*. Such was its influence on modern fantasy writers that it appeared in the celebrated Ballantine Adult Fantasy series in 1970. A theme of Meredith's writing, both fiction and poetic, is the concept of pantheism; that everything that is, is God. As such we are as one with all of nature and that God is within us. This belief caused a degree of confusion for Priestley, who wrote, "if everything is God, then nothing is God."[27] We shall discover later that this idea of a singular consciousness behind everything was to become of great interest to Priestley in his later years and is a theme that can be found in much of his writings on time, both in his plays and his novels. He was to call this source of creativity *"The Overmind"*. This is clearly a concept he first encountered in his readings of Vedanta in the years before the Great War. But to this was added esoteric philosophies of mind that had been developing in Europe over the previous thirty years.

It was in the early 1920s that he discovered the writings of Marcel Proust which stimulated an even greater interest in the true nature of time and memory. In *Man and Time*, he also describes how while looking at certain paintings, specifically those of the French Impressionists, he felt what he could only describe as "time shifts" or, as he later described it, "a different taste of time."[28] He is clearly struggling to find the right words to describe a clear altered state of consciousness. Later he was to write that he also was fascinated by the paintings of Pieter Brueghel the Elder because of the way in which, lurking behind Brueghel's scenes of peasant revelry, "somewhere just around the corner is a fairy-tale country. We are poised on the edge of marvels and miracles... feeling a trifle haunted."[29]

His Meredith book was published in 1926 and Priestley's world had changed again. In that year he married Jane, the former wife of D.B. Wyndham-Lewis, and had already a daughter by her, Mary, and acquired a stepdaughter, Angela Wyndham-Lewis. He was needing to broaden his writing horizons. Novel writing beckoned.

Jack's first attempt at fiction was a straightforward adventure story, *Adam in Moonshine* (1927). He wrote this quite quickly and really enjoyed the creation of fiction. The critics were less enthusiastic and, he admitted many years later, in *Margin Released*, that the work had many shortcomings. He described it as being a:

little coloured trial balloon. But the story does not move effortlessly like a balloon: it moves stiffly, creaking with self-consciousness. Not having any press-cuttings, I do not know exactly how it was received, but I have an idea it was called "an essayist's novel". I do remember, however, that Arnold Bennett dismissed it with scorn, saying that it had no substance. This was true enough, but it was rather like complaining that no slice of meat could be found in a meringue.[30]

He decided that his next novel would be far more intellectually challenging. In *Margin Released* he said that he was attempting to "transmute the thriller into symbolical fiction with some psychological depth."[31] He had long been interested in what he was later to call "the magical" and it comes as no surprise that his second book touched upon these topics. Ever since childhood his dreams had been powerful and vivid. Some of these remained with him for many years and were shown to be precognitive. For example, in his autobiographical series of essays *Rain Upon Godshill* he describes how, as a schoolboy, he had a vivid dream involving an uncle that he rarely saw. What was odd in the dream was that the uncle approached him in the dream in a very aggressive way and glared at him intensely. Many years later Priestley was in a public house with friends. Suddenly, his uncle entered the bar and glared at him in exactly the way he had done in the dream. For Priestley this was evidence that Dunne's hypothesis was correct.

In the same year as he wrote *Adam in Moonshine*, Jack published a collection of essays entitled *Open House*. These give an excellent picture of where Priestley's philosophical ideas were taking him at that time. It also gives an insight into how his perceptions of reality were beginning to broaden, specifically in his essay *The Berkshire Beasts*. Here Jack describes how, in one of his vivid dreams, he found himself walking in a park and encountering a herd of really strange animals with floppy ears and resembling elephants without trunks. They were all wearing spectacles with the lenses the size of dinner plates. In the dream he is accompanied by a family friend who explains that the animals in question are known as the "Berkshire Beasts". (Of course he describes many precognitive dreams in his other works. For example, in *Apes and Angels* he describes a visit to what he termed a *Strange Outfitter* who had a series of masks with moveable mouths. Many years later he encountered these peculiar masks in 'reality' as part of the stage props for his play *Johnson Over Jordan*.) In these dreams he described how he regularly met with those who had died. Atkins is particularly taken by how Priestley stated in *English Journey* that in his dreams the "dead move casually through them."[32] Of course it was, again, in *Johnson Over Jordan* that JBP was to describe the dream world inhabited by the dead, in this case the post-mortem experiences of its eponymous hero.

It is evident from this that he occasionally perceived a breakdown of this reality and the fleeting vision of what lies beyond. Many years later, in 1957, he was to describe himself as being a "time-haunted" man.[33] It is of significance that in this same year, 1927, Jack was to encounter a theory that for him offered a possible explanation for these experiences. That year a book was published that was to prove to be hugely popular and extremely influential. Entitled *An Experiment with Time*, it was written by an Anglo-Irish aeronautical engineer called John William Dunne. Being a man of letters Jack quickly acquired a copy and immediately realised that this was a work of great importance. In a subsequent review Jack described *An Experiment with Time* as being "the most important book of our time." So what was it about this book that had Priestley giving it such powerful praise? In order to understand this, we need to discuss, in some detail, who J.W. Dunne was and why his model of time intrigued Priestley, and many other writers.

## Chapter Two

# The 1920s: John William Dunne and the question of time

As can be suspected from his name, John William Dunne (1875–1949) was born in Ireland, into an upper-class Anglo-Irish military family based in County Kildare. He was the third son of General Sir John Hart Dunne KCB (1835–1924) and Julia Elizabeth Dunne. As what can also be suspected from his background, Dunne followed his family military traditions and after service in the Second Boer War of 1900 he returned to Britain and became interested in the military potential of aviation. In 1905, while based at Blair Atholl in Scotland he designed a tailless monoplane wing which so impressed Colonel John Edward Capper, the commanding officer of the Army Balloon Section in Aldershot, that he was given funds to develop his ideas and build a working model. Capper wanted a biplane which was subsequently built at Blair Atholl. By 1913 Dunne had developed a reputation as one of the major aviation designers in the world. It was Dunne who pioneered the 'V-Wing' design which can be seen today in almost all fighter aircraft.

As a military man and an engineer Dunne existed in a world of cold logic and rationality. Decisions had to be made on the facts and nothing more. He was therefore surprised when, in 1899, a very curious dream focused his attention on the power of dreams. Dunne was staying in a hotel in Sussex, taking a break before he joined his army associates down in South Africa fighting the Boers. One night he found himself experiencing a peculiarly vivid dream. In the dream he was having a heated argument with one of the hotel's waiters as to what was the correct time. The waiter stated that it was half past four in the morning whereas the dreaming Dunne was sure that it was the same time in the afternoon. In the dream he concluded that his pocket watch must have stopped and, on checking it, confirmed that was, indeed, the case. The hands were precisely on half past four. On seeing this he awoke. Filled with curiosity he reached out for the watch, which he always left by his bedside. It was not there. He got up and after a minute or so he found it lying on a chest of drawers. He was surprised to discover that the watch had actually stopped: at half past four.

He immediately concluded that the answer to the mystery was a simple one: the watch had stopped the previous afternoon at four thirty. He had, at the time, subliminally noticed this and his subsequent dream created a situation around this subconscious knowledge. Dunne simply rewound it and went back to sleep.

The next morning, he made his way downstairs to the nearest clock to confirm the correct time, assuming that if the clock had stopped the previous afternoon at four thirty it would be slow by the time difference between four thirty and the moment he rewound it and started its timekeeping again. What he discovered stunned him; he found that the watch was only two minutes slow. It had clearly stopped very close to the moment he had awoken after the dream, possibly when he was experiencing the dream. Again, he rationalized that the cessation of the ticking could have awoken him. But this did not explain how, in a totally darkened room, his dream had correctly anticipated the time.

But it was a dream that he experienced in South Africa in 1902 that was to change forever his attitude towards time flow and was, in turn, to have him create a whole new theory of time perception.

In the spring of that year Dunne was encamped with the 6th Mounted Infantry near the ruins of Lindley. It was here that the dream struck. In it he found himself standing on the side of a hill surrounded by little fissures with jets of vapour escaping. Looking across the landscape he realised that he was on an island. Not any island but an Island he had visited before, but only in dreams. From this 'memory' he was aware that the island was in danger from a potential volcanic explosion. For some reason he knew that 4,000 people were in danger. As is the way with dreams he then finds himself transported to a neighbouring island where he desperately tries to convince the French authorities that the volcanic island must be evacuated as soon as possible. In the dream he again repeats to the French officials that 4,000 people will be killed.

He then awoke with the images of the dream firmly in his memory. Because Lindley was a fair distance from any ports the arrival of British newspapers was sporadic and usually quite delayed. But when the next batch of newspapers were received Dunne was stunned to read a headline in the *Daily Telegraph* which announced, again in banner headlines, "Volcanic Disaster in Martinique. Town swept away. An avalanche of flame. Probable loss of over 40,000 lives." The article went on to explain that the main town of the island, St Pierre, had been totally destroyed when the local dormant volcano, Mount Pelée, erupted sending a cloud of poisonous gas across town killing virtually everybody. The date of the eruption was 8 May 1902.

The attentive reader will note a curious error in the dream's version of events. In the dream Dunne was convinced that 4,000 people were in danger of death and yet the newspaper precisely states 40,000, a figure that is now generally accepted as being accurate. Dunne himself picked up on this fifteen years later when, on rereading the headline, he saw the clear reference to 40,000. He realised that in his haste he had scanned over the number and had wrongly read it as being 4,000.

It was this discovery that stimulated Dunne to write a book describing his experiences. But, as a man of rigid logic, he also wanted to seek out an explanation for such time perception anomalies. It wasn't enough to simply discuss his experiences. He wanted answers.

And so it was in 1927 that Dunne's book *An Experiment with*

*Time* appeared in the bookshops. In this he suggested an answer as to how the dreaming self can access information from the future. He proposed that there is a whole series of times... serial time as he termed it. His logic was that time is perceived to have a physical presence. It seems to exist as a block out there, another dimension such as height, length and breadth. Dunne argued that in order for time to be perceived as "passing" its movement had to be measured by something else. And the only thing that time can be measured against is time itself. How long does a minute take to pass? Obviously a minute, but the first minute must be measured against the second minute, how else can we perceive the movement unless it is perceived to move against a static background? Of course this goes right to the roots of Einstein's theory of relativity... that the motion of any object is relative to other objects, which in turn are in motion. And so it is with time. Time One needs Time Two in order for it to be perceived to flow. In turn Time Two needs Time Three. Clearly this quickly turns into an infinite regress.

Dunne made his model even more complex by arguing that each "time" needs an observer in order for the time flow to be perceived. For Dunne the role of an "observer" was essential because, for him, without an observer nothing can be perceived:

Dunne suggested that in order for us to appreciate that time "flows" there has to be a way that this time can be measured. All measuring processes involve gauging one thing against another. We use a ruler to measure length or a set of scales to measure weight. Flow is similarly measured by comparing it against a static object. For example, a river's flow is measured as its relative speed in relation to a static riverbank. If there was no riverbank, then we would have no way of even knowing that the river was flowing at all. But time is different. We can only measure time's flow by using time itself. We cannot quantify the duration of a minute except by measuring it against the flow of a second hand against a clock face or by the changes on a digital readout. But a moment's reflection will have us realise that duration and time are the same thing.

In order to convey how any form of movement needs a frame of reference to define the movement Dunne used an analogy that I am sure many have experienced:

> We are [...] seated in the same carriage [...] standing at a railway station. Looking from the windows on the side remote from the platform, we perceive another train at rest upon the rails. As we watch it a whistle blows, and we become aware that our train is beginning to pull out. Faster and faster it goes; the windows of the opposite train are running swiftly across the field of view; but... a doubt arises... we miss the accustomed vibration of our vehicle. We glance towards the platform windows, and discover, with something of a shock, that our carriage is still stationary. It is the other train which is moving.[34]

This is what Dunne observed and he suggested that there must be a second time, a "Time Two", by which we measure time by. And, by implication, a third form of time by which the second time is measured. Clearly this implies an infinite regress but this did not concern Dunne. He also suggested that within each time is an "observer" that observes this duration. From this he extrapolated that during sleep our everyday observer (whom he called *Observer One*) can access the awareness of *Observer Two* whose perceptual framework uses Time Two as its source. In this regard *Observer Two*'s time perception is much broader. In other words, the 'present' for *Observer Two* may stretch out for a few days, or even weeks. As such this element of ourselves is aware of the contents of our immediate future. This is how he explained dream precognitions. Our dreams contain elements of our own future and, under certain circumstances, we can recall these precognitive elements and in doing so we "precognise" the future. However, what is more usual is that we only recognise a dreamed future event as we start to encounter it in waking life. We have a sudden recognition and have a dim recollection that this moment has been experienced before. Is this an explanation of the sensation popularly known as Déjà vu?

Priestley had long been looking for a logical and mathematical explanation of such anomalous perceptions and here it was. Jack mentally noted the ideas of Dunne and, as we shall discover, Dunne's "serialism" was to feature in many of Priestley's subsequent plays and novels.

Later, in 1929, *Benighted* was published. Although this play has no overt Dunne references, probably because it had already been effectively written by the time Jack encountered Dunne's ideas for the first time, it does contain subtle references to Priestley's fascination with the Vedanta idea of us all being part of a greater "overmind". In this novel three friends, married couple Philip and Margaret Waverton and Roger Penderel, are caught in a vicious storm while travelling in Wales. They are forced to take shelter in an isolated old house owned by the mysterious Horace Femm and his sister, Rebecca. As the weather conditions deteriorate they are joined by another pair of "benighted" travellers, Sir William Porterhouse and his young mistress, Gladys Du Cane. Initially the Femms will not allow the group to stay but eventually give in to their pleadings. They discover that upstairs is another member of the family, Sir Roderick, who is bedridden. There is also a huge manservant, Morgan, who wanders round the house like Frankenstein's monster. We later discover that there is another brother, Saul Femm, who is mad and has been locked up in a room at the top of the house.

It is easy to look back on this novel and see it as a cliché-ridden variation of the 'dark house' theme but it is more complex than that. There is a degree of psychological depth unusual for the period.

John Atkins speculates that JBP felt that the sense of the "magical" (technically 'numinescence') that is perceived in everyday "reality" has a link with our dream states. He references *Benighted* as an example. In one section of the novel Roger Penderel suggests that all his associates may be part of a dream of Horace Femm. Philip Waverton proposes that the opposite was possibly true and that his associates were dreaming Femm and his family. In an interesting observation Margaret Waverton reminds Roger and Philip that in *Through the Looking Glass* Alice was informed that she was simply part of one of the king's dreams.

The novel was later turned into a Hollywood movie, *The Old Dark House*, directed by James Whale and starring Boris Karloff. In an amusing comment in *Margin Released* Priestley describes how, many years later, he caught sight of a poster for the film outside a cinema in the Kasbah of Algiers. Many years later, in the early 1960s, Charles Addams, creator of the *Addams Family* franchise, based the butler Lurch on Morgan. Of even greater interest to the modern reader may be the fact that it was on watching a TV screening of the movie that unemployed actor Richard O'Brien was motivated to write the script that became the hugely successful movie *The Rocky Horror Picture Show*. This shows how Priestley may be considered to be an irrelevant writer of dated plays but he was an influence on one of the most culturally influential movies of all time.[35]

His next novel was a collaboration with another writer, Hugh Walpole. The advance Jack received for what was to become *Farthing Hall* allowed him the financial freedom to focus on his own work. A large picaresque novel entitled *The Good Companions*. This novel was to make his name and create riches beyond his wildest dreams.

Published in 1929 *The Good Companions* resonated hugely with the book-buying public. This was a bad time to be publishing a novel. It was the year of the Wall Street Crash and the start of the

Great Depression. Money was in short supply. But people wanted an escape, and this 600-page novel supplied it. After a very slow start the demand rocketed. Fleets of vans were hired to get the newly printed copies to the bookshops. It proved to be similarly popular in America. By Christmas of 1929 it was selling 2,000 copies a week. Within three years it had sold over a quarter of a million copies. Priestley was a success.

Although in no way can this be considered a 'time-related' novel, *The Good Companions* does contain a vaguely circular plot. The novel opens with the narrator swooping the reader down from the high Pennine Hills into the town of Bruddersford (a thinly disguised Bradford) and then focuses in on a crowd leaving a football ground. In a description that is cinemato-graphic in its depiction the narrator zooms in on one cloth cap, one a slightly different colour from the others. Underneath this cap is a person who will, in due course, become one of the *Good Companions*. Priestley's introduction is a classic movie opener – the sweeping down from on high to alight in one location accom-panied by a voice-over. For example, the film *American Beauty* does something similar. But remember, Priestley was writing this opening in the late 1920s when cinema was still in its infancy. Such a sweeping aerial vista would have been virtually impos-sible with aviation having not opened up to mass consumerism. It is as if Priestley's subconscious had precognised the cinematic techniques of the late 20th century. This is something I shall return to later. The novel ends with a crowd leaving a football match and within this crowd is the same character, but this time he is leaving the area to move to a new life in Canada. The narrator then reverses the opening scene by travelling away from Bruddersford and in a widening vista comments on the high Pennine Hills. The ending is a reverse image of the opening, as if time is reeling backwards. As John Braine observes in his biography of Priestley, "the journey has gone full circle."[36]

His follow-up novel, *Angel Pavement*, published in 1930, was a much bleaker affair but still contained hidden references to time. This suggests that JBP was intrigued by time as a novelistic device many years before the 'time plays' took his interest. For example, in the novel there is a moment of frozen time whereby the characters fall out of consensual time into a timeless psychological time. This takes place after a commercial traveller has visited the premises of Twigg & Dersingham's Angel Pavement offices in the City of London. A few moments before the firm's senior sales representative, Mr Goath, had announced how bad business was. The desperation of the commercial traveller leads the members of the firm to consider how financially damaging the future could be. Priestley describes how the office atmosphere changes and each individual sinks into a personal time-space:

> The faces of the three men, Mr Smeeth's grey oval, Goath's purple pulp, Turgis's tarnished youth, sank with the room, were half frozen into immobility, and seemed for a moment or two to be vacant, staring into nothing. Miss Matfield, who had risen from her table, saw it all for one queer second tangled with a whole jumble of deathly images; they were all under a spell, powerless to stir while sky rained soot, dust poured from every crevice, and cobwebs about them.[37]

This spell is broken when the typist, Miss Matfield, knocks over a box of paper clips. One can imagine how this incident would be depicted in a movie or stage version of the novel. Each person would freeze in time, immobile and staring into space. This is again an example of how Priestley writes in a profoundly cinematographic style at a time when such techniques were unknown.

The success of *The Good Companions* had led to a theatre production of the play, directed by Edward Knoblock, which opened at His Majesty's Theatre in London on the 14th of May

1931. The production ran for nine months and was very successful. Up until this point in his life Jack had been an avid theatregoer. From 1911 onwards he had regularly attended the Theatre Royal in Bradford and had seen many productions. He had a similar love for the music-hall, themes of which were to subsequently appear in his own plays. He was therefore delighted to work with Knoblock on the dramatization of the novel. In his 1957 book *The Art of the Dramatist* he describes how he insisted that the final scene, where Oakroyd boards the liner to take him to Canada, should be played out without dialogue. Knoblock did not agree and neither did the producer, Julian Wylie. But Priestley stuck to his guns and the subsequent audience reaction convinced Jack that he had:

An instinct, an insight, an intuition, worth more than years of experience and a knowledge of all the technical tricks.[38]

His inner self had spoken. He was going to try his hand at being a playwright.

## Chapter Three

# Before The Time Plays – 1930–1937

*Dangerous Corner*, Priestley's first play, was written in a week. The process of writing a play is very different to that of a novel but the speed in which Jack was able to write narrative showed that he was an instinctive playwright. Whereas a novel can take the writer's imagination anywhere in time and space, a play must follow a logical progression and each act needs to happen in 'real time'. There is also the issue of inner-narratives. In a novel the author can allow the reader access to the thoughts and motivations of the characters. This cannot be done on stage. All motivations and emotions must be conveyed by words, actions or by the skills of the actor. A novel can be read at various sittings, it can be put down and started again. If the plot becomes confused the reader can always go back and reread a section for clarification. A play does not allow such luxuries. It is watched over a finite period of time over a series of acts, usually no more than three. To create such a narrative flow, the playwright needs to write with speed and fluency allowing the plot to develop directly through the words and actions of the actors. His biographer and fellow playwright John Braine described this process to be like "riding on the Wall of Death or, more prosaically, whirling a bucket of water round one's head without spilling a drop."[39] This was an ideal writing process for Priestley for whom ideas simply flowed as if from another source outside of himself. He could visualise a scene and would simply allow the characters to converse. He would then write down what they said. In his later writings he stated that this skill was evidence of another personality buried deep within his subconscious, a second-self that had access to a far wider well of information.

He had made a considerable amount of money from *The Good*

*Companions* and *Angel Pavement* and decided to use some of this money to set up his own theatre production company. This decision, made so early on in his theatrical career, allowed him a considerable amount of freedom with regards to experimentation and innovation. It also was a brave decision because the world of the theatre in the early 1930s was not financially secure. Plays cost a great deal of money to stage and bad reviews or poor audience numbers could bring about considerable losses.

*Dangerous Corner* was to be produced by Tyrone Guthrie with a cast that included Flora Robson and A.V. Cookman. This proved to be a sound decision. The actors, all very experienced, had, within a week, learned all the lines and within two weeks the play was ready for presentation. This was a full week before the first performance so the cast was given a few days off before the dress rehearsal the night before the play opened.

The play begins in darkness with the sound of a muffled gunshot and a scream. The stage is illuminated and we are presented with a group of four women listening to a radio play. The gunshot and the scream were the final sequence of the broadcast. The play was entitled *Sleeping Dogs* and it will soon become clear to the audience that letting things lie is the sensible approach to life. Right at the start Priestley is playing games with what is reality and what is fiction. We have a small audience of four listening to a play while being watched by a greater audience who exist in the 'real world'. The women draw parallels between the radio play and the suicide the year before of a person called Martin Caplan. We discover that Caplan was Freda's brother-in-law and that there seems to be a great deal of sensitivity regarding the circumstances of Martin's death. The women's discussion is curtailed by the entry of three men, all in dinner suits.

We quickly discover the identities of all seven characters; Robert Caplan, a thirty-something managing director of a publishing company and brother to the deceased Martin Caplan,

Robert's wife Freda, Gordon Whitehouse and Charles Stanton, partners in the company, Betty Whitehouse, an excitable young woman in her early twenties, Olwen Peel, an executive in the company. Completing the ensemble is one of their authors, Maud Mockridge.

This opening sequence has all the hallmarks of a seemingly straightforward Country House whodunit with all the standard devices of the genre. Critic John Atkins points out that this is one of Priestley's "unveiling plays" whereby as the play develops more and more is discovered regarding the circumstances leading up to a series of exposures whereby the veneer of middle-class respectability is scraped away and unpleasant truths are uncovered. The "sleeping dogs" are not allowed to lie. As an aside, the use of a gunshot in the opening sequence of such a mystery play has become a cliché in itself, but it seems that this may have been the first time such a device was used.[40]

To avoid the subject of Martin's demise, the women discuss the play they have just listened to. Olwen realises that the title, the "sleeping dog", suggests that some things should not be disturbed. Stanton agrees, suggesting that being hell-bent on finding the truth is as dangerous as "skidding round a corner at sixty." Freda adds that life itself has many "dangerous corners." To lighten the mood Gordon attempts to tune the radio to a station playing dance music. He finds that it is not working. Changing the subject again Freda picks up a musical cigarette box and, on opening it, offers Olwen a cigarette. The room is filled with a thin, wispy tune. The tune stops Olwen in her tracks. She recognises that it belonged to Martin. This recognition, picked up by the others, brings about a sequence of revelations and admissions. The seemingly innocuous musical box has created its own "dangerous corner", and once turned there is no going back for any of the characters.

As the layers are worn away by each revelation the seemingly cosy world of the opening sequence is seen for what it is, a sham.

Robert is particularly affected being the one character for whom the "lying dogs" are particularly biting. In despair he goes into his room leaving Freda alone. She realises that he has a revolver in there. Off stage we hear a muffled gunshot and Freda screams. The stage blacks out. Immediately the lights come on again and the women are all sitting round the radio. The first act begins again.

Here we have Priestley addressing with our concept of what is real. We have a group of fictional characters on stage listening to a fictional murder story that mirrors what we have just witnessed in the previous storyline. This time the murdered man is very much alive. What we previously witnessed was a possible future, or maybe simply a dream of one of the characters. We have a circularity of time or a repeat of time but with crucial changes. For example, the events of this new version of Act I run quicker. This is because Priestley is manipulating our memory of the first act. We remember only sections of the original dialogue, specifically because we had not, at the time of first hearing, expected to hear it again. Priestley wishes to speed up this revisit and does so by omitting sections of the original script. In this way he makes time seemingly speed up second time round. The play swiftly gets back to the original "dangerous corner" involving the cigarette box. This time Gordon makes the radio work and, distracted by the music, Freda is distracted from noticing Olwen's recognition. The corner is successfully negotiated and the sleeping dogs remain undisturbed in their slumbers.

The play had its first London performance on Saturday 17 May 1932 at the Lyric Theatre. The audience reaction was not recorded but it is clear from the reviews that appeared in the press the following day that the theatre critics were far from impressed. One newspaper stated, "This is Mr. Priestley's first play and we don't mind if it is also his last."[41] This negativity worried all involved in the play and by the following Saturday, and after only five performances, Jack was considering closing it down. It was the second swathe of reviews that saved it. Ivor Brown of the *Observer* was complimentary and James Agate of the *Sunday Times* positively effusive:

> If this is not a brilliant device I do not grasp the meaning of either word, and if the plot is not a piece of sustained ingenuity of the highest technical accomplishment, I am not an impercipient donkey but an ass who has perceived too much.[42]

It was the theme of circularity that both fascinated and irritated the critics. It is important to note that much is made of the 'eternal return' elements of James Joyce's *Finnegans Wake* and, to a lesser extent, a similar device in Flann O'Brien's *The Third Policeman* but both these novels appeared in the late 1930s. In 1895 Robert Louis Stevenson had used a similar device in *The Song of the Morrow* and, a few years later, C.H. Hinton had a story *An Unfinished Communication* in the second book of his 1898 anthology *Scientific Romances*. But these were novels, not plays.

In a later review Victor Cookman of the *Times* was to echo this fascination by stating that *Dangerous Corner* was "probably the most ingenious play ever written."[43] Interestingly Jack himself did not share this enthusiasm, writing in 1948 that the play was no more than an "ingenious box of tricks."[44]

Such was the success of *Dangerous Corner* that it moved across the Atlantic and was first produced by Harry Moses at the Empire Theatre in New York. It was directed by Elsa Lazareff and opened on 27 October 1932. For this version Jack provided an alternative ending whereby Freda describes that she had seen a ghostly white owl visit the garden at night. Here we have evidence that although he may have considered the play to be simply a "box of tricks" Jack, in this rewriting, wished to introduce an element of the 'magical' and the mysterious. Was this harping back to his fascination with the writings of such authors as Lord Dunsany? As we have already discovered, back in 1922 Priestley's very first collection of short stories, *Brief Diversions*, contained elements of the uncanny. For example, in the story *The Uninvited Guest* a party is disturbed by the appearance of the personification of Death. In the American version of *Dangerous Corner*, we have an owl as a symbol of Robert's dead brother Martin. We shall also discover later that Priestley used offstage 'locations' such as a rose garden to symbolise the border between everyday reality and another reality that hides itself but can be perceived at certain times and by certain attuned individuals.

It is intriguing as to why this American version of *Dangerous Corner* was not, as far as I can discover, ever performed in Britain during Priestley's life. On 7 September 2001, a production directed by Laurie Sansom opened at the West Yorkshire Playhouse's small Courtyard Theatre in Leeds. Sansom had decided to use a hybrid text from both the American and British versions. The performance ended with the appearance of a huge white bird that appeared to fly towards the audience.[45] The impact of this was powerful, stimulating the *Independent*'s theatre critic Rhoda Koenig to write that the emotional impact "as beautiful as it is terrifying symbolises both avenging truth and Robert's dead brother, whose contempt of the others is unearthed by the cascade of confessions".[46]

The idea of a circularity of time, that we have already lived this moment before, is implied in *Dangerous Corner* in that at the end of the play the characters are all catapulted back to the start of the play with the potential of avoiding the outcomes of the previous version. This suggests that although time may be circular it does not have to repeat itself. This describes a spiral rather than a circle. That he used a circularity device in *Dangerous Corner* is clear, but this idea of eternal recurrence is also subtly referenced in the novel he was writing at the same time, *Faraway*.

On the surface the novel is a simple adventure story set in the

South Pacific with a strong ecological theme. But a series of small, and barely commented upon, uncanny incidents thread through it as a subliminal theme.

The first incident is peculiarly incongruous in that it lends nothing to the storyline and seems to have simply been dropped in for no reason. While planning the trip the central character, William Dursley, in discussion with the Commander, feels that he was reliving the circumstances that he had experienced in a dream:

> Perhaps he had talked to the Commander and listened to Mr Ramsbottom many a time before. And the island itself, was that really new? Had there not been an island before, nothing solidly geographical, of course, not a place you could recognize perhaps, only a shadow on a veil and seas breaking in and yet an island? Had they been there already?[47]

The sensation continues with William having a distinct image of "the three of them sitting on a rock, very hard, hot, jagged, talking earnestly." Priestley is keen to have his reader notice this by italicizing this phrase. What is peculiar is that later in the novel he has William's precognitive déjà experience come to pass but chooses not to remind the reader of this. He simply lets it pass by as if he wants only the attentive reader to pick up the nuance. It may be that at this stage in his career he was subtly including his own life experiences in his novel as a form of personal catharsis, caring little if his readers pick up on them or not.

I am surprised that this features in none of the references to the déjà experience in literature. This is again an example of how Jack's ideas are simply ignored whereas other writers gain the recognition of being revolutionary and of profound depth. For example, here is a much cited, and uncannily similar, section from Joseph Hiller's *Catch-22*:

For a few precarious seconds, the chaplain tingled with a weird, occult sensation of having experienced the identical situation before in some prior time or existence. He endeavored to trap and nourish the impression in order to predict, and perhaps even control, what incident would occur next, but the afflatus melted away unproductively, as he had known beforehand it would.[48]

This theme of a different sort of time that underlies our everyday experience occurs a few times throughout the novel. On each occasion it is used more as a scene-setting device than a narrative device. For example, while watching some tropical fish in a tropical lagoon William has a strong feeling of dislocation and the scene creates such strong images that later in his life they would spontaneously reoccur and instantaneously return him to the lagoon. Is this simply a powerful memory or is it an actual time slip where, for a split second, a past experience can be relived in the present?

The novel also has a strange section where another character, the down to earth and very practical Ramsbottom, encounters a Polynesian shaman who places him in a trance state. In this powerful dream Ramsbottom encounters an old girlfriend and they converse. Priestley describes how this dream is perceived by Ramsbottom as a state of super-reality in which he and his historical sweetheart have been translocated. Priestley describes this recognition of a reality behind this reality as being accompanied by a little "shiver."

This "shiver" effect intrigues John Atkins in his excellent book *J.B. Priestley: The Last of the Sages*:

It is the "shiver" that fascinates. It is mentioned by JBP on several other occasions – just as though everything is so delicately poised (perhaps the consciousness for one moment peering across the boundary?) that a mere shiver, a tiny breath of air, will upset the balance.[49]

Atkins then goes on to describe how back in 1927 Priestley had alluded to this feeling of disassociation in an essay entitled *Dissolution in Haymarket* published in his collection *Open House*. In this Priestley describes how, as he travels along Haymarket on a bus, he experienced a change of mood and atmosphere. The positive, happy environment is suddenly transformed into something brooding and threatening:

> The whole cheerful pageant of the street immediately crumpled and collapsed, with all its wavering pattern of light and shade, its heartening sights and sounds, its warm humanity, its suggestion of permanence, and I was left shivering in the middle of a tragedy.[50]

His use of the word "dissolution" is very well chosen. It is the dissolving or disintegration of something into something else. It is the pulling back of the veil to reveal what is hidden beneath. Priestley was later to discuss his fascination with the "magical". In my opinion this fascination was engendered by his own experiences. Although it would be many years before he was to read Russian philosopher Peter Ouspensky's *New Model of the Universe* the following passage describes quite precisely Priestley's "shiver" effect and the perception he has his character Dursley experience in *Faraway*. Ouspensky was on board a ship sailing across the Sea of Marmara in 1908 when he was overtaken by a "shiver". He felt as if he had:

> Entered into the waves, and with them rushed with a howl at the ship. And in that instant I became all. The waves – they were myself: the far violet mountains, the wind, the clouds hurrying from the north, the great steamship, heeling and rushing irresistibly forward – all were myself.[51]

This 'shiver' can also be described as an 'aura' in that both are created by a sudden cooling of the atmosphere similar to that brought about by a cool breeze on a warm summer's day. The word 'aura' has its roots in Greek and means exactly this, a 'breeze'. But aura is also associated with the altered states of consciousness brought about by migraine attacks and epilepsy. I am not for one minute suggesting that Jack was a migraineur or an epileptic but simply that such sensations can be associated with anomalous perceptions.

The following year, 1933, another work of fiction, *Albert Goes Through*, was published. This is a very peculiar little novel that is not mentioned by any of Priestley's major biographers. It is clearly influenced by the idea that we exist in one world but there are others that we can visit in our imagination. In this case Albert Limpley, a London clerk, is infatuated with the movies, still something of a novelty at the time. Albert has a high fever but he is keen to attend the premiere of a new movie starring his favourite movie actress, Felicity Storm. His kindly landlady offers to help and gives him some strong medication. Albert makes his way to the theatre but on arrival he blacks out and enters a state of delirium.

In a series of vivid dreams involving standard movie cliché environments, Albert is set the task of saving Felicity Storm from an ever-growing number of bad guys. What starts as an espionage adventure set during the Russian Revolution dissolves into the Wild West and then to contemporary Chicago replete with gangsters of various types. In each scene Albert notes the presence of a young woman, who seems familiar to him, in the background. His hallucinatory travels end in a musical farce set in a British country estate. In each environment he becomes the hero that has to save the permanently endangered Felicity Storm. Sadly, as adventure piles upon adventure he becomes disillusioned with Felicity and, in an ending in which all the 'bad guys' surround him he cries out, "You're not real Felicity Storm, you're just a silly fake."[52] As the villains attack him he wakes up in the office of the cinema manager.

On awaking he realises that the young woman in the background is a work associate and he decides that a real woman is far more interesting than any screen idol. He decides to ask her out on a date and the novel ends with them being engaged.

This is an often used plot line; for example, a few years earlier, in 1924, Buster Keaton played the role of a frustrated young man who, in a dream state, enters a movie screen (*Sherlock Jr.*). What makes Priestley's forgotten novel interesting is that there is a magical element in which the dreamer creates the dreamed, including the people who populate that dream. Here the dream ends when Albert realises that Felicity is nothing more than a creation of his own delirium.

Six years later he was to follow up on this idea of how we create fictional characters and in some way give them life in Act III of *Johnson Over Jordan* where Don Quixote explains that he is fading away because people no longer read Cervantes' novel and as less and less readers visualise him in their imaginations so his existence breaks down.

In May 1933 Priestley moved the family to the village of Godshill on the Isle of Wight. The success of his novels, particularly *The Good Companions*, had made him a very wealthy man and he was keen for Jane and the girls to have a taste of the country life. Although he was to term it his "country cottage", the house he actually bought, Billingham, was a seventeenth century manor house standing in fifteen acres of grounds. As he still needed a base in London he continued to own the house in Highgate. In effect this meant that the family divided their time between the two locations.

In the autumn of 1933 Jack embarked upon a journey across England. This resulted in his book *English Journey*. In the opinion of many this is his best non-fiction book in that it is, if anything, a political and sociological work that reflects Priestley's

socialism. Here we have none of his later speculations and observations on metaphysics and time. The book is simply a series of
observations as regards the state of English society in the early
1930s.

In the autumn of 1934 Priestley's new play, *Eden End*, opened
at the Duchess Theatre in London. This was one of the plays
which, in Priestley's opinion, wrote itself. He wrote it quickly and
easily, completing it on one perfect summer's evening with "the
tender light of the dying day on my final page."[53] Here we have,
yet again, Jack's fascination with the magic atmosphere of high
summer evenings and how creativity is evidence of something
greater within the mind of the creator. It is clear that *Eden End*
was Jack's attempt to write a play in the tradition of the great
Russian writer Chekhov. It is even reasonable to conclude that his
bucolic isolation at Billingham mirrored Chekhov in his estate on
old Russia. But there is another theme in *Eden End* which is
understated but nevertheless of importance: the idea of passing
time and how time changes us. It is also of significance that, yet
again, Priestley has the play take place in the early autumn of
1912. This year comes up again and again in his work and clearly
was of significance to him. Maybe it was a looking back over time
to a period of innocence before the carnage of the Great War. But
it is another theme that was to appear in many of his later plays:
the idea that we are more than simply a singular consciousness
inhabiting a mortal body. In a very subtle way Jack has his
character Dr Kirby suggest that we all have a deeper level of
consciousness that is detached from our everyday life:

Have you noticed – or are you too young yet – how one part
of us doesn't seem to be responsible for your own character
and simply suffers because we have that character? You see
yourself being yourself, behaving in the old familiar way, and
though you may pay and suffer, the real you, the one that
watches, doesn't seem to be responsible.[54]

We shall discover later that this concept of "the real you" will resurface in another of Priestley's plays, and in one particular monologue the location of this "real you" will be explained.

At the end of the play the family's nurse, Sarah, is saying goodbye to Stella, a young woman that she has looked after as would a mother. Sarah is old and senses that this may be the last time that they will meet. She says, "I am an old woman now, a'most past my time. Happen I shan't see you again." Stella responds that, "Yes, you will, you must," to which the old lady replies, "Oh, I'll see you sometime. There is a better place than this, love."[55]

This very moving final sequence had a profound effect on the audiences. Many years later, in his biography of Priestley, playwright John Braine was moved to comment why this exchange had such emotional power:

Why do these last words of Sarah move us so much? ... Because she is not frightened of death and so rises above being merely an ageing body, rises above the materialist definition of a human being – so much water, a handful or so of chemicals, a machine made of quickly perishable materials, an electric light bulb which will burn itself out. There will be a better place, and those who know how to love will find it.[56]

As Braine so eloquently states, for Jack death is not the end but the start of another adventure. This is not the usual Christian viewpoint of life after death but something far more profound: the idea of survival in another form of existence. As we shall discover these ideas, based to an extent upon Priestley's interest in Eastern philosophies such as Vedanta, were to be placed in stark focus by his discovery of another philosophy, that of Peter Ouspensky.

*Eden End* was a reasonable success, running for over 150 performances before being picked up by small theatre companies across the country. Buoyed with this success Jack agreed, against his better judgement, to personally supervise a New York production. Jane's sister Bubbles died in June 1935 followed in August by his stepmother, Amy. These sad events made Priestley decide that the family should accompany him over to America. In autumn 1935 Jack sailed to New York on the liner *Aquitania* while Jane and the six children travelled via the Panama Canal to the West Coast. The plan was that they would make their way to Phantom Ranch in Arizona and Jack would join them as winter set in. As Priestley suspected, the New York audiences and critics did not take to *Eden End* and its short run was a total failure. This hit Priestley hard, both financially and emotionally. It was an emotionally frail Jack Priestley who made his way across America to meet up with his family at a rented ranch in Arizona.

In his autobiographical book *Midnight on the Desert* (1937) Priestley describes how it was he first encountered the writings of Ouspensky. He had returned to America in the autumn of 1935, specifically to supervise the Broadway production of *Eden End*. Sadly, although there had been a great deal of enthusiasm for the play from Americans based in London the play simply was of no interest to American audiences. Resigned to the failure Priestley returned to his ranch in Arizona where his wife and family were spending the winter having travelled ahead of him.

During this time, he made frequent visits to Hollywood to work on various screenplays. These were happy days where he spent time playing tennis and enjoying fascinating dinner parties with the likes of Charlie Chaplin and the Marx Brothers. His problem now was that he really was unsure as to what direction to take his future plays. Clearly the failure of *Eden End* suggested that a radical rethink of his approach was needed. As we have already discovered, Priestley believed that there were other forces at work in his life and, in times of need, these forces would point him in the right direction. And this is exactly what happened one warm evening in Santa Barbara.

When in Los Angeles his base was the Biltmore Hotel at Montecito Beach, just outside Santa Barbara. He needed to find a place to eat so he decided to walk into the centre of Santa Barbara. He soon came across a section containing a selection of old Mexican buildings. As well as an old restaurant called "El Paseo" he discovered a tiny bookshop run by an American who amusingly informed Jack that he wanted to retire to the Cotswolds. In this bookshop something that Jack knew well took place, something he later described as a "familiar minor miracle". By this he was acknowledging that many times in his life he felt that he was being guided to discover things of importance to him. On this occasion he begins by dismissing such sensations only to acknowledge their existence. He writes:

> I am not a man of destiny; I follow no star; no angelic voices guide me; I live, like the majority, in an earthly muddle. Except in one small particular. If I begin thinking about a book that I do not possess, a book that is out of print or not easily accessible, that book will turn up, often in a most unlikely place. This has happened to me over and over again; and if it is by Chance then Chance is bookish and biased in my favour.[57]

He goes on to describe how for some weeks before going to Santa Barbara he had been wanting to find a copy of Ouspensky's *A New Model of the Universe*. Jack had seen many references to this book but, at that stage, knew little about it. As far as he was aware this book had never been published in England. In less than two minutes in this bookshop near "El Paseo" he had spotted a copy of this book. It was a solitary copy and, according to the owner, had been there many years. He had in no way been looking for this book, in such a small bookshop. JBP makes the point that this was an unusual book to be found in stock in such a small shop. If it had been purchased in order to sell on to some "rich old theosophy ladies", as he describes it, then it would have been long sold. But it was there, seemingly waiting for the illustrious English playwright to pick it up.

In his *A New Model of the Universe* Ouspensky proposed that we live our own life again and in doing so we can, with great effort, realise that our actions will have outcomes. This suggests an extreme solipsism whereby other people are simply players in a huge drama that evolves from actions made by the "observer" consciousness. However, what Ouspensky fails to explain is the mechanism by which this 'remembering' works. If each of us will, after death, be reincarnated into the past to live our lives again what can be the agent of change? If we are ignorant of the fact that we are living our life again how can we possibly change anything? All the other 'minds' that we encounter will blindly follow the same plot as they did the last time. It is as if we are doomed to act a role in the same extended 'formation novel', or 'bildungsroman' as described in German literature. We are ignorant of the fact that this is a 'rerun' and as such we will react in the same way to the lines as they are fed to us by the other 'actors' in the drama. Ouspensky recognised how this would involve a genuine repetition of events as described by the stoics; a simple rerun of a life as unchanging as the storyline of a movie on a DVD. He described this life by using a Russian term called Byt. Ouspensky described this as a "deeply rooted, petrified, routine life." For Ouspensky this was the lot of the vast majority of humanity. They are simply trapped in an endless cycle of repetition.

Ouspensky believed that certain "advanced" human beings can break out of this mindless repetition. By a process that he never explains these people become aware of the fact that they are living their lives again, indeed not only this but they remember what happened last time. In this way they can correct any errors they made last time and follow that outcome to its conclusion. This theme of "self-awareness" is central to his 1905 novel *Kinemadrama* and its subsequent rewrite *The Strange Life of Ivan Osokin*.

Jack read *A New Model of the Universe* in, of all places, Death Valley. Many of us are heavily influenced by the circumstances and environment by which we first encounter certain ideas. I am sure that the desolation of Death Valley coloured Priestley's opinion of Ouspensky's work, particularly Ouspensky's concept of Recurrence. In 1972, in his book *Over the Long High Wall* he states quite categorically that he "rejects" Ouspensky's idea that we return to live our lives over and over again.[58] In this regard he applies his own version of J.W. Dunne's theory. He gives an example of the "afterlife" of a fictional character he calls John Smith. Smith's allotted life span was between 1890 and 1970. After his death (which, as Priestley had acknowledged earlier in the book, was to do with running out of time rather than a "death" as it is usually understood to be), Smith finds himself in Dunne's concept of "Time Two". This will "in one sense (be a) dream world in which every experience of those eighty years is represented and may be relived."[59] I am confused as to why this is not a simple reworking of Ouspensky's "recurrence". Priestley describes how this will be perceived in exactly the same way as it was the first time, for example the duration of time will pass in the same way. Later he again reiterates how Smith will perceive this existence:

Such a man would identify his Time 2 self completely with the 1890-1970 John Smith spread out along the fourth dimension, and would simply experience it all over again, and perhaps over and over again until his Time 2 self, developing at last some detachment, was heartily sick of it.[60]

Immediately after the above quotation Priestley does mention Ouspensky in a very oblique comment which to me makes no sense. Here we have Smith living his life over and over again. He explains that he used such a concept in his 1960s BBC Television play, *Anyone for Tennis?*,[61] a play we will return to later.

In this discussion he suggests that Smith may decide to relive specific episodes in his life:

> After more rides on the misery-go-round, perhaps he might begin to relive earlier episodes, wondering where he went wrong but unable at this stage to put anything right.[62]

I find his term "misery-go-round" to be particularly powerful. It is interesting to note that Smith is viewing his life from a location in Time 2. This suggests that his actual consciousness is his own "Observer 2" watching the life of "Observer 1". This suggests a form of bicamerality in which both "observers" are the same person but with Observer 2 being immortal. This is uncannily similar to my own model of the Daemon-Eidolon Dyad applied within a first-person video-game analogy.

Priestley then turns his attention to the wicked and evil people. He contends that they too experience their lives many times from a location in Time 2. In some process that he does not explain, these individuals in some way share the suffering of those to whom they inflicted pain and distress. How the "observer" can share such things must be explained in order to make this work. They will also live over and over again the futility of their final moments.[63]

In my opinion the best book explaining Priestley's early metaphysics is *Midnight on the Desert*. In this he discusses Dunne and in his explanation of Dunne's sometimes confusing prose clarifies matters:

> On this view of time the past has not vanished like a pricked bubble. To understand this dimension of things we move in Time as a blind man's finger moves over a piece of carving. Our consciousness travels along the track as we might travel

on a rail journey. Then the past is the station we have just left, and the Future is the station we are approaching. The past has not been destroyed any more than the last station was destroyed when the train left it. Just as the station is still there, with its porters and ticket inspectors and bookstall and its noise and bustle, so the Past still exists, not as a dim memory, but in all its colour and hum.[64]

His interest in the source of his creativity also continued throughout his life. In his essay *Outcries and Asides*, he wonders if some other intelligence takes over at these times. In *A Teasing Riddle* he seems to describe a hypnogogic sensation when a thought enters his mind whilst travelling on a train. He postulates that this thought is not his own. It is just as if "he had picked up some strange programme on his receiver".

While the ideas of Ouspensky were mingling with the dream theories of Dunne another great thinker was to impose his ideas on Jack: the great Swiss psychoanalyst Carl Gustav Jung. As we will discover, Jung and Priestley were to meet in 1946, but at this stage Priestley's interest was purely through the reading of Jung's work in English. Dunne's ideas of the precognitive aspects of dreams involved something that Priestley had great difficulty with, the idea of an infinite regress. This was something that Jack found impossible to accept. The idea of an endless number of observers existing in an endless number of times made no logical sense. For him the model could be made to work with two or, at most, three levels of time and observers. The extended temporal knowledge available to *Observer Two* or *Observer Three*, located in another, even higher level of time perception, could be accessed by *Observer One* – the everyday self – during dreams. And it is here that Jung's theories came to his rescue. Jung suggested that we all have two aspects to our consciousness; again the everyday self that exists in linear time, is born and dies in time, and another, universal consciousness that lives forever and exists outside of time. We are all simply mortal aspects of this greater consciousness, a consciousness that contains all the knowledge acquired by humanity over all time. As we shall discover, Jung called this the "Collective Unconscious".

Jung argued that we can access information from the collective unconscious in our dreams and during altered states of consciousness. Of course, this is simply a Westernisation of the Vedanta model that Jack had been aware of since his teenage years. But Jung added something new, something that really resonated with Priestley. Jung argued that the dream-information presents itself as symbols perceived in the altered state. Many of these symbols are *Archetypes*, as Jung termed them. Jung introduced this concept in 1919 joining the Greek words *'arche'* signifying beginning, cause, origin, and *'type'* to create a new word. These archetypes have to be interpreted and their meaning can be buried in symbolism. Priestley could see how Jung's Archetypes could be used to support Dunne's contention that precognitive dreams are symbolic and the actual information may not be that clear.

Priestley believed that Jung's model could be used to explain his own dreams, for example the mysterious "Berkshire Beasts" he described in his 1927 collection of essays, *Open House*. Indeed, some of his other dreams could be used as evidence that in dreams we can access the perceptions of others, even others who are long dead. Two years later, in 1939, Jack published the first of his series of biographical essays, *Rain Upon Godshill*. In this he describes a very peculiar "Big Dream", as he termed them, in which he seems to experience the dying moments of somebody else. In the dream he found himself in a foreign city viewing its scenes and locations through the eyes of what to him felt like a much younger and smaller man, possibly a student of some sort. This young man seemed to be involved in some form of political resistance to the authorities. He finds himself creeping into a military institution, presumably to discover some secrets that will be of use to his associates. To his horror he is discovered in the act and is approached by two soldiers. He tries to run away through an open doorway, but as he does so he is shot several times and is mortally wounded. He feels his life ebbing away:

> I will swear that that swaying progress from the office into the street and the blind weakness that washed over me there were somebody's last moments and that my consciousness had relived them.[65]

It is of significance that this dream took place sometime in 1938, soon after he discovered the theories of Jung. Jack interprets this as an event in the past. However, it could have been an event that was about to happen as the world was about to plunge into another awful world war.

Jung's concept of the "collective unconscious" really resonated with Jack. As a writer he knew that sometimes ideas and stories just seem to occur as if out of nowhere. In his 1947 collection of biographical essays, *Rain Upon Godshill*, Priestley wonders about the true nature of this "muse". He speculates that he may have accessed this when going under with a whiff of nitrous oxide at a dental appointment. He felt that he had "apperceived" into the "heart of all things."[66] He argues that this sensation does not come from the gas but that the gas releases a part of the mind that is buried very deep. He was convinced that he perceived a much higher level of reality. As he writes:

> The effect was of life but of some higher order of life, no more to be fully comprehended by me than the organization and performances of the Philharmonic Orchestra could be understood by a gnat.[67]

He also sensed this presence when he was working, particularly during states of high creativity. He states that at these times, "For a brief while we had been attached to a mind infinitely richer and greater than our own."

It is curious that he never makes reference to the writings of George Meredith in this regard. As we have already discovered, in 1926, Priestley wrote a biography of this enigmatic Victorian writer and was known to be a great admirer. Meredith had regularly discussed his belief that we are all part of a greater consciousness and that under certain psychological conditions we can sense this presence.

Jack also describes examples of seeming precognition, or information gained using extrasensory means. One such incident took place in January 1937 when he and his wife Jane visited Egypt on a holiday. Whilst there, Jane decided to visit a fortune teller. Most was rubbish but she was told that shortly someone very near to her would be in great danger and she would have to travel half across Europe to help this person, a female. On their return to England they discovered that their 17-year-old daughter, Angela, had taken ill in Italy. Jane rushed half across Europe to tend to her daughter who was convalescing in a nursing home in the small Italian town of Fiesole in the hills above Florence. The illness turned out to be measles. Jane subsequently sent for Jack and he travelled with various serums for his daughter.[68]

It was while staying in Fiesole that he experienced a very curious time slip and one that clearly supported his growing conviction that time, or at least our perception of time, was far more complex than our modern science would like us to believe. He describes it in this way:

I had gone up to my wife's room after lunch, to see if she was ready to go out, and found her sleeping. I sat in an arm-chair near the bed to wait, and then began to doze. I saw her open her eyes, smile slowly, rub her eyes, yawn and stretch and then sit up. I stared harder, and the room gave a little quiver, and then I was wide awake and saw that she was still sleeping. Within a minute or so, however, she opened her eyes, smiled slowly, rubbed her eyes, yawned and stretched, and then sat up, just as I had seen her do in my tiny dream a few moments before.[69]

Was it a short-term precognitive dream, an equivalent of a déjà vu? Or was it some form of time slip? What is particularly intriguing is how Jack describes how the "room gave a little quiver" as if reality was settling itself down. Was this an equivalent to the "shiver" effect that he described his character Ramsbottom encounters in Polynesia in his 1932 novel *Faraway*?

Experiences such as the ones described above can really shake one's faith in the modern materialist-reductionist model of science. I suspect that it was these experiences, all, sadly, anecdotal in nature and therefore inadmissible evidence as far as modern materialist-reductionist science is concerned, that stimulated Priestley to write the following condemnation of modern science's assured dismissal of such experiences later in 1937:

The hand is forging ahead by leaps and bounds while the brain is developing its faculties with exasperating slowness... We are cave-dwellers going for a joy-ride in a Chevrolet...[70]

For Priestley this summed up the 20th century dilemma. He saw humanity at that time at a huge crossroads with two negative options: scientific materialism or pseudo-mysticism linked with militant nationalism. His hope was that a third road could be found that opened up the human mind to its own inner potentials. He believed that the key to this other route was an understanding of the mysteries of time:

If we could find a key to fit this lock, we may open a door to a new universe. And we could do with a new universe.[71]

These are incredibly forward looking and, in many ways, quite revolutionary. These were not the words of a reactionary writer caught in an Edwardian way of thinking, but a radical intellectual pushing the boundaries of what it is to be human. For example, here Jack describes how in 'modern' science books the role of man, and consciousnesses, is belittled and marginalized in the vastness of the universe. He goes on to add that the belief that science may, one day, be able to reproduce life does not in any way make consciousness mechanistic. He writes that modern man can:

> now triumphantly announce that life is simply an affair of radio-electric cells, the difference between the amoeba and man is a simple arrangement of cells whereas man is a large and complicated one. But why this particular collection of radio-electric cells should have spent its life on this research, it does not explain. At what stage do the cells develop a sudden selfless passion for Truth?[72]

This short period in Italy, staying in a nursing home run by Irish and Australian nuns in the small village of Fiesole overlooking Florence, proved useful. It allowed Jack to spend more time wrestling with the plot of his Ouspensky-inspired play, *I Have Been Here Before*. This was not proving easy. In the end he rewrote the play five or six times before he was in any way happy with it. His problem was a simple one: how to dramatise complex ideas in a way that an audience can follow the ideas without losing the plot. The final draft was completed while he was staying in the nursing home.

When the play finally appeared on stage at the Royalty Theatre in the autumn of 1937 it was received with a degree of confusion from both critics and audiences alike. An example of this was what the economist and social reformer Beatrice Webb wrote in her diary after attending one of the early performances:

Went to Priestley's play *I Have Been Here Before* based upon Dunne's hypothesis that you can, if you have the gift, see forward as well as backward in time and (this seems self-contradictory) by knowledge alter the happening. The metaphysics of the play as expounded by the German philosopher were absurd but he and four other characters were clearly conceived and admirably acted.[73]

Although it was premiered after his subsequent play, *Time and the Conways*, I would like to discuss *I Have Been Here Before* first as my account is about how Jack's ideas developed rather than the dates his plays actually first appeared on stage.

*I Have Been Here Before* is set in a rural Yorkshire inn called the Black Bull. The proprietor Sam and his daughter Sally are awaiting the arrival of three female guests. An elderly East European gentleman arrives and asks if a room is available. He is somewhat confused when he is told that the inn is fully booked. He asks questions about who is booked in, specifically asking about the two couples. He is informed that there was only one couple staying that night and the other guests will be three ladies. This adds to his confusion and he leaves. The phone rings and Sam is told that the three have cancelled. Almost immediately the phone rings again and another booking is taken, this time from a Mr and Mrs Ormund. Sam and Sally are puzzled. Their guest list now reflects accurately what the mystery gentleman had stated earlier. A few moments later one of the other guests, a schoolteacher called Oliver Farrant, arrives back from his walk followed by the elderly East European looking a good deal more relieved now that his predicted guest list is accurate.

We discover that the mysterious East European is a German refugee, the Ouspensky-like scientist, Dr Görtler. He spends the rest of the play asking very leading questions of the other characters, specifically whether any of them have any sensations of déjà vu about their present circumstances. All agree that they do. In Act II, Görtler explains to the assembled cast the doctrine of the eternal return and how we may all live the same life over and over again. In echoes of Ouspensky's exposition on "Byt" people discussed earlier, Görtler explains:

> I said you might live the same life over and over again. But not all... some people, steadily developing, will exhaust possibilities of their circles of time and will finally swing out of them into new existences. Others – the criminals, madmen, suicides – live their lives in ever-darkening circles of their time. Fatality begins to haunt them. More and more of their lives are passed in the shadow of death. They gradually sink.[74]

Later Görtler explains how some people manage to escape from the circle by turning it into a spiral:

> We do not go round in a circle. That is an illusion. WE move along a spiral track. It is not quite the same journey from the cradle to the grave each time. Sometimes the differences are small, sometimes they are very important. We must set out each time on the same road but along that road we have a choice of adventures.[75]

Later that day, Oliver and Mrs Ormund go out for a walk leaving Dr Görtler and Mr Ormund alone together. Görtler then asks a series of searching questions of Ormund regarding his life. On their return from the walk Oliver and Mrs Ormund agree that they both have a huge sense of foreboding and that in some way this is related to any actions they may make in the near future. It is clear that both are very attracted to each other and at the end of scene two they embrace.

In Act III Farrant and Mrs Ormund announce that they are to leave together. It is here that Görtler explains why he planned to be in the inn that particular weekend. He points out that the overpowering feeling of déjà vu that was being experienced by all concerned was because they all had lived through these events before. He was there to ensure that events did not spiral out of control as they did last time when, on hearing the news of the affair, Mr Ormund commits suicide. This led to the closing of the school and the ruin of all their lives. Because of Görtler's intervention and discussions with Ormund in Act II the husband was mentally prepared for the news and his reaction is not as extreme. With Görtler's subtle help he has been able to come to terms with the circumstances and accept them. With the suicide averted the school does not close and a better outcome for all concerned takes place.

Curiously Priestley has Görtler claim that his future knowledge of events was received through a precognitive dream rather than simply an example of Ouspensky's "self-remembering". In many ways this reflects Dunne as much as it does Ouspensky.

The play was not well received and the ideas were simply too complex for the general theatre-going public of the late 1930s. In 2016 the Jermyn Street Theatre in London revived the play for a short run. Sadly, the critics again failed to appreciate the underlying themes, giving Anthony Biggs' production generally negative reviews. This is surprising as modern audiences, used to some of the more challenging movies coming out of Hollywood in recent years, should appreciate fully the "metaphysics" that Beatrice Webb thought to be so "absurd".

Priestley was keen to present Ouspensky's theories in a way that would be understood by an educated but not necessarily philosophically sophisticated audience. He uses his characters as ciphers and has the stage directions hint at a deeper meaning. For example, he has a series of time-related effects such as clocks ticking and chiming at crucial moments in the play.

In Act II Görtler attempts at an explanation as to how life

cycles work:

> Some people, steadily developing, will exhaust the possibil-
> ities of their circles of time and will finally swing out of them
> into new existences. Others – the criminals, madmen, suicides
> – live their lives in ever-darkening circles of their time.
> Fatality begins to haunt them. More and more of their lives are
> passed in the shadow of death. They gradually sink –[76]

Later, in the same act he explains that such lives are more like
spirals than circles:

> We do not go round in a circle. That is an illusion, just as the
> circling of the planets and stars is an illusion. We move in a
> spiral track. It is not quite the same journey from the cradle to
> the grave each time. Sometimes the differences are small,
> sometimes they are very important. We must set out each time
> on the same road but along that road we have a choice of
> adventures.[77]

Adding:

> What has happened before – many times perhaps – will
> probably happen again. That is why some people can
> prophesy what is to happen again. That is why some people
> can prophesy what is to happen. They do not see the future, as
> they think, but the past, what has happened before. But
> something new may happen. You may have brought your wife
> here for this holiday over and over again. She may have met
> Farrant here over and over again. But you and I have not
> talked here before. That is new. This may be one of those great
> moments of our lives.[78]

Earlier, in an exchange with Janet Ormund, Görtler responds to

Janet's question. If the future is preordained, and it must be if it has already been experienced by somebody else (in this case Görtler), she says to Görtler, we are not all marionettes: "We can make our own lives, can't we?"

> **Görtler:** Once we know, yes. It is knowledge alone that gives us freedom. I believe that the very grooves in which our lives run are created by our feeling, imagination and will. If we know and then make the effort, we can change our lives. We are not going round and round in hell. And we can help one another.
>
> **Janet:** How?
>
> **Görtler:** If I have more knowledge than you, then I can intervene, like a man who stops you on a journey to tell you that the road ahead is flooded. That was the further experiment I had hoped to make. To intervene.
>
> **Janet** (pointing to the notebook): Recurrence and Intervention.
>
> **Görtler:** Yes. That seemed possible too. I discovered some things I did not know before. Two of you, troubled by memories, were instantly attracted to one another. That I expected. But the third –
>
> **Janet:** You mean Walter?
>
> **Görtler:** Yes. The one I had not met before. I soon discovered that he was a man who felt he had a tragic destiny and was moving nearer and nearer to self-destruction –
>
> **Janet** (startled): Suicide?
>
> **Görtler:** Yes, that was why the great business collapsed, why so many were ruined, why everybody knew the story. You told me when you left him, your husband went into the garage and shot himself.[79]

In many ways the difficulties that Jack had with the play can be evidenced in its performance. The characters tend to talk in order to explain the ideas rather than having natural conversations. Priestley's keenness to convey the complexities of Ouspensky's spirals deflects from the human elements.

He had no such problems with the writing of his next play, *Time and the Conways*. This involved a direct contact with his muse and was written quickly and effectively and, curiously, ended up being performed before *I Have Been Here Before*. It is to this intriguing piece of theatre that we now turn our attention.

## Chapter Four

# Time and The Conways (1937)

On his arrival back from America and, after wrestling for months with the plot of *I Have Been Here Before*, Priestley had been experiencing a period of melancholy stimulated by the worsening European situation and events in his own life. In the depths of this he was:

Blown away by the arrival, like a flash, of what seemed to me a "glorious idea": to make Dunne's theory of time the basis for a new dramatic structure.[80]

Adding later

Suddenly I saw that there was a play in the relation between a fairly middle-class provincial family and the theory of time, the theory chiefly concerned with J.W. Dunne, over which I had been brooding for the past two years.[81]

Such was the fervour generated by this "glorious idea" Priestley wrote his new play, later to be entitled *Time and the Conways*, in just ten days. In his 2012 article *J.B. Priestley and the Theater of Time*, Jesse Matz does draw similarities between *Time and the Conways* and George S. Kaufman and Moss Hart's 1934 play *Merrily We Roll Along*, which has a central character, Richard Niles, going backwards in time from his empty if successful life in 1934 back to 1916 and the idealism of his graduation day. Priestley may or may not have been inspired by this play, if he was, he never acknowledged it, but, as Matz observes, the inclusion of Dunne's philosophy creates a far more effective structure.[82]

According to Vincent Brome, during this stay at Billingham on the Isle of Wight Priestley came to believe that he was under the guidance of another intelligence. He was later to write that his subconscious "shot up" solutions to some of the real technical problems that he encountered on writing *Time and the Conways*. These came as "fast as they were needed". He called this his "Old Fairy Godmother Inspiration". He then described how he tapped creative energy from a "much greater mind". This mind took over his everyday mind bringing about a temporary union that was "the sudden arrival of what seemed to be wonderful ideas".[83] John Braine was fascinated as to the differences in modes of creation between *I Have Been Here Before* and *Time and the Conways*, even though they were written one after the other. The former did not come easy to Priestley. There were at least three drafts, the final one being written in a nursing home in Italy. The latter flowed through him and on to the page. Braine suggests that whereas *I Have Been Here Before* was written by Priestley's conscious brain, *Time and the Conways* flowed directly from his subconscious in an act of spontaneous creation:

> To say that he wrote it is, of course, inaccurate. It would be better to say that he released it. If he hadn't released it, if there had been any question of conscious invention, he couldn't have written the second act first.[84]

The Dunne book in question is, of course, *An Experiment with Time*. Or is it? Something must have rekindled Jack's interest in the writings of J.W. Dunne. As we know he first encountered Dunne's work back in 1927 when Dunne's book was first published. But in none of his subsequent plays or novels can there be found any real Dunne influences. *Dangerous Corner* involves a circularity of time and *Faraway* discusses incidents of déjà vu but these are not really Dunne-related issues. Indeed, the major focus of *An Experiment with Time* was precognitive dreaming and this features nowhere in Priestley's fictional writings between 1927 and 1937.

In 1934 Dunne had published his third book (his actual first book, published in 1924, was on fly fishing). Entitled *The Serial Universe*, this expanded on the time-model first introduced in *An Experiment with Time*. This book was published in 1934. This discusses in much greater detail, and in more accessible text, Dunne's concept of "serial time" and the role of the "observers". I suspect that it was the publication of this book, or possibly a talk that Dunne gave on 22 April 1936 at the Foyles Literary Luncheon in central London, that rekindled Priestley's interest.

The Foyles Literary Luncheons were annual events and had started six years previously in October 1930 when Christina Foyle responded to her customers' requests to meet authors. At the time Foyles was recognised as being the largest bookshop in the world. That Dunne, an esoteric and somewhat eccentric writer, had been invited to speak was a reflection of his fame. That over 1,200 people attended was proof of this fame. It is reasonable to suggest that Priestley may have been a guest at this presentation. His advocacy of Dunne's work was well known and the two men had stayed in touch over the previous decade. Is it not possible, maybe even probable, that Dunne would have invited Jack to this event?

What may be of even greater significance is that in his later work, *The New Immortality* (1938), he includes a transcript of the full lecture, a lecture that was subsequently given to the cast of *Time and the Conways* in the summer of 1937 and in the autumn of that year a further audience of 1,500 watched him present it at the National Book Fair. Here we have a direct link between Dunne, Priestley, *Time and the Conways* and Dunne's lecture at Foyles. This is far more than simple coincidence.

Throughout the play there are references to Dunne's concept of "second level observers". As discussed below we have Kay's Act II 'time slip' where she observes the future, and we also have a series of clever theatrical devices that hints at perceptions outside of linear time. For example, in Act I there is the game of charades in which the youngest Conway sibling, Carol, dons, as Priestley described it in his stage directions, "an old shawl... some white hair – for the old lady." They discuss how odd such old-fashioned and ridiculous the clothes look. Later fashion and changes in clothing are the clue that the audience are given to the time slip into Act II. The audience will also be dressed in the fashions of their time and will no doubt be of the opinion that Edwardian fashion was similarly "ridiculous". During the game of charades, the children wonder if they could ever "see round the corner, into the future." This is exactly what the, at that point, unsuspecting audience do in Act II.

This idea of future knowledge influencing decisions made in the past is an intriguing idea and one that has become a standard plot device of many modern movies and TV series. If part of our subconscious already knows the outcomes of decisions we make now, then it is perfectly reasonable to conclude that that part of us will warn us and instigate evasive action. Furthermore, the element of us that views time from a position within the fifth dimension may also be able to act as a muse or a source of inspiration. Is this the guiding force active in Priestley's life, his "Old Fairy Godmother Inspiration" as he termed it?

Although it was written after *I Have Been Here Before* it was *Time and the Conways* that reached the stage first, having its opening on 26 August 1937 at the Duchess Theatre in London's West End. It was a huge success.

One can assume that this was because the plot can be followed as a simple story of the effect that time has on the characters. A major theme is the idea of how small incidents can shape the future and make it take one direction rather than another. It also focuses in on shattered dreams and unfulfilled potentials. These were themes that both critics and audiences alike could relate to. In an interesting theatrical device Priestley uses the three acts to convey a form of time slip. The first act takes place in the

Drawing Room of the large home of the Conway family. The year is 1919 and the family have come together to celebrate the birthday of one of the daughters, Kay. This sets the scene and introduces all the characters. They are a very happy, if somewhat privileged group who seem to have no worries in the world. The war has just finished and there is great optimism for the future. The first act ends with Kay reading a letter and going into some form of trance state. When the curtain opens for the second act the room is the same but a good deal more austere. We discover from a radio broadcast that the year is 1938, nineteen years on from the first act. Through the dialogue of the characters we discover that each one, with the possible exception of the eldest Conway, Alan, have become bitter and worn down by time. It is clear from her reactions that Kay is a little confused by some of the things that are said. It is as if she feels that she is an observer of the events even though she is part of them. As the act unfolds, resentments and tensions explode and the Conways are split apart by misery and grief. As Act II comes to an end Kay ends up alone on stage with her brother Alan, the only character who seems to be aware that time is playing tricks. He quotes an excerpt from William Blake's *Auguries of Innocence*:

Joy and woe are woven fine, A clothing for the soul divine.
Under every grief and pine, Runs a joy with silken twine.
Man was made for joy and woe; And when this we rightly know
Through the world we safely go.

Priestley was very careful in his choice of poem. Blake's *Auguries of Innocence* opens with the famous lines: "To see the world in a grain of sand and heaven in a wild flower, hold infinity in the palm of your hand, and eternity in an hour". In many ways the last few words of this opening section of the poem even more accurately reflect the philosophy presented in *Time and the*

*Conways*. Time is an illusion that we are fooled by. As Alan states later, "all our time will be us, the real you, the real me."

The discussion between Alan and Kay at the end of Act II is probably the most important section of the play and may even be one of the most important pieces of writing of Priestley's career. It contains a series of observations and comments by Alan that can be referenced back not just to the works of J.W. Dunne but also Priestley's time at Cambridge attending the lectures of the philosopher John McTaggart.

In his 1964 book *Man and Time* Priestley suggests that McTaggart was almost alone among the idealist philosophers in acknowledging that although one can deny the reality of time and therefore avoid the major philosophical problems it creates, one cannot avoid having to explain the appearance of time to consciousness.[85] In this regard Jack has Alan explain to Kay that in his opinion time is simply a form of dream:

> If it wasn't it would have to destroy everything – the whole universe – and then remake it again every tenth of a second. But time does not destroy anything. It merely moves us on – in this life – from one peep-hole to the next.[86]

Later adding:

> But the point is now, at this moment, or any moment, we're only a cross-section of our real selves. What really is the whole stretch of ourselves, all our time will be us – the real you, the real me. And then perhaps we'll find ourselves in another time, which is only another kind of dream.[87]

Alan's use of the words "the real you" may stimulate a recognition in the attentive reader. We have encountered this phrase in Priestley's earlier play *Eden End*, a play that is not generally associated with his 'time plays'. In my opinion it is more than coincidence that Jack used this term again. In *Eden End* the character Dr Kirby felt that part of him was an "observer" existing outside of space and time.

The second act comes to an end with Alan saying that he will get her a book that will explain how time really works. This is clearly a reference to Dunne's *An Experiment with Time*, adding that the error is thinking that time is snatching our lives away, but that we are immortal beings, in for a "tremendous adventure". Kay repeats these words and the act suddenly comes to an end. The next act opens with Kay on her own, back in the room as it was in 1919. She is clearly confused and thinks that she has been asleep and experienced a dream involving Alan and the others. It is at this point that part of the audience will spot Priestley's clever device by which the whole of Act II may have been a dream experienced by Kay. However, because audiences are used to time going backwards and forwards in plays the going back in time is not so strange.

There are many clever forwards and backwards in time references that could be described as premonitions. A particularly effective usage of this is an incident in Act III where Kay Conway states that it wouldn't be too bad to fall in love in one's own home, much better than to be desperately unhappy and in love miles away, and in a strange house. As she says this she shivers but does not know why. As we already know from Act II we have viewed the circumstances, from the viewpoint of Dunne's "Observer Two", and as such we know that this is a premonition. It is interesting to reflect that Kay is also experiencing a déjà vu sensation as she subliminally remembers her experiences from Act II. The issue here is how much of it she remembers and what the nature of the Act II experiences are. It is suggested that they are a dream, implied from the fact that she seems to either fall asleep or have some form of seizure at the end of Act I. In Act III her "recognitions" of the circumstances suggest that the memories are fleeting recognitions rather than clear images.

In Act III there is also a sequence towards the end where the characters discuss where they think they will be in the future. It is during these optimistic discussions that Kay recalls her dream of the future. She becomes tearful and tells Alan that there is "something you know that can make things better." She then asks Alan if he "remembers" quoting Blake to her. Alan clearly does not know what she is talking about. In an echo from the second act she restates the lines as Alan had done in the future. When they are again alone Kay says to Alan that there is something he can do to change things. In this she is clearly referring to her half-remembered memories of the dream. It may be that Alan also feels a memory of the future when he responds to Kay's question with the words, "There will be something one day, I will try, I promise." With this the play comes to an end.

Dunne was very excited that his theories were, at long last, being given a dramatic twist. He asked Priestley if he could give a talk to the cast before one of the performances. It was evident that the elderly aviator believed that an even more powerful performance could be elicited if the actors fully understood the principles behind the play. Priestley described (in various books and articles) how Dunne filled a blackboard with mathematical formulae and esoteric diagrams in his attempt to explain the theories of Hermann Minkowski and the discoveries of the Michelson-Morley Experiment. The actors all gave the impression that they understood exactly what Dunne was trying to get across. Priestley believed that their collective performance in front of the dapper little Irishman was as good as anything they subsequently did on the stage. But the reality was they didn't understand any of it.

This gave Dunne food for thought. How was he best to present his complex ideas to an audience not used to thinking geometrically and mathematically. A few months later he unveiled his solution. On 2 December 1937 he gave a short talk on BBC Television. In the ten-minute presentation Dunne attempted to show exactly how his concept of Serial Time worked. Next to him was a pianist sitting in front of a grand piano. Dunne requested that the pianist play each note, in sequence, from the top to the bottom. "That," he said, "is what everyday life is, just one damn thing after another." He then requested that the pianist play Mendelssohn's *Spring Song* and Beethoven's *Funeral March*. For Dunne that was the way his 'Observer 2' sees time. This being can choose what notes to play and in so doing make a thing of great beauty. For Dunne, accidental access to the perceptions of the higher entity, either through dreams or precognitions, are equivalent to pushing down the notes in a totally random way. Perceptions through dreams are thus a cacophony made up of perfectly good notes.[88]

I was surprised to discover that shortly after completing *I Have Been Here Before* and *Time and the Conways* Priestley wrote another play that met with very little success and quickly disappeared. *People at Sea* was, according to its creator, cliché-ridden and the characters to be, as he termed them, "shop soiled". It is reasonable to conclude that Jack was exhausted after a year of stress and creativity, and the clouds of war looming over Europe could not have helped his mind-set. But the play does have one interesting theme, and this is that Jack continued trying to get across Ouspensky's ideas through the voices of his characters. In this case it is the character called Professor Pawlet, another version of Dr Görtler.

Priestley had now attempted a play presenting the ideas of J.W. Dunne and another using the theories of Peter Ouspensky. But there was one area of interest to Jack that he had not attempted to place in a stage setting, and this was the survival of consciousness after death. To do this would be a real challenge and, at long last, prove to his critics that he was far from an 'Edwardian' playwright. What he created has been considered by some to be the most ambitious play ever attempted on the British stage, *Johnson Over Jordan*.

# Chapter Five

# Johnson Over Jordan

The idea that human consciousness may, at a deeper level, resonate directly with a collective mind and, in doing so, allow the mind to access information from other times and places had been an ongoing area of interest to Priestley. In the mid-1930s, while staying at the Phantom Ranch in Arizona, Jack had started reading the works of Carl Gustav Jung, the Swiss analytical psychologist. Jung's ideas resonated with him and presented answers to his questions.

In 1916 Jung wrote an essay that introduced to the world a concept he called the *Collective Unconscious*. This was a very different concept to the then general understanding of the unconscious which was, according to Jung's teacher and friend, Sigmund Freud, a direct part of the individual personality that contained repressed images and sublimated memories. Jung's Collective Unconscious was something far greater than the individual; it was an internalized aspect of the collective mind of the human species. The idea that we all can, under certain circumstances, attune into a greater mind, a mind that contains information far in excess of our own experiences, was something that Priestley could really appreciate. It explained his creativity and his feelings that humanity was part of a greater something. Given his interest in Jung, I am sure that even if he had not attended, he would have known about Jung's lecture delivered to the Abernethian Society at St Bartholomew's Hospital in London on 19 October 1936, a presentation which chronologically and significantly coincides perfectly with Jack's discovery of Jung's work.

In his 1936 London lecture Jung defined what he meant by the *Collective Unconscious*:

My thesis then is as follows: in addition to our immediate consciousness, which is of a thoroughly personal nature and which we believe to be the only empirical psyche (even if we tack on the personal unconscious as an appendix), there exists a second psychic system of a collective, universal, and impersonal nature which is identical in all individuals. This collective unconscious does not develop individually but is inherited. It consists of pre-existent forms, the archetypes, which can only become conscious secondarily and which give definite form to certain psychic contents.[89]

This process by which a personal, aware, consciousness can illicit information from a deeper, collective unconscious was but one facet of Jung's elegant and intuitively satisfactory model. Jung also argued that regular consciousness was a dynamic in which four sometimes conflicting "personalities" overlap. These are known as the Ego, the Persona, the Shadow and the Self.

The ego is that which we call "I" or "me". This is considered to be the centre of consciousness, the something that does the perceiving, the point where perceptions all come together. But this centre of consciousness is not, according to Jung, what we really are. It is simply an organizing principle that gives us sense of identity and uniqueness. Although in this role the Ego is the centre of the personality it is part of a greater awareness that Jung called the Self.

The Self can only be perceived through the Ego. For this reason, it can never be fully understood because the Ego colours all perceptions with its own prejudices, fears and desires. The Self is transcendental and the totality of body and mind. It is this embodied force that guides the person through life. This has profound teleological qualities as the Self knows far more than the ego ever can. The Unconscious watches from a background and endeavours to keep us in balance.

In turn each Ego also has its "animal" side. Jung termed this "the Shadow". It is the source of both creative and destructive urges. The Shadow may appear in dreams and carries with it the memories and fears of the Ego. Jung believed that the Shadow was made up of a series of layers, with the lowest layer merging into the Collective Unconscious, and it is here that it interacts with the Archetypes.

The Jungian Persona is the social face that the Ego presents to the world. The word Persona is from the Latin word persona which means mask or character. Jung's choice of terminology was quite precise in this regard. It is a façade we hide behind and we use it to role play and to conform to the demands of society.

Jung argued that the human psyche exists in this world to achieve self-realization. This is reached when we become aware of our true Self by the integration of both the individual and collective elements. This normally takes place in the second half of life when we are forced to come to terms with our own death. Jung shared with Priestley a fascination with Vedanta and it is clear that the Jungian Collective Unconscious has many similarities with the Vedanta concept of Brahman, the universal mind.

But it was Jack's encounter with another philosophy that was to give a structure to his understanding of the Jungian theory of personality, and this yet again involved his fascination with Eastern belief systems. As we know the Hindu Vedanta had long been of interest to Priestley. But it was ideas emanating from the mountains to the north of the Great Indian Plain that was to now capture his attention.

In 1919 an American anthropologist Walter Yeeling Evans-Wentz met with Major W.L. Campbell in Darjeeling in Northern India. Campbell had just returned from a period in Tibet and had brought back with him a collection of Buddhist blockprints. Campbell gave the prints to Evans-Wentz who, in turn, asked a local teacher, Kazi Dawa Samdup, to translate the works. One of the books, a small volume entitled *Great Liberation on Hearing the Bardo*, was of great interest to both Evans-Wentz and Samdup.

Two months later they had a full translation of what was to become known as *The Tibetan Book of the Dead*. The book appeared in 1927 and generated a great deal of interest. Legend has it that the book had originally been written in the 8th century CE by the great teacher Padmasambhava and later buried on Mount Gampodar. Campbell had discovered the manuscript when he had visited the Tibetan town of Gyantse in south-west Tibet. It was soon to also be known by its Tibetan title of the *Bardo Thodol*.

Like Priestley, Evans-Wentz had been intrigued by the Vedanta model of reality and his interpretation of this ancient work had a Vedantist underpinning. Central to *The Tibetan Book of the Dead* is the belief of life after death.

Given his lifelong interest in Vedanta it is not at all surprising that Jack read *The Tibetan Book of the Dead* soon after its publication. He had been particularly interested in Evans-Wentz's description of the Bardo State:

> ... a prolonged dream-like state, in what might be called the fourth dimension of space, filled with hallucinatory visions directly resultant from the mental-content of the percipient.[90]

Jack quickly drew links between the Buddhist, Vedanta and Jungian interpretations of the after-death state. But being ever the pragmatist what he saw here was an opportunity to use the Bardo State as a structure whereby which he could apply his own interpretation of Jungian analysis within a dramatic context. In *All About It* he makes this quite clear:

> I hardly set foot inside the Tibetan *Bardo* [...] I imagined for my hero a far more modest and westernised *Bardo*.[91]

He believed that this end-of-life state could be the place where the Jungian concept of Individuation would come to pass. This is again powerful evidence of what a perceptive thinker Jack was.

Many years later, in 1957, Jung himself was to make similar links. In that year the third edition of *The Tibetan Book of the Dead* was published containing a commentary by Jung. In this he commented that, "The *Bardo Thodol* is in the highest degree psychological in its outlook."

But there was an even grander ambition here. Priestley saw that the Bardo State, with regards to its timelessness, could also be explained by the time theories of J.W. Dunne and, similarly, Ouspensky's concept of the eternal recurrence, with its idea of reliving one's life again and again, also had Bardo-like elements. He realised that an uber-play could be written that would incorporate all of these disparate themes. And so it was that this fermentation of ideas led to the writing of Priestley's most ambitious play, *Johnson Over Jordan*.

In a curious way *Johnson Over Jordan* seems to have its source in Jack's own subconscious. In 1937 Jack embarked upon a huge lecture tour of the United States. This involved the travelling of vast distances across featureless countryside which allowed him to daydream as he looked out of the train window. During these interludes he spontaneously perceived "odd scenes and fragments of dialogue"[92] that seemed to just well up from his Jungian unconscious. These hypnagogic images and sounds were so powerful that by the time he arrived back in Arizona he was able to begin the first draft. As we shall discover later, *Johnson Over Jordan* has one scene in which a hypnagogic interlude facilitates contact between two characters, one of which is dead.

By January 1938 he had written the second draft and the play was almost ready to go but work on another play, *Music at Night*, had taken his attention. Both plays have similarities and it is clear that there was a degree of cross-fertilisation of ideas between the two. They both involve an inner-world of experience that is shared by the audience and are both extremely Jungian in their respective themes. We shall return to *Music at Night* later.

*Johnson Over Jordan* was first produced on 22 February 1939 with Ralph Richardson playing the title role. It started at the New Theatre but after two weeks was moved to the smaller Saville Theatre. The audiences in general were good, but the experimental nature of the production attracted a younger, and less wealthy, sector of society. This meant that the more expensive seats were not sold in the numbers to ensure a profit on what was already a very expensive production. Ralph Richardson, playing the title role, was already a very famous actor and it was his performance that impressed the critics. Sadly, the rest of the production did not receive such positive reviews. Even though the major cost of Richardson's wages were deferred the play simply could not continue losing money every night. After a two-month run it closed.

It is clear that Priestley felt that the context of the play may confuse many. In recognition of this potentiality he added to the published play an essay entitled "And All About It" which does exactly that. He explained how the play reflects very accurately Dunne's time theories in that Robert Johnson is existing in a timeless place. This cannot really be a play about life-after-death because, as Dunne argues, time is a continual present in its purest form. Priestley adds that he started writing notes on this play before either *Time and the Conways* or *I Have Been Here Before*.

In "And All About It" Priestley explained that *Johnson Over Jordan* was a complete change of method for him:

What I wanted to do was take my characters out of time… you can do it in a dream play… because in our dreams we do actually lead a genuine, if very confused, four-dimensional existence. In dreams not only are we free of the usual limitations of time and space, not only do we return to our past and probably go forward to our future, but the self that apparently experiences these strange adventures is a more essential self, of no particular age.[93]

Here we have an acknowledgement that this play was still using the time theories of J.W. Dunne, specifically in reference to Dunne's concept of the layered "observers" all existing in different dimensions of space-time.

But we also have here a reference to the underlying unity of consciousness found in Vedanta; that at a deeper level of reality we are all one unitary consciousness experiencing itself subjectively. As we shall see, Jack carried this through in a subtle way within the confines of his seemingly non-mystical post-war play *An Inspector Calls*.

The play starts with the curtain rising on the hallway of a large pleasant house somewhere in the London suburbs. The furniture places the period as being contemporary to the play's writing, that is, the late 1930s.

The use of music immediately informs the audience that a funeral is taking place. This is reinforced by the entry of a maid dressed in black accompanied by an undertaker and confirmed by the entry of an elderly clergyman in funeral robes. We discover that the deceased is a businessman by the name of Robert Johnson who has recently died just before he reached his 51st birthday. He is survived by his wife, Jill, and two children, Richard and Freda, who are in their early twenties. The service is to take place in Robert's family home before his remains are taken to the cemetery. The family and close friends follow the clergyman and the undertaker into a location off stage, presumably another room in the house. We hear the vicar begin the service. It is then that we see Johnson appear in a state of total confusion.

It is important at this point to refer to Priestley's own comments on the play as outlined in that essay "And All About It" which accompanied the 1939 printed version of the play. Here Priestley stresses that the version of Robert Johnson that we see on stage is a "self that [...] is a more essential self, of no particular age."[94] This is of great importance as it is a reflection of the ideas central to *Time and the Conways*, written a few years before; that at each moment in time we are but a slice of our true self that exists within a place outside of the four dimensions of space and outside of the present moment. It is important to revisit the words spoken by Alan at the end of Act II of *Time and the Conways*:

> But the point is now, at this moment, or any moment, we're only a cross-section of our real selves. What really is the whole stretch of ourselves, all our time will be us – the real you, the real me. And then perhaps we'll find ourselves in another time, which is only another kind of dream.[95]

And it is the "real" Robert Johnson that we see on stage. This "self" exists in a form of dream state that moves him from location to location within "the whole stretch" of himself as Alan Conway terms it. Priestley attempts to clarify what he means by this:

> What he really is doing is moving freely in and out of the past and recreating the experiences he finds there, as we do often in dreams.[96]

The stage directions demand that Johnson, in these opening sequences, acts "like a man in a delirium." [97] It is important at this point to clarify the meaning of the word "delirium" as it was used in the late 1930s. It was defined as a stage of consciousness between alertness and coma that is perceived by the patient as being "dream-like".[98] The word has its origins in Latin with the verb *delirare* – literally 'to leave the furrow' (in ploughing), the furrow being normal cognition of the world. And this is exactly the state Johnson finds himself in. As far as he is concerned he is still alive and deeply within the fever state of the pneumonia that had killed him. But he is no longer sure exactly who he is. He makes a series of disjointed statements reflecting an agitated state of mind, reflecting his concerns regarding his illness and the effect this will have on his family. It is clear that from now on we will be viewing events from the hallucinating mind of a person who seems to be alive in his world and dead in that of the other characters. But we soon realise that Johnson's world has no logic to it. He calls out for his secretary and suddenly four seemingly identical young women appear and dance around him, all of whom are his PA, Miss Francis.

We then witness a series of dance sequences involving a working day of a typical office. Dancers come on and off the stage and a loudspeaker system barks out orders and instructions regarding the work processes to be followed. Johnson is clearly in a very confused state whereby his personal concerns are being mixed in with his career in a small London shipping company. The dancers part and we see a large desk with two elderly men sitting either side in formal business dress. Johnson approaches them and asks for their help. He explains that one minute he was lying in bed not feeling very well with a high temperature, and the next he finds himself in this strange location. One of the old businessmen informs him that he will need money to leave this place, but in order to receive money he will need to successfully fill in some forms and convince "The Examiners" that he should receive a payment. He then meets the two "examiners" who do reject his form and insist that he cannot leave.

In an excellent essay published in The J.B. Priestley Society Journal, Priestley scholar Lee Hanson suggests that in Act I we also see how Priestley applies Jung's model of the Psyche. As we have already discussed, this has two aspects; the conscious Persona and the unconscious Shadow. Hanson directly quotes Jung in this regard:

The persona is a complicated system of relations between individual consciousness and society, fittingly enough a kind of mask, designed on the one hand to make a definite impression upon others, and, on the other, to conceal the true nature of the individual.[99]

His perception starts to move around. He sees his wife, Jill, destitute, clearly a potential future scenario and then, suddenly, he is back at school being scolded by one of his schoolmasters. The next second he has moved forward twelve years or so and is starting his career in shipping and is again being told off, this time by one of the business partners, Mr Clayton, somebody the audience has already encountered in the opening sequence. He then interfaces with another known character, his wife's mother, Mrs Gregg. Again it is a discussion regarding his worthiness to marry Jill and his ability to keep her in the manner she had become accustomed.

Priestley is here using elements from, among other writings, Dickens' *A Christmas Carol*. He is being shown snapshots of his own past life. What is intriguing here is that a modern audience would not find such a device at all strange. Many modern movies have the central character relive elements of their own past. It has become something of a trope. But what is of more significance is that Priestley places this within the hallucinations of a dying, or dead, person. This is, in effect, a Near-Death Experience (NDE). However, NDEs were not to become known about for another thirty-six years when Raymond Moody published his hugely influential book *Life After Life* in 1975. Central to the NDE is something known as the "panoramic life review" and this is exactly what Priestley has Johnson experience.

In his article Hanson argues that the "flashback" sequences are far more than simply scenes from Johnson's past:

Johnson does not receive flashbacks, he actually is back in the time and the place of the characters that meet and greet him. He does not see these scenes through a screen or projected against some backdrop, he is actually part of them, whether real or imagined.[100]

All through the play we have situations in which the contemporary Johnson, or more accurately, the self-consciousness of the contemporary Johnson, becomes lost and he becomes an earlier version of himself living in that moment of time. Each time this occurs the audience is warned of a temporal shift by the bathing of the stage in a hard white light. An example of this is when he finds himself back in his school days in Act I. Priestley's stage direction shows Johnson's initial confusion and then a realisation that he is not a schoolboy but somebody older observing the world from the body of a youngster:

> But then as he stares at the table in front of him, he is at first puzzled and then relieved, suddenly remembering that he is not a schoolboy any longer. No, he certainly isn't a schoolboy, but how far does that take him? What is he now?[101]

It is clear from this direction, which has to be conveyed non-verbally by the actor, that Johnson is in a state of ego-ness in that he does not know who he is. He is simply an 'observer'. But he is still aware that he is "Johnson" in that this is the name by which he is addressed by the schoolmaster. As he considers what he should do next the loudspeaker announces that there are only a few minutes left for the forms to be completed. This snaps Johnson out of his childhood persona back into 'the present', whatever that may mean within the confused and mercurial timescape that defines his new perceptual world.

All of the characters appearing in Johnson's post-mortem world are not real, they are projections from his own subconscious. His family members and business associates act out scenes from his past but at no time are we given to believe that they are anything but hallucinations with no present existence except in his mind. It is important to note that Priestley has each act open with a sequence that is outside of Johnson's perceptions. This is a reflection of the 'real' world as it is perceived by the living. It is only when Johnson is on stage, and is therefore the 'observer', whose act of observation creates the perceptions of the audience, that the hallucinations begin. In this way we, as the audience, share Johnson's delirium. The introduction of reality at the start of each act allows the audience to understand that time is passing in a different way when we are in Johnson's world to the reality perceived by the living characters. Johnson flits in and out of linear and sequential time throughout the play.

Act I is full of anxieties and fears. This is a reflection of the Jungian Ego. The office environment represents the individual trapped in a place that they have no real control over; they are at the whim of faceless bureaucrats and pointless procedures. We also can detect elements of Jung's Persona as Johnson projects into the environment what he believes to be the correct responses to the questions and challenges thrown at him. But there is something lurking behind the Ego-driven personae. In a very curious section another 'inner and deeper self' that is not fully Johnson comments on his situation. This something is aware of the strangeness of the circumstances. It notices a musical refrain that the audience also hears. It says:

That music does not belong to this place. But then neither do I. Who does? I've lived in a world where that music was, but not for long – no, never for long. Not my fault. It comes and goes so quickly, just gleams and fades, that other world, like the light at sunset on distant hills.[102]

Here Priestley is introducing the Jungian Self. This other personality is aware that Johnson is existing in two worlds: this strange world of delirium and another world that is just beyond his comprehension. Of course, we as the audience know that this world is the world of the living and that Johnson is already dead. But it is important to note that for Johnson time itself has become non-linear. He seems to flit back into time both for many years and a few seconds. Wherever he is located within this state seems to share the same moment in time as the few days after his death.

As discussed earlier the Shadow is the Jungian equivalent of the Freudian Id. It represents all the elements of the personality that the Persona does not identify with. These elements are nearly always perceived to be negative and reflect the animalistic urges that bubble just below the surface. According to Jung the Shadow can be encountered in dreams and in states of altered consciousness. The liminal state between life and death that Johnson finds himself in is exactly where Jung would expect the Shadow to manifest. At the end of Act I the Shadow comes to the fore. It takes over from the Persona and has Johnson snatch some money and dive into the entrance of the "Night Club".

As Act II progresses the Shadow comes more to the fore. Initially the Persona holds on to a degree of control. As he interfaces with the disturbing characters whose world consists of the passing pleasures of the Night Club he makes grandiose statements about himself and how he deals with others. These are clearly untrue and as the circumstances erode away his fragile ego the Shadow looms ever larger. It suddenly breaks through and all Johnson wants is immediate self-gratification, achieved at any cost to both himself and, more importantly, others. The subsequent attempted rape of his daughter and the murder of his son are evidence of these bestial and murderous tendencies.

Priestley, through his characters, suggests that death may simply be a continuation of the dream state that we experience most nights throughout our lives and that in this dream state a person would be unaware that they had actually died. At the start of Act II Johnson's daughter, Freda, in a conversation with her brother, Richard, speculates:

Well, supposing the dreaming goes on. Then you wouldn't know even know you'd died, would you? And it wouldn't be so bad for him as it is for us – would it? I mean, because he could be dreaming about still being with us, and wouldn't really know the difference.[103]

This conversation continues with Richard saying that there were things he would have liked to have said to his father but that it was too late. Freda suggests that if her brother thought these things then maybe the message would get through to their father "somehow."

As we have already noted, the start of each act is a snapshot of 'consensual reality', the world in which time runs linearly and perceptions can be shared. For example, at the start of Act II Johnson's daughter, Freda, and son, Richard, discuss how sad it was that their father will never know how much they appreciated him and they have a precise conversation about this.[104] But in Johnson's perceptual universe, also shared by the audience, time has no meaning. We hear this exact conversation again later in the act but this time it is heard by Johnson who receives clearly the emotions of his children. With regards to the linearity of the play, both conversations happened at different times. In a form of telepathy, the children's wishing to have their father receive a communication from beyond the grave is facilitated.[105]

After we hear the conversation between Freda and Richard for the first time, their mother Jill appears, having just taken a nap. She is in a state of confusion. She describes to the children how she had just experienced a semi-dream state in which she found herself looking for her husband. She says:

I was – half asleep. Then I had a hateful sort of dream. Frightening, horrible. I suppose it was really a nightmare. I dreamt I was trying to find your father. I knew I had to find him. And I had to look in the strangest of places – all vague –

but – frightening.[106]

Priestley is quite precise that Jill was "half asleep" when she experienced this vision. This is a state known as hypnagogia and although Priestley never uses this term, it is evident from his autobiographical writings that this altered state of consciousness intrigued him. As we have already discovered, the play itself had as its genesis a series of hypnagogic images and dialogues that invaded Priestley's mind while he was on a lecture tour of the United States in late 1937. Was this what stimulated this curious interlude?

Hypnagogia is a liminal state whereby dream images are drawn up from the subconscious and are played out as images in three-dimensional locations within the visual field of the 'observer'. To be technically correct Priestley may be referring here to hypnagogia (just before going to sleep) or hypnapompia (on awaking from sleep) as it is not clear whether the dreamers are falling asleep or waking from sleep.

In the play Jill's dream search is later perceived by Johnson within his Bardo state. While within the night club Johnson sees his wife enter, an incongruously dressed figure surrounded by masked revellers. This could easily be understood as being simply another creation of Johnson's subconscious. For example, as Jill calls out his name he shouts back that, "He is not here, go away."[107] But Priestley's stage directions make a direct link between what Johnson sees in his near-death experience with the "reality sequence" at the start of the act. When Jill initially is seen in the night club looking for her husband the stage direction demands that:

A single white ray picks out Jill who has just entered below, on the other side. She looks exactly as we saw her when she came into the hall to tell the children about her dream.[108]

It is suggested here that Jill's dream has somehow transported her into Johnson's Bardo. This should be picked up by attentive members of the audience but it is not stressed in any of the subsequent onstage character discussions. In this, Priestley suggests that both perceptual realities have a degree of consensuality in that they are shared by both Jill and Robert.

In the Don Quixote sequences in Act III we have Priestley suggesting that all conscious beings are, in the final analysis, mere shadows, similar in many ways to the fictional characters, such as Quixote, created by our writers. He has Quixote say:

Your great poet once said that the best of our kind are bit shadows, though I think he knew that your kind too – who appear so solid to yourselves for a little time – are also only shadows. And perhaps you do take life from the mind that beholds you and your little tale, so you live as we must do, in another greater being's imagination, memory and affection.[109]

This idea that our existence depends upon an act of observation of another, higher sentience brings in elements of quantum physics and mysticism. From a reference made earlier in the play, when, in Act I, the examiners accuse Johnson of not having tried hard enough to acquaint himself with:

The Mendelian Law, the Quantum Theory, Spectral Analysis, or the behaviour of Electrons and Neutrons.[110]

This suggests to me that during the writing of the play Priestley had been aware of, and possibly even reading about, quantum theory. It is clear from the quantum physics sections of his 1963 book *Man and Time* that by the late 1950s Priestley had a very good working knowledge of the mysteries of wave-function collapse and the "observer effect."[111] If this interest had started in the 1930s, when Niels Bohr, Louis de Broglie, Paul Dirac and

Erwin Schrödinger were creating quantum theory, then it is reasonable to conclude that this reference to existence being in the perception of a "beholder" was very current and amazingly advanced. Of course, Priestley's interest in mysticism, specifically Eastern mysticism, would have introduced him to the idea that everything that is exists because it is being observed by Brahman.

The play ends with Johnson walking into an intense blue light that becomes bluer and bluer. The drums roll and the cymbals clash and the audience sees, beyond Johnson, the curve of the Earth and a backdrop of stars. Johnson disappears into the blue light and the curtain comes down. This was, and still is, one of the most spectacular ends to a play ever witnessed in London's West End theatres.

Sadly, the theatre critics were not impressed. The *Times* felt that the use of masks was very distracting and *Tatler* was similarly disturbed by the choreography.

But it was events in Europe that were soon to focus the attention of most people away from the metaphysical aspects of survival after death to a very real danger that death itself was to become all too commonplace, a new war in Europe.

## Chapter Six

# The War Years – 1939–1946

In the late 1930s the threat of war was an ever-looming presence. With this in mind Priestley embarked upon a novel that was to become *Let the People Sing*. Fearing the worst he was keen to write something that could raise the spirits of the population and offer a form of escapism. His intention was to write something similar to *The Good Companions*. On first approaching this the novel and circumstances offer nothing with regards to time anomalies or Priestley's fascination with the 'magical'. But a careful reading of the novel and the strange set of circumstances surrounding it suggest otherwise.

In *Margin Released* Priestley describes what his life was like those few weeks before the outbreak of World War One in June 1914. It seems that he was filled with a need to experience as much he possibly could. He writes:

During the first eight months of 1914, one might say I was running around at a standstill. I was cramming the hours with experience, tasting this and gulping down that, widening acquaintance, making a few new friends; but in the centre of all this nothing much was happening. My life was like a round-about with the gilded cars and cockerels flashing by, the bray of the organ, the drums and cymbals, never silent, while the man in the middle wipes his hands on an oily rag and yawns. I have never been much of a planner, but at this time I was not visited by even the ghost of a plan. Not only did I not know which way I was going, I never even looked to see if there were any signposts, any paths. I had not the least notion what I was going to do, and now – or so it seems, if memory is not cheating – at last nobody, not even my father, asked me.[112]

Atkins, in his *J.B. Priestley: The Last of the Sages*, suggests that Priestley may have had sublimated precognitive and retrocognitive abilities and cites this great need to experience to the full in 1914 evidence that in some way Priestley knew that within a few short weeks his life and indeed the world in general would change forever. In *Margin Released* Priestley suggests that the unconscious, when manifest in dreams, is concerned with the future, not the past, and that what seem like dreams involving the deep past may actually be about the future. With regards to his own "cramming the hours" with experiences in the early summer of 1914 Priestley states:

> I believe I know now what was happening that summer. I believe I did nothing but enjoy what could be enjoyed because we were soon to be at war. Consciously of course we never entertained a thought of it; but deep in the unconscious, which has its own time and a wider now than consciousness knows, already the war was on, a world ending.[113]

Is it possible that Priestley's unconscious had already precognised the outbreak of this new war? Indeed, is there evidence that at a subliminal level he actually knew the date?

For some undisclosed reason Priestley agreed to have a pre-publication reading of the book to be serialized on BBC Radio. The first reading was planned for Sunday 3 September 1939 and, quite surprisingly, Priestley agreed to be the person doing the reading that evening. In her book *Priestley*, Judith Cook creates a powerfully evocative image of Priestley and his wife Jane driving through beautiful late summer sunshine and clear blue skies on their way to the BBC studios in London to record the programme. On coming down from the ridge of the North Downs at Bagshot they see cars loaded with people and luggage heading out of London.[114] Earlier in the day Neville Chamberlain's dream of peace in our time was shattered by Nazi warplanes bombing

Warsaw. Great Britain and her Empire had, that afternoon, declared war on Germany and her allies. On arrival in London Priestley describes how he groped his way through:

> An appalling blackness, my very first taste of it, and almost felt I was back in the First War when in Broadcasting House, I found myself among sandbags, bayonets, nurses in uniform.[115]

One could argue coincidence here, but this is a coincidence of huge significance. Germany invaded Poland on 1 September 1939 bringing about World War Two.

The novel that was published later that month seems, on the surface, to be simply a feel-good story about normal everyday folk, building a new world. It exists in an alternative Britain in 1938/39 where the dictators and the other ills of mid-19th century Europe are still present but offer no threat, a place where optimism prevails. As it was written after the Munich Agreement it exists in a world where "peace in our time" has been achieved. Of course the irony is that on the day it was first broadcast that peace was lost forever.

It seems to contain none of the themes that preoccupied Priestley in 1937 and 1938. He was focusing his attention on *Johnson Over Jordan*, a play that we have already discovered was as experimental and as time-related as *Let the People Sing* was prosaic and predictable. The novel, as it draws to a conclusion, has Priestley recreating his own preferred past into the future as when the old-style music hall comedian Tommy Tiverton appears top of the bill at "the good old Palace, Birchester."[116] But dig deeper into the novel and we find running through it many, if not all, of Priestley's esoteric themes.

For example, although *Let the People Sing* seems to have no aspects involving time, a careful reading shows that this is not the case. We know that Priestley experienced throughout his life powerfully vivid dreams. In *Let the People Sing* one of the minor characters, Candover, has a very powerful dream-life and has an ability to recall, in detail, the contents of his dreams. Furthermore, he travels in time in his dream states, moving both into the future and into the past. His dreams take him into the Fifth and possibly the Sixth Dimensions. Later in the novel Candover ends up in court, an event and set of circumstances that he had already encountered in his dream world. He informs the judge that he has already lived the circumstances and knows what will happen.

In the novel Priestley has Candover be the voice of an alternate world within his alternate world, a person perceiving information from the real 1939 existing outside the confines of the novel. In his dreams he sees:

Fleets o' ships sinkin' an' cities all on fire, an' hundreds of thousands o' people running about an' screaming an' then dropping down dead.[117]

This prognostication, reminiscent of Nostradamus at his best, seems to foresee the Atom Bomb attacks on Hiroshima and Nagasaki waiting quietly to come about six years later in the reader's reality, a place somehow accessed by Candover's dreaming self. But of course, Candover's words are simply Priestley's.

The play has its own Ouspenskian 'Görtler' in the guise of Professor Ernest Kronak and it is Kronak who believes that Candover's dreams are evidence that the old man is accessing the universal mind. For Kronak this explains how Candover's dreams can span such huge time scales, for example he interprets one dream as being the Sack of Bagdad by the Mongols in 1258.

In *Margin Released* Priestley suggests that maybe what we consider to be dreams of the past are, in fact, dreams of the future. Early in the book he discusses how, around 1911 or 1912 (note the 1912 link again), he had become haunted by the idea that he had in some subconscious way links to the mythic continent of Atlantis. This preoccupation became so overpowering that at that time he wrote a short poem entitled *Evensong to Atlantis*. He readily acknowledges that the poem was "very bad indeed."[118] Reflecting upon this infatuation he suggests that maybe all legends and myths contain memories of the future, not the past:

> We assume that legends and myths, so far as they have any connection with historical time, point back to some remote age when they themselves took shape. But what if a few of them point the other way? Suppose the destruction of Atlantis had not happened but was going to happen? We were not leaving it behind but rushing towards it, perhaps; so that sitting up there in my attic, before life claimed too much of me, closing the little window still open then in the shadowy half of my mind, I found myself wondering over and over again about Atlantis. There are patterns of cause and effect we do not understand, so we pretend they do not exist, keeping even a glimpse or a hint of them out of all textbooks.[119]

As the war began Jack focused his attention on an idea for a new play that would not be performed until 1946 after many revisions. In its final version *Ever Since Paradise* opens with a character, Helen, suggesting that in a dim way we all can sense what is about to happen in our lives. In this play Priestley pricks his own bubble in that he makes fun of his own metaphysical interests. He has the characters discuss ideas very similar to Dunne in which they discuss the "Big Now" behind the "Little Now". This brings about a response whereby one of the characters states, "not just now thank you, some other time."

He also has a famous medium called Madame Rubbishky who discusses a version of Ouspensky's theories in a talk entitled "*I*

*Am the Great All"*. Why he chose to do this is unclear. Was it an attempt to deflect his critics? A way of saying that "I don't really believe all this stuff, you know"? This is particularly intriguing in that the play itself contains many metaphysical aspects. In one section there is an out-of-body experience whereby one of the characters steps out of her body to watch the performance of the others. The audience is also occasionally acknowledged by the cast. This approach is a form of post-modernism years before such a concept had been created. As Innes states, this work:

Anticipates Samuel Beckett's self-reflexive works, *Film* and *Play*, being based on the same contradiction between *cogito ergo sum* and *esse est percipi* – 'I think Therefore I am' versus 'To be is to be perceived.'[120]

There are six characters and in this I am reminded of Pirandello's work. These consist of three sets of couples: Helen and William who are the narrators, Paul and Rosemary who act out the storyline behind them, and Philip and Joyce, the accompanists.

Priestley linked *Ever Since Paradise* with *Johnson Over Jordan*. In his 1973 book *The Art of the Dramatist* he explained that with both plays he wanted to suggest that from the location of the fourth dimension life can be perceived in a non-linear fashion with:

Childhood and adult life interrupting each other, all of which can bring a piercing sweetness, a queer poignancy, and, again, dramatic experience a little different from what one has known before.[121]

The following year, 1940, Priestley began writing a play called *The Long Mirror*. Although never stated as such in academic papers and books on Priestley, he himself considered this to be one of his "time plays". He felt that this was "the Cinderella" of his more serious plays and he acknowledged that the idea of the play was so powerful that he somewhat hurried the script. His son, Tom Priestley, is also of the opinion that this is one of his father's best works and that it is sadly neglected.

The play has a very interesting background. Tom Priestley has informed me that it was based upon an actual event that took place in the life of Jane Priestley's sister, Ena Holland. Ena subsequently turned this into a novel entitled *The Undercurrent* published under the pseudonym of Ruth Holland, published in 1926. In 1936 Edith (Ruth) was also to write a novel based upon her brother-in-law's play *Dangerous Corner*, followed in 1936 with a novel based on his other play, *Laburnum Grove*.

This play takes place in a very similar set of circumstances as *I Have Been Here Before*. The location is an isolated hotel with a small number of guests, one of which seems to have prior knowledge of the life of another. Waiting upon the guests are colourful 'locals'. In this case the location is North Wales, whereas in *I Have Been Here Before* it was Priestley's own Yorkshire.

It opens with a conversation between a waiter, Thomas Williams, and an elderly guest, Mrs Tenbury. The uncanny atmosphere is set from the start when Mrs Tenbury, on being awoken by the entry of Thomas, comments that she had only been dozing and how much she enjoys her dreams but at the same time finds them to be a great mystery:

> I often dream of places I have never seen before, and they seem quite real and sensible. I don't see how I could invent them. So much convincing detail too. I don't believe that I am as clever as all that. And all the people too, where do *they* come from?[122]

A few seconds later Thomas discusses how his wife, Mrs Williams (who is never seen), experiences a reoccurring dream involving being lost in a wood and that over the years she has associated this dream with impending trouble and that the very night before this dream had reoccurred after a long absence. We know that Priestley was fascinated by dreams; their source and their messages. He had been studying Jung at the time of writing this play and his interest in the works of J.W. Dunne meant that precognitive dreaming was one of his major themes.

Mrs Tenbury and Thomas are joined by another guest, Branwen Elder, who claims that she has just seen a ghost; a little old woman in grey who "flits about the drive, staring and muttering."[123] This is a curious comment because, like Mrs Tenbury's earlier observation regarding dreams, this ghost, indeed ghosts in general, are never discussed again in the play.

Priestley has Branwen present an explanation for ghosts and hauntings. She suggests that the ghost is not actually a person but an impression created in the past by powerful emotions that leave a form of residue that can be picked up by sensitive individuals, "like footprints in sand, or the mark of one's finger on a glass."[124]

We discover that Branwen has recently returned to the UK from South Africa and that something had prompted this return. She seems aware that there will be a visitor to the hotel and she knows who this visitor will be. She is proven right when composer Michael Camber turns up with his wife, Valerie. We discover that for five years, ever since attending a concert in which Michael was the conductor, Branwen has been able to share his thoughts and perceptions. This seems to be a form of telepathy, remote viewing and an out-of-body experience. Branwen attempts to explain what happened:

I was listening to your work, I began to drift away from myself, but my mind was merely wandering, as people's minds often do when they're listening – or half listening – to music. I began to feel almost that I were conducting the orchestra. I felt I knew what was coming next on the score.

She then finds herself back in her body. This section has elements of remote viewing and a form of déjà vu. Later that evening she has a full-blown out-of-body experience while sitting in front of the fire in her flat:

> Quite suddenly I wasn't in my flat at all. I was in a restaurant – I think it was Manzoni's but I was never sure – looking down on a little supper party. It was being given by a heavily-built, oldish man with a sallow tired face, and you were there, with Rachel Flower, the pianist.[125]

I am intrigued as to why Priestley decided to describe Branwen's perceptions of the dinner party in this way. If he was simply trying to convey a form of telepathy, why did he not simply have her perceiving the dinner party from the viewpoint of Camber himself. Priestley doesn't. He has Branwen fall into a form of hypnagogic state in front of the fire in her house and then she is 'viewing' a scene from a vantage point above it. He precisely has Branwen state that she was "looking down on a little supper party." This is exactly how OBE perceptions are described. We know that JBP's dreams were very vivid. Could it be that he was describing incidents in his own life? This would certainly explain the peculiar dream discussion at the start of the play, something that contributed nothing directly to the plot itself.

It seems that Camber may share these perceptions. On arriving in the hotel he confuses Branwen with his wife. There is a strong physical resemblance between the two women. We later discover that it was the resemblance that Valerie had to Branwen that subconsciously stimulated his initial attraction to his future wife. His sensitivity is far less than Branwen's; but later in the play, a crucial event takes place in which he remotely perceives something that Branwen says to Valerie that has him drive off into the night in a fit of anger.

At the end of the play the two main characters agree that it was in a dream that they met. "It was a kind of dream, but we were real in it."

The idea of time and death is touched upon earlier in the play. Michael references a dead friend of his called Hugo Stander. Branwen replies that Hugo is not dead but simply "out of our time, and we are still in it" suggesting that we lose communication with the dead because we are still trapped within linear time whereas the dead move to a different temporal tune. This is a curious piece of dialogue because it adds nothing to the storyline. Stander is never mentioned again, and neither is the location of the dead. Again, it seems, Priestley has certain bees in his bonnet and he simply wishes to free them within the confines of the play. The final discussion regarding the mirror returns to the theme of birth, death and time. This is another attempt by Priestley to explain to an audience the ideas of J.W. Dunne. The sequence is an excellent analogy of the "long body" and explains the idea that we are "all our lives" not just how we are at any one moment. This mirrors, pun unintentional, Alan's speech in *Time and the Conways*. It seems that JBP wanted to have another go at this in another play. Sadly, the introduction of time confuses rather than enlightens and this, together with other seemingly unnecessary references to ghosts, confused audiences. Although it had several provincial theatre performances during the Second World War, and was staged in London in 1945, after a run of 13 performances at London's Royal Court from 29 October to 9 November 1952, the play was not again performed professionally until February 1996 when it had a short run at North Wales' Theatr Clwyd. Indeed, Ian Shuttleworth's review of the production for the *Financial Times* suggests why:

> that the kind of mysticism which would be easily acceptable in late Strindberg is for some reason harder to swallow in a twentieth-century British setting.[126]

I would like to suggest that the reason such mysticism is not accepted within a "twentieth century British setting" is that audiences do not accept Priestley as being an experimental or original playwright. I am sure that if a Strindberg play was located in a similar time location the reviews would be glowing and positive. The issue is simply that the play was written by Priestley and this alone is enough to have its ideas dismissed.

Priestley was to echo his own words, placed in the mouth of Mrs Tenbury, nine years later when he wrote his 1949 book of essays, *Delight*. In this he discusses the things that he really enjoys in life and one of these is dreaming. In this he asks exactly the same questions as his elderly fictional character: where do they come from? What are they? He stated that people say to him "It's only a dream" but he would respond with "But why *only*?" He was convinced that there are two types of dream – precognitive and "unsatisfactorily, ordinary dreams". The vast majority of dreams are the latter but, sometimes, we experience the significant ones.

These are of a different order of vividness and power. Intriguingly he fails to give reference to his own earlier work.

In 1946 British theatre critic Eric Bentley wrote the following with regard to both Priestley the man and his work, making specific reference to the plot device in *The Long Mirror*:

Mr Priestley finds what may be the only exit into speculation that is open to a certain class of mind: occultism. In the early thirties he wrote phony plays about eternal recurrence as expounded by the English magician J.W. Dunne. Today he offers us a play about "an extrasensory or second-sight relationship" and three socio-political plays calculated to make us feel cheerfully "progressive". Anyone interested in the drama of ideas should compare them with Bernard Shaw's plays. In Shaw ideas flash, roar, and reach the target in one long fascinating battle fought with the most efficient ordnance from the poison phial to the bomb. In Priestley they fizz and flop like damp fireworks. The inadequacy is at once imaginative, intellectual, and, probably, moral.[127]

His next play, *They Came to a City*, is a very curious piece that was subsequently turned into a movie that also reflects the slightly uncanny atmosphere that surrounds the characters and how, indeed, they came to a city. The play opens with the appearance of a group of individuals, another of Priestley's "cross-sections" of British society, arriving at the gate of a mysterious city none of whom have any idea how they got there. This suggests that either they are all sharing a collective dream or that they are involved in a collective version of what we would today recognise as a near-death experience. The stage directions and the overall atmosphere are reminiscent of *Johnson Over Jordan*. Unlike *Johnson Over Jordan*, *They Came to a City* was quite successful having a long run at London's Globe.

In the summer of 1943 Jack found time from all his war-related work to write what I consider to be one of his most interesting plays, *Desert Highway*. In his introduction to volume three of his *Collected Plays* he states that it was "a gift for the army."[128] It is, on the surface, simply an ensemble work whereby another group of clichéd representatives of British society (the chipper cockneys, the dour Yorkshireman, the West Country farm boy and the Oxford educated dilettante and the Jewish outsider) are members of a tank crew trapped in the Syrian desert when their tank breaks down. Out in open space they are then attacked by a German aircraft and one of the group, the young country lad, is seriously wounded. However, as with much of Priestley's work, this analysis is simplistic in the extreme. A careful review of this rarely performed and virtually ignored play uncovers another time play, but one that takes a very different approach to the mystery of temporal flow.

Soon after the attack by the German aircraft two of the group stumble across an ancient stone monument. The Oxford educated member of the group, Corporal Philip Donnington, suggests that this was some form of shrine left by the countless number of people who, over the centuries, would have passed along this "desert highway." He says:

> I believe this is an old desert road. Thousands of years ago men were travelling this way, and probably some of them often spent the night in this very place. I don't suppose they were very different from what we are. They were on the road too, far from home, wondering what was happening back there, wondering what it's all about, laughing and cursing and crying out and dying.[129]

It is here that the play moves away from cliché into something far more interesting and, if analysed correctly, shows that this much-neglected play is thematically linked to Priestley's time plays.

In a sequence very similar to the end of Act II of *Time and the Conways*, Priestley has his soldiers fall asleep as they contemplate how, over thousands of years, warring armies and common migratory tribes passed the very spot that they occupy now, in 1943. The stage direction suggests a change from everyday reality to something far more extraordinary:

> They are now asleep. The stage is almost dark. A rushing wind is heard. A spotlight, like a shaft of moonlight, comes on to the stone monument, which slowly begins to rise, revealing the figure of a roughly carved stone idol. When the idol is at its full height, the light opens out, and we see HUGHES, no longer in uniform but with the hair, beard and dress he has in Act II, come creeping out of the tent. As the wind still howls, he goes forward to the idol and elaborately prostrates himself before it, holding his position as the curtain slowly falls.

With this strange scene Act I ends and we enter what the stage notes call an "interlude". When the curtain rises it is the same scene and all the characters are no longer British Tommys but a group of desert nomads, part of a caravan crossing the Syrian desert. Time has dissolved and we are now in 703 BCE. Again we can draw parallels between this and Kay's 'time slip' whereby her *Observer One* is allowed a short-term glimpse of a future that may, or may not, come to pass. But while here the nomads may look the same as the soldiers we have just left in Act I, it is clear that this similarity is simply surface. These characters are not like Kay in *Time and the Conways*, there is no residue of, in this case, the future personalities. They are simply people of their time. But they are dealing with very similar issues. We discover that the threat of the Nazis has been replaced by the invading Assyrian armies. Times may be very different but humanity remains the same, including the gift of precognition. In one discussion the ancient version of Corporal Donnington, now an Egyptian scribe, describes how, in Egypt, he met an old man who by fasting was able to gaze into the "far future." This man saw:

> ... strange and incomprehensible things – horseless chariots going as fast as the wind – men inside great metal birds – men making wars – for always there were wars, as today – with thunder and lightning and vast invisible javelins – but even so, Egypt was still there – and the great pyramids still cast their mighty shadows – and the noble Sphinx still gazed across the desert. That – is Egypt.[130]

Here we have Priestley introducing Dunne's idea of parallel times in which the future as presented in Act I is perceived by individuals referenced in Act II and also a clever reference to Carl Jung's concept of the Collective Unconscious. This is a level of sophistication far above what should be expected of, in effect, a play quickly written to assist the war effort. This is again evidence of just how neglected and ignored Priestley's genius has been.

In one link with the future the Jewish officer, Ben Joseph, is now an Israelite guide. Another link is that the character who looks like the young soldier, Wick, is about to die – this time as a human sacrifice.

The second act opens and we are taken back to 1943. According to the literary critic Holger Klein the suggestion is that the group have experienced some form of collective dream.[131] In this version of time Wick dies of his wounds. This parallels the death of the ancient Wick many centuries before. The play ends with the approach of a mysterious aircraft that may be the Germans coming back to finish off the business, or an Allied craft that offers safety.

For me *Desert Highway* says it all about how Priestley is perceived by many, including his biographers. None of them take the time to explore this play in greater detail. The literary critics do better, but not excessively. The most exhaustive review of Priestley's work is Gareth Lloyd-Evans' 1964 analysis *J.B. Priestley – the Dramatist*. *Desert Highway* has one reference and this is simply to state that the critic James Agate abstained from seeing the play because he believed he would not like it.[132] Holger Klein, in his later, 1988, analysis, *J.B. Priestley's Plays*, is very positive. He was impressed with the characterization and the use of regional dialects and felt that the "interlude" was both "bold" and "admirable".[133] I disagree with Klein that the interlude was some form of "collective dream" because in Act II Priestley has none of the characters comment on this nor do any of them seem confused or intrigued. It will be recalled that in *Time and the Conways* Kay is clearly remembering her precognitive dream in Act III. In my opinion this play also applies the Jungian concept of the Collective Unconscious in that the Second World War soldiers can be seen as being part of a collective humanity reliving, in a timeless present, the same experiences. We know that Jack had been aware of Jung's concepts for a few years by this stage. It is possible that he may have attended Jung's famous lecture at the Abernethian Society in 1936 and we know that one of the first major broadcasts he did after the end of the war was an interview with Jung himself. I believe that *Desert Highway* was a very brave attempt by Jack to incorporate time into an ostensibly propagandist work. Whether it succeeded in its aim to subliminally generate interest in his own time theories and the work of Jung is not clear.

As the war drew to a close he moved back to novel writing, emerging in 1946 with the book *Bright Day*. In his book *Margin Released* Priestley stated that this was his own favourite novel.[134]

The novel opens with the narrator, Gregory Dawson, staying at the Royal Ocean Hotel in the fictional Cornish seaside town of Tralorna. It is just after the Second World War so totally contemporary at the time of writing. Like Priestley, Dawson is originally from Yorkshire and had spent time in Hollywood as a scriptwriter. He was suffering from a slight case of writer's block and, on the advice of an associate, had decided that the comparative isolation of this hotel would be ideal to re-stimulate his creativity.

In the dining room he notices two of his fellow guests, a distinguished, upper-class English couple in their late sixties. He feels he knows them from somewhere but he cannot quite place where. It is then that the trio of musicians hired by the hotel to entertain the guests begin to play the slow movement of Schubert's *B Flat Major Trio*. As the "cello began the exquisite quiet tone" Dawson found unbidden memories spontaneously appearing in his mind:

> I was far away, deep in a lost world and a lost time. I was back again – young Gregory Dawson, eighteen, shy but sprawling – in the Allingtons' drawing room in Bruddersford, before the First World War, years and years ago, half a good lifetime

away. The thin ribbon of sound pulled back curtain after curtain.[135]

In his waking dream he finds himself vividly remembering events that took place in 1912 and 1913, specifically to another house owned by the Allingtons, two cottages that had been knocked into one house on the edge of the Yorkshire Moors. He describes how he could smell the lilac and bitter scent of wool samples. He was, effectively, reliving parts of his past.

Here again we have Priestley's preoccupation with time and memory. He clearly believed that music could open a portal to another area of consciousness, an area usually sublimated by the clamour of everyday living. In *Bright Day* his approach to this subject is subtle in the extreme. It is implied that Schubert's music is responsible for his flashback and it is left to the attentive reader to draw such inferences. We quickly discover that the association is, indeed, the music and through this he is able to identify who the mysterious elderly couple are. Many years previously, in the summer of 1913, he had been invited to an event hosted by the well-to-do Allington family in one of the cottages whose image had been evoked by the music (p. 116). He realises that the very same piece of music had been played that day.

The way in which music acts as memory-stimulant has striking similarities with Marcel Proust's much respected *Remembrance of Things Past*. In Proust's work long-lost memories of the central character are evoked by the taste of a madeleine cake. Like "Marcel", the narrator in *Swann's Way*, the first volume of *Remembrance of Things Past*, Gregory finds himself in, as Priestley has his central character describe it: "a lost world and in a lost time." Indeed, it may or may not be of significance that the literal translation from the French of Proust's work is not *Remembrance of Things Past* but *In Search of Lost Time* (*À la Recherché du Temps Perdu*). Is it simply coincidence that Jack has Gregory use exactly the same term to describe his music-facilitated past-life memories? Whatever the link here we have the much-denigrated Jack Priestley applying very similar themes to those of the intellectually feted Marcel Proust. Is it simply that Priestley's novel was published 32 years after Proust's masterwork and as such *Bright Day* was considered to be derivative? If so it is curious that I can find no associations between the two works in any books, papers or articles. For me the answer is far simpler; as I mentioned earlier with regards to Priestley and Strindberg, it is simply to do with the fact that Jack Priestley was just an outsider whose work continues to be seen as popularist and dated. As such, the self-proclaimed arbiters of what is intellectually significant and what is merely artisanship have had their say. Hopefully this will soon change.

In my opinion *Bright Day* is an incredibly clever novel. It plays with time and memory in ways that Proust does not. For example, we later discover in detail the events leading up to the summer's evening at the Allingtons' rented cottages on Broadstone Moor. Here we have a group of well-to-do folk discussing, among other things, the political situation in Europe. We shall discover later another work in which Jack has his characters in a very similar set of circumstances discussing European affairs and coming to similar conclusions. He sets his characters within the confines of a high summer evening, a time of year that we know fascinated him. He believed, like Shakespeare, that the hazy days of summer were when the "magical" can be perceived; when the barrier between this world and others is at its weakest. As we shall discover, he returned to this theme in his 1950 play *Summer Day's Dream* and again in his very last play, *Time Was, Time Is*.

It is during the liminal light of high summer that Priestley introduces the "magical" into the narrative. You will recall that in *Time and the Conways* Priestley has his character Alan Conway explain to his sister, Kay, that at any one moment we are all just slices of our greater self – our body as it is viewed from a location in the fifth dimension. In *Bright Day* Jack has Gregory glimpse the "greater self" of one of the Allington daughters, Bridget:

> What I saw, as I stared in my bewilderment, was Bridget herself as I have never seen her before. It was as if I saw her not only as she was at that moment but as she soon would be, with the woman added to the girl.[136]

Later in the novel Dawson has a similar perception when he encounters his old friend Eleanor Nixey 30 years later when she had become Lady Harndean. He is walking along a cliff path when he recognises the elderly person walking towards him. He perceives not a person in time but as if he is viewing her from a location outside of time, from Dunne's Time Two:

> What I perceived then, in a blinding flash of revelation. Was that the real Eleanor Nixey was neither the handsome young woman I had been remembering nor the elderly woman I saw before me, both of whom were nothing but distorted fleeting reflections in time, that the real Eleanor Nixey was somewhere behind all these appearances and fragmentary distortions, existing outside time and change; and that what was true of her was of course true of us all.[137]

This is profoundly Dunnian in that we have here Dawson's Observer One having a glimpse of time as perceived by his Observer Two, existing in Eternity. Gregory seems to have glimpses of the perceptions of his alter-ego located in Dunne's Time Two, what we would now term the fifth dimension.

Although Priestley strongly denied that Gregory Dawson was based upon himself one thing that cannot be denied is that Priestley described in his own autobiographical writings similar experiences to the one he describes above. In *Over the Long High Wall*, published in 1972, he describes how throughout his life he had experienced odd moments of "delight" as he terms it when, thinking about a person or a set of circumstances from his past, that there is a "little click".

Priestley was sure that time was simply the process whereby the eternal present is kept from us. In *Over the Long High Wall* he writes the following:

> On these occasions I have been recalling a person or a scene as clearly and as sharply as I could, and then there has been, so to speak, a little click, a slight change of focus, and for a brief moment I have felt as if the person or scene were not being remembered but were really there *still existing*, that nobody, nothing, had gone. I can't make this happen; either it happens or it doesn't, and usually it doesn't.[138]

He goes on to explain that he can never force this state of consciousness, it happens spontaneously and without any form of personal control. He was of the opinion that this was similar to the state of mind brought about in times of high stress or the taking of psychedelic substances.

*Bright Day* is a classic *bildungsroman*, the literary genre discussed earlier in relation to the theories of Peter Ouspensky. You will recall that in such novels the central character goes on a journey, inner or outer, in which they grow and develop as a person. This was to become hugely popular with the young intelligentsia of the 1960s and 1970s where Hermann Hesse, Harper Lee, Thomas Mann and J.D. Salinger all became the authors that one had to be seen reading. Yet again Priestley was so far ahead of his time that this book went under the radar. Had it been published in 1956 under another name, something French or German, it would have been recognised as a work of genius. But this was stuffy old bourgeois Jack Priestley, not some working-class 'angry young man' trying to make his mark on the world.

Ironically it was one of these 'angry young men', John Braine, who found the book to be of great significance. He tells how he bought the book in 1951 and read it again and again. In his biography of Priestley, Braine likens *Bright Day* to Rainer Maria Rilke's *Sonnets to Orpheus*.[139]

What I find of significance is that it was a rereading of *Bright Day* that had author Colin Wilson reassess his opinion of Priestley. According to Braine, Wilson read Priestley's 1957 essay collection *Thoughts in the Wilderness* and this started his rediscovery of Jack's work. Wilson read this while staying at Braine's house and had, until his reading of the work, made a series of "off-handed and derogatory remarks" about Priestley.[140] Unfortunately Braine does not give a date to this event but as his Priestley biography was published in 1978 one can but conclude that this was many years before. Indeed, by September 1972 Wilson was writing a glowing review of *Over the Long High Wall* for the *New Scientist* and in this he opens the review with a conversation he had had with Priestley twelve years before, presumably in 1960.

In the review Wilson makes a curious observation with regards to Priestley's time plays and time-related novels. He explains how Priestley started his career as an essayist, an author of short, chatty pieces known as "middles". From this Wilson adds:

> Mr. Priestley became very good at it, and his training served him well when he came round to write novels and plays full of crackerbarrel philosophers.[141]

Is this the source of Wilson's long-held belief that Priestley was a confidence trickster? Priestley did not reciprocate this opinion having given a very positive review to Wilson's first book, *The Outsider*. In his 1956 *New Statesman* review Priestley wrote that the book was a "remarkable production for a young man of twenty-four."[142]

That Wilson is so dismissive of the sources of Priestley's "crackerbarrel" philosophy surprises me. I can only assume that this is a reference to J.W. Dunne and Peter Ouspensky. And yet, over the years Wilson had written extensively about both philosophers, and had in these writings shown a huge intellectual respect. Indeed, in his review he echoes my own observation above with regards to Priestley's powerful observations on altered states of consciousness.

Indeed, by 1988, four years after Priestley's death, Wilson was discussing Priestley's ideas on time and altered states of consciousness in a hugely positive way in his book *Beyond the Occult*. Indeed, the "little click" that Priestley also called his "delight".

Wilson and Braine were representatives of a new form of literature that was to develop in the 1950s in Britain. These 'angry young men' were to become the vanguard of a new form of theatre and novel, something quite alien to Priestley's gently intellectual approach. Their day was still a few years in the future. For Jack, the ending of hostilities opened up new opportunities as an international man of letters and a total change of life.

## Chapter Seven

# The Post-War Years

The period after the Second World War was not a good one for Jack. His daughters and stepdaughters had all, to a degree, left home and young Tom was away at boarding school. His relationship with his wife Jane was not good and a series of financial investments in farms had proven problematical. But what really depressed Jack was that the social optimism by which he was able to write such plays as *They Came to a City* had evaporated in the post-war austerity. Britain had won the war but lost the peace. As a socialist he had great hopes for the new Labour Government but, again, realism had tempered any ideas of a real change in society.

In August 1946 his good friend H.G. Wells died. Wells had been one of the few who really appreciated *Johnson Over Jordan* stating that it was one of the most impressive productions seen on the London stage for many years. Wells and Priestley shared a friendship with J.W. Dunne and an abiding interest in time. In Well's novel *The Shape of Things to Come* (1933) the narrator acquires his knowledge of the future by a form of dreaming similar to that suggested by Dunne, and Wells had for decades written about time being a fourth dimension. So lost into the fifth dimension was somebody he felt he could talk to.

Fortunately, he had a new time-related play to take his mind off things, *An Inspector Calls*.

As we have discovered, Priestley long argued that his creative abilities seemed to spontaneously occur, unbidden, out of his subconscious. He trained himself to react to these thoughts and images and, like Dunne with his notebooks, would write them down quickly for future reference. In the late 1930s a reoccurring image kept flashing in his mind's eye. This involved the appearance at a family gathering of a mysterious police officer. Although he felt this was of significance at the time, the war put it to the back of his mind. Fortunately, he had, at the time, discussed this image with his friend, theatre director Michael McOwen. It was McOwen who reminded him about it in a meeting they had in 1944. This reminder was to bring about a creative fugue by which, in one week in early 1945, Jack wrote a new play, a play that was to prove to be his most popular, *An Inspector Calls*.

The three acts all take place in the dining room of a large house in the fictional North Midlands town of Brumley. The house is owned by Arthur Birling, a wealthy factory owner. The curtain rises on a social get-together. Birling is there together with his wife, Edna, his children Eric and Sheila and Sheila's fiancé Gerald Croft, the son of Birling's major business rival. We discover that the party is to celebrate the engagement of Sheila and Gerald and the implications of the joining together of two major family businesses. The conviviality is soon destroyed when the front door bell rings. The maid answers the door and then enters the room to announce that "an inspector called". This is a peculiar way of stating the facts because, in actual fact, the inspector was calling and is subsequently invited in. The use of the past tense in this regard is, in my opinion, a clue to what is about to take place. The policeman is brought into the room by the maid and introduces himself as Inspector Goole. We discover from Goole that two hours before a young woman had died at the local infirmary after drinking disinfectant. He announces that her name was Eva Smith. It is here that Priestley introduces the crucial element on which the whole play revolves, a photograph of the young woman. This fulfils a similar role to the cigarette box in *Dangerous Corner*. The inspector shows the photograph individually to each member of the Birling family and Gerald Croft. By doing so Goole has each cast member confess to their involvement in the events that drove the young woman to commit suicide. It is here that Priestly introduces his subtle model of Vedanta – that we are all, at a deeper level of consciousness, linked. In a powerful speech Goole states:

> We don't live alone. We are members of one body. We are responsible for each other. And I tell you that the time will soon come when, if men will not learn that lesson, then they will be taught in fire and blood and anguish.[143]

This could be interpreted as a usual statement that we are all members of society and we should look after each other. But this is not the point Priestley is making. His use of language is quite precise. We are "all one body" is not the same as we are all a single society. To be embodied is to be linked in a far more visceral and physical way than simply sharing a culture, location or even common humanity.

With this statement the inspector leaves the house. What we then have is a series of self-protecting statements by all the characters, all using this to avoid responsibility for Eva's death. Then they try to convince themselves that Goole was not a real police inspector. A phone call to the local police station confirms this. Then they check the infirmary to discover that no young woman had died that night. They then realise that although each recognised the photograph there was never a time that more than one of them was looking at the picture. They convince themselves that the bogus inspector had a series of different photographs, each of which was recognised, but were of different young women. There is also a supporting confusion on names. Eva Smith had changed her name to Daisy Renton. This was to be another lifeline to self-announced innocence for all the responsible parties. But as they start to relax the phone rings, Birling answers it, responds to somebody on the other end of line and puts the phone down, turns to the group and says:

That was the police. A girl has just died – on her way to the infirmary – after swallowing some disinfectant. And a police inspector is on his way here – to ask some – questions –.[144]

With this the curtain falls. Just like *Dangerous Corner* we end up in a form of time-loop. The chime of the doorbell and the ring of the telephone are substituted for the sound of a gunshot which carefully links the end and start of the earlier play. But here time is not a circle. We know that Goole was not a real detective and that the detective that will subsequently arrive will not be the same person. But Goole was aware of something that had not happened when he arrived at the house. Eva/Daisy had just died at the end of the play. Indeed, another interesting point, which may be an error on Jack's part but somehow I doubt it, in the first version of her death Eva/Daisy dies at the infirmary whereas in the second version of the event she dies "on her way to the infirmary". I suspect that Priestley did this in order to confirm that there was no possibility that Goole could have known the circumstances in advance.

The similarities in the writing speed between *An Inspector Calls* and *Dangerous Corner* are interesting. Both plays seemed to erupt from Jack's subconscious and, once active in his mind, played themselves out in his mind's eye with the characters and their conversations simply being transcribed by Jack the observer.

Both plays use a similar plot device, a circularity whereby the beginning of the play is the end of the play. In *Dangerous Corner* this is obvious and it is implied that in this new version of events the characters will avoid the "dangerous corner" that brought about such trauma in the initial version. In *An Inspector Calls* this Ouspenskian recurrence is used in a very different way. Time is about to repeat itself but the characters have no opportunity to change the course of events because the source of their discomfort has already taken place in linear time. In many ways this is similar to the time slip in *Time and the Conways* in which Kay is given a glimpse of the future and then finds herself back at the point where bad decisions were made. Kay's knowledge is of no help to her because Carol will still die young and her mother will still make the bad business decisions. So it is with the Birlings. The knowledge that the mysterious inspector has given them is useless. Events will carry through regardless.

But *An Inspector Calls* has another theme, a very subtle one, that shows evidence of a writer incorporating ever-increasing sophisticated ideas into his work. Most critics and audiences pick up on the overt message that in the fullness of time all actions have consequences but there is a second, covert message in which actions taken damage all of us because, in the final analysis, humanity is a singularity.

As we have already discovered, Jack, from his teenage years, had been fascinated by the Indian philosophy known as Vedanta. In *Man and Time*, he describes what this system tells us about the nature of individual consciousness. Looking back to his late teenage readings, no doubt in or around the year 1912, he describes how he:

> Read that if we go deeper and deeper into the self we can arrive at last at the recognition of Atman, the essential self; and that if we go deeper still into the not-self, the world that seems so solid and real, pulling aside the veil of illusion, we shall find Brahman, the ultimate reality; and that Atman and Brahman are identical.[145]

This philosophy suggests that no man is an island and our actions have consequences not just for others, but ultimately ourselves as well. When we injure others we are injuring ourself. This is the central, but very subtle, theme of *An Inspector Calls*. But for most audience members and, indeed, many critics, the play is a very standard three-act play with no elements of expressionism, experimentalism or symbolism. It seemed to many that Jack was returning to normality after the disaster that was *Johnson Over Jordan*.

This play had its opening night in Moscow because no theatres were available in London at the time. It is set in 1912. Priestley's work was popular at that time in the Soviet Union and *An Inspector Calls* was seen as an anti-capitalist play. Productions by the Kamerny Theatre and the Leningrad Theatre were shown in Moscow, followed by a European tour ending at the Old Vic in London.

As with *Dangerous Corner*, Priestley again plays with the standard detective story tropes and creates something truly disturbing. We again have his standard 'unveiling' of facts and characters as the play progresses but this play is far more about guilt and consequences of actions than simply about motivations. Both plays also have the ending reflecting the beginning, but here the philosophical and metaphysical implications are carried through. It is possible that the storyline of a customer bullying a shop assistant leading to a potential suicide was inspired by one of the untied threads found in Priestley's unsuccessful 1936 play *Spring Tide*.

The play is specifically set in 1912, a year that we know has particular resonance for Priestley. Jack cleverly places references to future events contained in a future that the 1945 audience had lived through. There is a mention of the unsinkable Titanic and a wonderfully mind-bending but almost throwaway comment by Inspector Goole when he points out that in "twenty or thirty years' time – let's say in 1940, when you may be giving a little party like this." This is in no way mystical but it does break through the invisible barrier between the audience as knowing and future-living observers of an event in the past.

This is worth following through. For example, in *Time and the Conways* the 'observer' of time-fractured events, Kay Conway, is actually in the scene and on stage and part of the action. She can be seen by the others and has a three-dimensional existence in this world. However, it is located in the future with regards to the previous act. This is not in any way strange in that audiences happily accept that a subsequent act may be taking place many years after the end of the first act. This is how narrative story-telling works. There is a suspension of belief. We happily accept that a decade or two has mysteriously disappeared from our 'audience viewpoint' but accept that the onstage characters have lived through these years. This belief is reinforced when the actors comment on events that have taken place and, in doing so, assist us in understanding the thematic development of the plot. But with *Time and the Conways* Act II is a deeply rooted metaphysical exercise with regards to the audience-actor relationship couched within a time anomaly. Kay has an initial advantage over the audience in that she knows that it is 1938 whereas we don't (assuming we have not read the programme). Our only reference to the progression of time are the fashions, both clothing and furniture, which are of the late 1930s, not Edwardian. But she is, like us, now a slightly detached observer. She subliminally knows that something is not quite right. Like Martin Cheveril in *Jenny Villiers*, she is perceiving events from a location outside of time, from the fourth, or maybe fifth, dimension. But she is not 'outside' in that she interfaces with the future people. This can be paralleled with the audience who also view events from outside of both space and time. The audience watch the events on stage from a similar omniscient fifth dimension.

In his wonderful book *J.B. Priestley – The Dramatist*, Gareth Lloyd-Evans echoes my sentiment that *An Inspector Calls* is a play about how we all share our experiences and all of our actions have a cause and effect that changes the lives of others:

> Although *An Inspector Calls* is technically a return to the taut 'thriller' method of *Dangerous Corner*, the play, in theme, is

perhaps the clearest expression made by Priestley of his belief that 'no man is an island'.[146]

But as I have already commented, Jack's approach to the idea of a linking between us all was far more than a simple statement of togetherness, it was an expression of a deeply held belief that we are, in a very fundamental way, a single consciousness.

In her book *Playing for Time* Geraldine Cousin notes an uncanny coincidence with regards to *An Inspector Calls*. On 11 September 1992 a new production of *An Inspector Calls* opened at the National Theatre in London. In the final scene a doll's house on stilts pitches forward and collapses. This is director Stephen Daldry's way of showing that the world of the Birlings is collapsing in the same way that the social world that the Birlings inhabit will also soon collapse as the world of 1912 is destroyed by the political and social impact of the First World War. Exactly nine years later the optimism engendered by the collapse of the Soviet Union and the end of the Cold War was to similarly be destroyed by the collapse of the Twin Towers in New York.[147]

In the year the play was first performed (in the Soviet Union it will be recalled) the post-war optimism was to quickly fade as the Cold War took hold. But for a time it was hoped by all, including Jack himself, that a brave new world, the "city" described in his play *They Came to a City*, would rise from the ashes. Not wishing to sit back Jack became heavily involved in post-war reconstruction including taking senior positions in the organizations set up by the new tool for world peace and cooperation, the United Nations. Unknown to Jack's *Observer One* this was to set his life off on a totally different course. However, there is evidence that Jack's *Observer Two* had been preparing for these events for some years.

With the work done on *An Inspector Calls* Jack needed something else to fire his enthusiasm. This came in the shape of a very peculiar little play called *Tober and the Tulpa*.

It seems that while living on the Isle of Wight one of his neighbours was a Dutch writer called Jan de Hartog. Due to de Hartog's relationship with his stepdaughter, Angela Wyndham-Lewis, they had become friends. They shared many interests and clearly one of these was Tibetan Buddhism, as was the creation of a movie script. From this came the idea of *Tober and the Tulpa*.

The final film outline, which still exists in the J.B. Priestley Archive at the University of Bradford, tells the story of a lonely double bass player who finds a way to create a companion to give him company. He creates what is known as a "tulpa". This is a thought-form that can be brought into physical reality by applying certain mental techniques. When the tulpa appears it is in the form of a beautiful woman. This is simply a disguise. It really is a monster that is using this portal into this reality to destroy the world.

In a wonderful piece of obscure information, the British comedian/actor Norman Wisdom was very keen on the script and the Priestley Archive has a letter from 1963 in which Wisdom was offered the film rights. He was keen to retitle it as *Adam and Evil* and even up until his death in 2010 he was still working on getting it filmed.

In the story Tober walks past a perfume store and in the window he sees a photograph of a beautiful woman. While this image is in his mind he visits a funfair and plays on a fortune machine. He then enters some form of altered state of consciousness and he awakens in an alternate universe where he encounters a man selling pamphlets. One catches his attention. It states "A Lifelong Pal for Sixpence: Why not find an ideal companion from another world?" He decides to try this. In the new world he gets a job in an orchestra and sees the girl from the photograph and discovers she is called Hilda. He then creates the tulpa and to his horror finds he cannot control it. It runs berserk and kills Hilda. He tries to kill the female tulpa in a series of attempts reminiscent of the many processes the Russian aristocrats did to kill Rasputin. He then discovers that because she is a creation of his mind she can only be eradicated if he kills himself. He is considered to be insane and he is taken to a mental asylum. The tulpa appears to him and says that she represents the great elemental forms of darkness and that she plans to go to America and use atomic bombs to destroy the world. In a desperate attempt to stop this happening Tober throws himself to his death from the asylum balcony only to wake up and find himself back in this world. He goes back to the fairground to find it shut.

The outline story was submitted to the British Board of Film Censors (BBFC) in November 1947 by Sydney Box of Gainsborough Pictures who were keen to turn it into a movie. Such was the furore that the script was initially refused any form of certification but was eventually given an "H" (for horrific) certification. Because of this Box abandoned the whole project.[148]

In October 2002 it was announced in the *Sunday Times* that work on *Tober and the Tulpa* would begin in spring 2003. Indeed, in his 2003 autobiography Norman Wisdom stated that he had persuaded the actress Bo Derek to take the role of the tulpa.[149] According to the BFI website the film is still reserved with a director named as Anthony Simmons but the film has still to be made.

Priestley's interest in writing about tulpas is again evidence of his wide reading. As we have already discovered, Jack believed that the reality we perceive around us is directly related to our mind. Although he never mentions in detail his knowledge of quantum mechanics, he was clearly very aware of its implications. Central to the Copenhagen School of quantum physics is the idea that subatomic particles, the building blocks of our material universe, are brought into existence by the act of measurement and, from this, the act of observation of an "observer." The ultimate meaning of this, something that has been proven countless times in experimentation, is hotly debated. But it does suggest that the world presented to us by our senses is, in some way, created by those senses. This is the central belief of Buddhism and, to a lesser extent, Vedanta. We know that Jack had been fascinated by Vedanta since his late teens. But here we have evidence that Jack was also interested in Buddhism. We know that he regularly wrote he believed that reality, both in its ·physical and temporal manifestations, was a mind-generated hallucination and that the mind can, under certain circumstances, change it. Is this why he was interested in tulpas, the thought manifestations reputedly created by Tibetan Buddhist lamas?

One cannot help but surmise that this work was inspired by Jack's research of the Tibetan Buddhist Bardo state for his play *Johnson Over Jordan*. In the same way that the tulpa is created by the mind so it may be that the Bardo state is similarly mind-generated. As such all the characters that Johnson encounters as he travels "over Jordan" are, in a sense, tulpas.

Priestley was now in a new, post-war, world. His role in the war had been of crucial importance and, for a time, he became the voice of a Britain and her Empire facing the might of Nazi Germany. Sadly, his involvement was not to reap any real rewards. He stood for Parliament as an independent in the first election after the war. He failed to be elected. The country wanted change and in a surprise election result the Labour Party was elected to power. Jack was seen to be a figurehead of the pre-war establishment. The new order wished to look forward, not back. Jack was facing a crisis, but it was a crisis of a personal nature that was to change his life forever, a crisis that he had probably been subliminally aware of for at least a decade. Had Jack's own 'Observer Two' been preparing him for what was about to take place?

# Chapter Eight

# After the War – Dunne & Jacquetta

As we have already discovered, Jack had been reading books on Eastern mysticism since he was a teenager. Of particular interest to him was the idea of the 'oversoul', a part of us that exists outside of linear time and perceives all of our life from a location in Dunne's "Time Two". In September 1968 Priestley had his little-known time play *Anyone for Tennis?* performed on BBC Television. We will return to this play later, but what is of interest to us at this stage is Jack's revision of Dunne's serialism that is found in the accompanying article on the play which was published in the *Radio Times* the week before.

In the article he specifically states that he "believes" that the human mind exists in three different dimensions of time. The first is linear time: the journey from cradle to grave. For most people this is the only life there is, a belief that Jack argues "has done much harm". Making reference to this in the play he writes:

In Time Two, everything that happened along the line of Time One would still exist, though each of us would have access only to what happened in our own Time One. The old name for Time Two was Eternity, which is too often regarded as an ever-lasting Time One. But eternal joy and eternal sorrow are not joy and sorrow going on for ever and ever: they are states of mind in Time Two. Time Three is like the third dimension completing a cube. If Time One hurried events along a single line and Time Two shows us those events recurring, Time Three – so to speak, the thickness of the Time cube – allows us to bend the line of Time One, giving us the chance to change events, to bring into actuality different possibilities [...] I may add that we all exist here and now in all three of these dimensions of Time, but we concentrate almost all our waking attention on Time One.[150]

If this is the case, then this can present an explanation for precognitions. Here Priestley is suggesting that our Observer Two, existing in Eternity (Time Two), has a total overview of our whole life from the moment of our birth to the moment of our death. Occasionally Observer One can gain a glimpse of what Observer Two knows, an event that soon appears in Time One, already existing in Time Two but in the future within Time One.

I have noted earlier with regards to his play *The Long Mirror* that Jack Priestley had, in some way, precognised some of his future works. With regards to *Johnson Over Jordan* we may have evidence that Priestley had dreamed elements of the production years before. In his autobiography *Rain Upon Godshill* he describes how he experienced a reoccurring dream involving people in curious, flexible masks. It was this unusual design of mask that became a feature of the first production of *Johnson Over Jordan*.

Priestley claimed that he had long forgotten this particular dream but had been reminded of it when, just before he wrote this section on *Rain Upon Godshill*, he had looked at one of his old essays. He used to write these as articles once a week. Three of these essays featured dreams. One particular essay was called *The Strange Outfitter*. This describes a dream where he visits an outfitters shop. (He included this essay in a later book called *Apes and Angels*.)

The dream started as quite a mundane set of circumstances in the shop which has JBP trying on a cap. Suddenly the shop assistant and another woman are seen to be wearing large masks. "The most frightening thing about them was that they had moveable mouths." They went out into the street and there was a whole crowd of people wearing masks. Many years later, in the second act of *Johnson Over Jordan*, the crowd all wear masks, particularly expensive masks because they had moveable mouths.[151]

Priestley suggested that this may be pure coincidence but clearly from his description of the dream this is not what he believed.

So what, I hear you ask, has this got to do with Jack in the years immediately after the Second World War? Well I believe that Priestley's interest in time took a different direction in the late 1940s. This was reflected in his fictional writings and also in his non-fiction. Something took place at that time that was to reinforce his developing belief in precognitions and to give him a framework to take the ideas of Dunne, Ouspensky and Jung to create his own model of reality, something he was later to call *Future Influencing Past* (FIP). By this he means that emotions generated at a time in the future can leach back into the past. I believe that there may be an example of this in his own life to which he has given a series of clues in his writings.

In his introduction to the play in his 1944 collection *Three Plays* he writes:

I wrote this play early in 1940, before Hitler set his avalanche in motion. It suffers from the defect of having a central and all-important situation that seems to many people wildly unreal. The fact is, however, that although the setting and the characters of the drama are imaginary, its central theme, based on an extra-sensory or second-sight relationship between a girl and a man, was taken straight from life, one of the two persons concerned being very well known to me. Nor did I heighten the real story, but, if anything, I tended to modify some of its more fantastic features.[152]

This comment has long intrigued his friends and associates. That the source events in question were even more fantastic than those depicted in the play suggests something of extreme strangeness. Also his comment that "one of the two persons concerned" is well known to him suggests a very close personal relationship.

Can the clues be found in the play itself?

As we have discovered, in the play the characters Branwen Elder and Michael Camber seem to be linked in some way. They discuss various possibilities of how they may have met in the past and can find none. They then consider the possibility of having met in dreams but Branwen argues that she also seems to have a form of telepathic link with Michael that suggests more than simply a shared dream. She feels that they are linked in another form of time.

In her attempt to explain her belief Branwen shows Michael a long mirror. At first the two of them see themselves reflected. Then Branwen steps to one side and Michael can only see himself. However, he still knows she is there. She then says:

> I think this outward world in time, where you and I are going to say goodbye and vanish from one another's sight, is only like a long, long mirror, full of twists and cracks and corners, stretching from the cradle to the grave. All you see are the images. What is real and true – and alive – is here, not in there.[153]

The observer of the "long mirror' is Observer Two looking at life from a location in eternity. This is more than simply Priestley applying Dunne's concept of The Long Body, as he did in his earlier play, *Time and the Conways*. In this model the awareness of Observer Two can be shared with Observer One. In this model people can be subtly aware that certain individuals will have a great impact on their future life. This can be sensed before these individuals have been encountered in Time One. I believe that Priestley had created a play based upon his own future memories, future memories that were, in turn, to contain evidence of another form of precognition. If this is the case, then Jack was quite right to say that he had "modified some of the more fantastic features."

Why do I suspect this? Well, Jack was usually stunningly honest in his writings. In his various autobiographical books, he is very straight about his thoughts and feelings. But in his 1964 book *Man and Time* he had a section that suggested he was hiding something. In this he tells a tale of a man that had a feeling about a person he had never met. He says:

Dr. A had begun to receive official reports from Mrs. B, who was in charge of one branch of a large department. These were not personal letters signed by Mrs. B, but the usual duplicated official documents. Dr. A did not know Mrs. B, had never seen her, knew nothing about her except that she had this particular job. Nevertheless, he felt a growing excitement as he received more and more of these communications from Mrs. B. This was so obvious that his secretary made some comment upon it.

A year later he met Mrs. B and fell in love with her. They are now most happily married. He believes, and so do I after hearing his story, that he felt this strange excitement because the future relationship communicated it to him; we might say that one part of his mind, not accessible to consciousness except as a queer *feeling* (italics mine), already knew that Mrs. B was to be tremendously important to him.[154]

Priestley argues that Dr. A was, in some way, influenced in his decision, from the future. As this can only be discovered in retrospect it is rarely recorded and usually goes unnoticed. He adds that it seems that such effects usually relate to circumstances which involve, or will in time involve, close, personal, relationships. It also usually manifests in waking life when a person is suddenly overcome by profound emotion.[155]

This is a fascinating story and seems to be the basis for the plot of *The Long Mirror*. But if it is why did Jack specifically state that the real events were even more fantastic than those presented in the play? Is there another element to this story that is not immediately clear?

The answer may lie in an extraordinary admission that Priestley makes in his 1972 autobiographical series of essays, *Over the Long High Wall*. Dr. A was, in fact, Priestley himself.[156] For some reason, eight years earlier, when he wrote *Man and Time* he was not willing to go public and admit that Mrs. B was the archaeologist Jacquetta Hawkes who became his wife in 1953 after a very messy divorce.

But here lies another mystery. We know that *The Long Mirror* was written in 1940 and that Priestley would have received the official reports from Jacquetta in 1947 when they were both working for UNESCO. Could it be that in some way Jack's *Observer Two* subliminally facilitated in his *Observer One* the plot device of two people sharing a profound link?

According to Judith Cook, Priestley and Hawkes first met at a UNESCO event in Belgravia in early 1947 with a second meeting in July 1947 at another UNESCO meeting in Paris.[157] They had dinner together and confided in each other about their respective lives. Later they travelled together on the Queen Mary to New York en route to Mexico City. It was here that the fires were kindled and an affair began that was to last for six years. In his *Man and Time* comment regarding Dr. A and Mrs. B, Priestley goes on to state that "a year later" the couple met and they fell in love." This suggests that Jack felt his FIP in 1946, at least six years after writing *The Long Mirror*.

As Jack is no longer with us to confirm or deny my conjecture we will never know the set of circumstances that led to his writing of *The Long Mirror*. The "close friend" will, sadly, remain an unknown person, similar to Shakespeare's dark lady of the sonnets.

These ideas that human consciousness may, at a deeper level, resonate directly with a collective mind and, in doing so, allow the mind to access information from other times and places had been an ongoing area of interest to Priestley. As we have already discovered, in the mid-1930s, while staying at the Phantom Ranch in Arizona, Jack had started reading the works of Carl Gustav Jung, the Swiss analytical psychologist. Jung's ideas resonated with him and presented answers to his questions. It was again to do with a Jungian concept that Jack found particularly intriguing: the *Collective Unconscious*.

You will recall that Jung's *Collective Unconscious* was something far greater than the individual; it was an internalized aspect of the collective mind of the human species. The idea that we all could, under certain circumstances, attune into a greater mind, a mind that contains information far in excess of our own experiences, was something that Priestley could really appreciate. It explained his creativity and his feelings that humanity was part of a greater something.

During the years after his introduction of the *Collective Unconscious* and the *Archetypes*, both of which Priestley regularly referred to in his "Time Plays", Jung had developed a theory of personality types that was to become the basis of all modern psychometric testing. In his pioneering 1921 work *Psychological Types* he introduced the world to the idea of the extrovert and the introvert, and to these he added his four cognitive functions: *Thinking, Feeling, Sensation* and *Intuition*. In this model each of the four cognitive functions can be modified depending upon whether the personality in question is an extrovert or an introvert.

By the end of the Second World War Jack had read all Jung's work that had been published in Britain and was fully aware of the power of these models. Throughout the previous decade Priestley had been frustrated that the British public had not picked up on Jung's work in the same way they had done the theories of Jung's erstwhile associate Sigmund Freud. As many of the themes of his plays involved Jungian models he was aware that much of his subtlety was being missed. His attempts to communicate to his audiences Jungian themes in his plays *Johnson Over Jordan* and *Music at Night* had met with failure and, with regards to the former, an expensive failure at that. He was keen to try again, whatever the cost.

During the War, Priestley had become a national symbol of resistance against Germany and her allies. Indeed, for a time his popularity was greater than Winston Churchill himself. This gave him a particular level of power with regards to the BBC. He approached a mutual friend of Jung, Gerhard Adler, and requested that Adler write to Jung on Priestley's behalf. Much to Priestley's delight Jung replied that he would be happy to meet with the British playwright. In May Priestley travelled to Jung's home in Küsnacht, near Zurich, and a meeting of minds took place. This was the start of a friendship which lasted until 1955, when Jung went into decline after the death of his wife, Emma.

Although Priestley never wrote an account of this meeting he did do a radio broadcast on the 18th of June 1946 on the BBC Home Service in which he gave his impression of the effect Jung made upon him. This was the first time that Jung's work had been introduced to the British public. This was enormously successful and Priestley received many letters of congratulations from British psychologists keen to introduce to Britain Jung's analytical psychology. Priestley sent a transcript of his broadcast to Jung who responded that it was the best summary of his ideas he had ever seen.[158] After some initial misgivings, and after a direct request from Priestley himself, Jung agreed to do a BBC radio talk which was broadcast on the *Third Programme* on 3rd November 1946. The transcript, under the title of *The Fight with The Shadow*, was subsequently published in Jung's Collected Works (1964).

This initial meeting stimulated an ongoing correspondence

between the two men. In Jung's collected letters there is one dated 8 November 1954 in which Jung acknowledges receipt of two articles by Priestley on his work. In this letter Jung writes:

> You as a writer are in a position to appreciate what it means to an isolated individual like myself to hear one friendly human voice among the stupid and malevolent noises rising from the scribbler-infested jungle.[159]

This shows how isolated and attacked Jung was feeling at this time. It is reasonable to conclude that Priestley felt similarly embattled with the British and American intelligentsia similarly denigrating his work. However, as a Yorkshireman, he was not going to give up that easily. In 1946 he produced another play with a 'time' theme. This was *Jenny Villiers*, which ran for two weeks at the Theatre Royal in Bath. Priestley then failed to find another venue so rewrote it as a novel which appeared the following year.

Atkins discusses this little referenced piece. He points out that this is a mystery in itself as it is rarely mentioned by any other writers who discuss Priestley's work. He suggests that it is not just a ghost story but also a story ghost. The central character, Martin Cheveril, is a 50-year-old playwright supervising a performance of his play, *The Glass Door*, in the Old Theatre in the fictional northern English town of Barton Spa. In 1940 Priestley wrote his play *The Long Mirror*. In 1940 Priestley himself was 46. I cannot help but notice the similarity of the titles. Was this some form of wish-fulfilment piece?

Cheveril has become disillusioned with the play and falls out with the producers over his extremely pessimistic last act. He discusses this with his leading actress, who accuses him of having become jaded by his success. He is left alone in the "Green Room" and whilst brooding over his life, and possibly facilitated by the drugs he is taking for his depression, he experiences a state of altered consciousness. The "Green Room" is the term used to describe the room the performers use when they are not actively involved in the performance.

In the darkness he perceives a series of events that took place in the theatre in the 1840s and specifically a tragedy involving a young actress called Jenny Villiers.

Priestley had regularly discussed how the theatre environment is one of those places in which a border can be crossed between this reality and another. It is therefore significant that he chose a theatre to have his time slip take place.

In 1947 he was to publish the next instalment of his autobiography, *Rain Upon Godshill*. This is a fascinating insight into what issues were on his mind at this time and it is clear that, yet again, it was dreams and altered states of consciousness that were still intriguing him. In *Jenny Villiers* the "Priestley-like" playwright Martin Cheveril, in a dream state, slips back in time and in doing so witnesses a series of events from the 1840s. In *Rain Upon Godshill* Jack discusses how, in his own dreams, he seems to receive glimpses of other lives and other times. He observes that sometimes his dreams are really mundane. This is surprising to him as he earns his living as a writer who, by his very nature, embroiders life and makes it more exciting than it really is. On stating this he observes that it is odd that many of his most vivid dreams do not reflect this in any way. They are really boring. As he writes:

> It may be that my alter-ego wishes to discover what it is like travelling in wholesale silk in Exeter or organising a bridge drive in Skegness or going on a cruise nowhere in particular with a shipload of dreary strangers.[160]

He suggests that these mundane dreams are, in fact, a glimpse of another real life that is being experienced by somebody. He makes the point that there is a consistency of realism about these dreams that make them believable. He cites a particularly vivid dream in which he sees the "world" through the eyes of a much *"younger and smaller man, really somebody else, a student or something of that kind"*. The dream takes a nasty turn in which his alter-ego is shot by two uniformed men. Wounded badly he staggers into the street and feels his life ebb away.

Priestley finds it unbelievable that his subconscious could create such a sensation, something he had never experienced in waking life. He was absolutely sure that he was reliving the final moments of somebody else's life.

This idea that we exist in multiple versions of ourselves located in alternate dimensions of reality is an intriguing, if hardly original, one. To this can be added Priestley's speculation that we may also be able to communicate with our own future. This suggests a seemingly peculiar nature of reality, but one that is now supported from our understanding of quantum physics and cosmology. I am reminded here of the experiences of American researcher Robert Monroe who argued that he regularly found himself in his dream state (which he was fully self-aware of) perceiving another version of Earth through the eyes of another person. This is exactly what Jack described he experienced in his dream.

Of course Jack believed that his muse came to the fore during his waking-dream states. He cites many examples in his autobiographical material of storylines, plot devices and dialogue spontaneously appearing in his mind. These were particularly powerful when he was in the state known as hypnagogia. We have already referenced this liminal state between sleep and wakefulness a few times. In his pre-war play *Johnson Over Jordan* the central character, Robert Johnson, seems to be in an ongoing hypnagogic state as he goes through the process of dying, and in the play his wife also slips into this state whereby other realities seem to be available. Indeed, as we have already discovered, Jack reported that he was inspired by a series of hypnagogic images and sounds to write *Johnson Over Jordan*. Whilst writing *Johnson* Priestley also wrote another play that has a similarly dreamlike quality whereby all the characters drift off into hypnagogic states. As with *Johnson* this play, *Music at Night*, contains many themes that intrigued him, specifically the idea that we are all simply elements of a greater super-consciousness and that that super-consciousness can be perceived during hypnagogic states.

*Music at Night* was written in 1937, after his return from his extensive American lecture tour. A series of curious hypnagogic images experienced as he travelled across the vastness of the American Midwest on a Pullman train had inspired him to write *Johnson Over Jordan*. Jack was an immensely creative individual and was able to conceive of multiple plot lines that could accommodate his ideas. This was the case with regards to his Jung-inspired material. *Johnson Over Jordan* allowed him to link Jungian psychology with the time theories of J.W. Dunne and the recurrence model of Peter Ouspensky but he failed to fully develop the Jungian concept of the Collective Unconscious in this play. Although adding to his workload he embarked upon a play that would put this right. And this is how *Music at Night* was written whilst he was still working on *Johnson Over Jordan*.

As a great lover of music Priestley knew through his own experiences that the listening to music can facilitate altered states of consciousness, specifically hypnagogia and that in these states the Collective Unconscious can be experienced. In *Music at Night* Jack was keen to show how music can move consciousness to deeper and deeper levels of awareness until the point is reached where individual personality melds into the Jungian Collective Unconscious.

It is reasonable to suggest that this play was influenced by one of the incidents Priestley describes in his earlier play *The Long Mirror* (1940). As we have already seen, in this play one of the characters experiences an altered state of consciousness while listening to a piece of music. In *Music at Night* he creates a whole play based upon such internal reveries and does so with an ensemble of characters.

The set is the sitting room of a large house in the late 1930s. A small group have been invited by their upper-class hostess to listen to a performance of a new concerto. Each member of the group reflects a particular strata of the British class system, allowing the play to comment on aspects of social conditions both at that time and for the two decades before. Priestley does this by having all the characters fall into a semi-hypnotic state as the performance progresses, and as they do their dream states conjure up images and situations from their respective pasts. This is the classic hypnagogic-hypnopompic state as discussed earlier.

One of the known effects of the hypnogogic-hypnopompic state is the dilation of psychological time in relation to consensual or 'clock' time. Priestley subtly refers to this by having the dream sequences last far longer than the three movements of the concerto. The dreamers also seem to move out of the confines of their own bodies and in some way become other people, sharing a viewpoint of other characters. Time and geography also become blurred with flash-forwards and flash-backs across both time and space. In this way Priestley suggests that we all share a greater consciousness that is both within us and outside of us and that this awareness fills all time and space creating a single perceptual unity. In his stage notes Priestley tries to convey this collective world-spirit when he describes to the producers how the stage set should be presented as the music draws to a close:

> The lights change so that the room seems to have vanished and we see a wide sky behind and in front of two columns that might be part of some dateless temple. The whole effect should suggest humanity itself outside of time. At the same time the dead should be grouped on one side, in such a way as to suggest there are countless numbers of them, that we are

only seeing the beginning of a vast crowd.[161]

Priestley underlines this Jungian idea that humanity has a common collective unconscious that contains the species memory of all mankind, going back deep into prehistory. In a series of short statements in Act III all the characters had their perceptions of a lost past converge into a mélange of memory. For example:

**Ann:** I have gone down, down, and I am alive and awake, but I do not know who I am. And it does not seem to matter, for I am alive, awake and have no sorrow.

**Peter:** I am remembering... To crouch in the cave and see the great deer in the knobs and hollows of the stone and then to paint the great deer and the other creatures on the wall of the cave.

**Kath:** It was hard at first to come down from the bare hills into the thick forests, with the children afraid of the shadows... but afterwards it was better.

**Lady S:** When the men with dark faces who came for the metal went back to their ship we went with them, and afterwards when it was calm on a blue sea we sat and combed our yellow hair which the men loved.[162]

In recent years hypnotic regression into past lives has become very popular. Here we have Priestley describing how the phenomena may actually work over 70 years ago. But for Priestley such regressions into the past can be seen as evidence of one simple truth, that we are all one consciousness experiencing itself subjectively. He has one character, Peter, announce with great joy the revelation that:

There cannot be you and I, or any separate selves, and we are walled in no longer but are free. Free![163]

Although I suspect totally unaware of this, popular American stand-up comedian Bill Hicks became famous for an uncannily similar statement from one of his routines:

> Today a young man on acid realized that all matter is merely energy condensed to a slow vibration, that we are all one consciousness experiencing itself subjectively, there is no such thing as death, life is only a dream, and we are the imagination of ourselves. Here's Tom with the Weather.[164]

Of course, and totally unfairly, Hicks was considered to be one of the most intellectually challenging and revolutionary comedians of his generation, whereas to that same generation J.B. Priestley is an irrelevant playwright who wrote old-fashioned Edwardian drama. Curious isn't it?

The play ends with a very peculiar set of circumstances; one of the characters (Bendrex) has actually died during the performance and is taken to the next plane of existence by his already dead manservant, Mr Parks. This incident contains a handful of the classic near-death experience (NDE) themes, for example the encounter with those who have already passed on.

The play also suggests that more than one lifetime can be articulated from the viewpoint of Ouspensky's sixth dimension. Twenty years later, in an attempt to explain a well-known mystery of quantum mechanics, young PhD student Hugh Everett III introduced to the world his "Many-Worlds Interpretation" whereby every potential outcome of every decision is actualised within what has now become known as the "multiverse". This idea has, in recent years, been refined by, among others, Stephen Hawking and his associate, James Hartle, in something known as the "Top-Down" Hypothesis. This is again evidence that Priestley was a revolutionary rather than reactionary thinker, one who was, in many ways, ahead of his time.

As is with many of Priestley's intellectually demanding plays, *Music at Night* suffered bad reviews and has rarely been performed since its first production at Malvern. For me this is a stark reflection of the general public and the conservatism of the press rather than evidence that the play is in any way a failure. Some critics have returned to this play and seen it as an additional Time Play and, in doing so, have given it the recognition it deserves.

In his biographical work *Margin Released* Priestley stated that he was, in both *Music at Night* and *Johnson Over Jordan*, trying to create a "four-dimensional drama."[165]

By now Priestley was leading a double life. His affair with Jacquetta Hawkes had begun but he felt tied to his wife and family. This strain was reflected in his creativity. His output of books and plays dropped away and what he did publish was not up to his usual standard. In 1949 he published a collection of essays entitled *Delight* and then, in 1951, his large novel *Festival at Farbridge* appeared in the bookshops. In this period he did create one fascinating play, one that may well have reflected his own wishing to escape into a bucolic haze of summer sunshine. This was his 1949 play *Summer Day's Dream*.

In this little-performed play Priestley suggests that life itself is a form of dream-illusion. It is set in 1975 in a post-nuclear war Britain that has reverted back to a pastoral economy, its largest city being Shrewsbury. Tom Priestley is of the opinion that this is one of his father's most underrated plays.

The title was chosen deliberately to echo Shakespeare's *A Midsummer Night's Dream*. And the play follows that subtext. As we have already discussed, Priestley was fascinated by the mysterious quality found in evenings in high summer and commented upon this in his essays. We again have an older time supervening on the present, the idea that all times have equal value and equal reality from the viewpoint of Time Two. We again also have another of Jack's tropes: the magical garden. But again we have more evidence that Priestley was years ahead of his contemporaries. Here is a play that is profoundly ecological and probably has a message for the 21st century rather than the 1940s.

The atmosphere reminds me of Woody Allen's popular 1982 movie *A Midsummer Night's Sex Comedy*. Of course, the critics have cited Ingmar Bergman's 1955 *Smiles of a Summer Night* to be Allen's major influence. Well, we wouldn't want to reference old-fashioned J.B. Priestley, would we? That *Summer Day's Dream* was performed five years before the Bergman 'classic' is of no consequence. Bergman is an auteur, Priestley simply an artisan. Of course Priestley is also from Bradford rather than the much more exotic and intellectually credible Uppsala in Sweden.

In *Summer Day's Dream*, the central idea is that the whole of our life is a dream sequence. This was again a theme that had long interested him. In the same year as *Summer Day's Dream* had its premier Jack published a series of essays under the collective title of *Delight*.[166] In this he stated that he enjoyed his dreams but asked where do they come from.

The end of the decade was taken up with the writing of a film script about a man who is told he is about to die and he decides to withdraw all his money from the bank and go and live the high life in an expensive hotel. He then discovers that there had been a mix-up with the diagnosis and he is not going to die after all. Sadly, he is then killed in a car accident on his way back to the hotel after been given the good news. The film was released in 1950 with the title *Last Holiday*. Even with a star such as Alec Guinness playing the central character George Bird, British critics "shrugged it away" as Priestley was later to describe the reception in his book *Particular Pleasures*. One can only assume that the depressing nature of this story was yet another reflection of Priestley's mental state at that time. Things were becoming very emotionally difficult for him and were about to become a great deal worse.

## Chapter Nine

# The Post-War Period – 1950–1960

According to Judith Cook in her 1997 biography *Priestley*, it was in 1950 that Jane realised that there was another woman in Jack's life.[167] He was distant and irritable and had ceased to confide in her. In the late spring of 1950 they took a holiday in Paris. Jane had hoped that this may have rekindled some affection but this was not to be. During the stay Jack wrote to Jacquetta how much he wanted to get back to London. Things came to a head during the vacation and the Priestleys agreed that their relationship was at an end. For some reason Jack did not want a divorce but wished to continue the façade of a marriage.

On their return to England rumours started to circulate. In the summer of 1950 Priestley and Jacquetta were seen on a walking holiday in the Yorkshire Moors by friends of his stepsister, Winnie.

In late 1951 Jack was in negotiations with New York theatres about two possible productions of his plays. This necessitated a visit to the city. Coincidently Jacquetta was on an American lecture tour so they arranged to meet up on the 9th of October in Manhattan. During their stay they saw a performance of the *Don Juan in Hell* section from George Bernard Shaw's *Man and Superman*. This production was unusual in that it used no scenery, no standard stage lighting and the actors, wearing evening dress, pretended that they were reading the play. This inspired them to write a play together using a similar set-up. Jack had introduced Jacquetta to Jung's theories and they were both fascinated by the psychoanalyst's concept of the *four cognitive functions* discussed earlier in relation to Jack's pre-war interest in analytic psychology.

The play was premiered at the 1952 Malvern Festival under

the title of *The Dragon's Mouth*. The sparse stage setting consists of four mikes with high chairs behind them. The mikes are linked by a length of white rope which suggests the rail of a ship. Four characters, two men and two women, walk on to the stage and seat themselves in front of their respective microphones. We discover that the four are in quarantine awaiting blood tests for an unknown illness. They have been isolated on a yacht somewhere in the West Indies, trapped within a small cove full of rocks – the 'dragon's teeth' of the title. Matthew is a businessman, Nina is a follower of the latest fashions, Stuart, an academic and Harriet, a personnel manager.

With regards to the Jungian cognitive functions, Stuart the academic symbolises *thought*, the emotional Harriet symbolises *feeling*, the lover of high fashion, the stylistic Nina embodies *sensation* and Matthew uses his *intuition* in his business dealings. Jacquetta wrote the Nina and Stuart sections and Priestley Harriet and Matthew.

In his prologue Priestley explains in detail the genesis and influences of this "platform" play and discusses Jung's theories of personality. As we have already discovered, Jack had first been attracted to the work of Jung back in the late 1930s and this initial interest was not personality theory but Jung's interpretation of dreams and dreaming.

The play ends with the sound of the returning motorboat carrying the results of the tests. We therefore never discover who is to live and who is to die. This ending has echoes of a similar cliffhanger in Priestley's 1944 play *Desert Highway*. Again we do not know if the sound of an approaching aircraft represents survival or death.

The play received a mixed reception. Undeterred Priestley embarked upon a punishing tour of single performances at fifty-two different venues across the UK. The tour was a financial disaster and was cut short. It then ran at the Winter Garden Theatre in London and was also performed in New York. But the real success was that it formalised the public relationship of Jacquetta and Jack.

One of the lines in *The Dragon's Mouth* echoes strongly Jack's belief in the Jungian *Collective Unconscious* when one of the characters says "… there is something in us, belonging to another order of being that cannot be identified with all this political stuff and its processes." But are we correct in assuming that these are simply Jack's words? We know that Jack had been discussing Jungian analysis with Jacquetta for a few years, but there is evidence that Jacquetta herself had experienced profound mystical perceptions and that she shared Jack's belief that this model of consciousness was true.

In 1932, as Jacquetta Hopkins, she assisted at a dig on the slopes of Mount Carmel in Palestine. In her 1955 book *Man On Earth* she describes how, during one of the digs, a skeleton of a Neanderthal woman was uncovered. As she watched her fellow archaeologists brush away the soil around the skull she was overcome with a sensation of the unity of all human beings throughout time and space:

> I was conscious of this vanished woman and myself as part of an unbroken stream of consciousness, as two atoms in the inexorable process to which we belonged. I saw us as two atoms, but also, a little sickeningly, as two individuals; myself, the inheritor of a consciousness that seemed so profoundly and subtly personal, and this one-time mother of the tribe who must have lived and died hardly aware of past or future, yet who would surely have known fear, and even sadness, when at last her shambling body weakened and she had to lay it down.[168]

She puts this in context by adding that with imaginative effort "it is possible to see the eternal present in which all days, all the seasons of the plain stand in an enduring unity."[169]

A few weeks later she was overcome with an even greater experience of the mystical:

> One night when the land was still fresh from the rain, I was wandering near our camp enjoying the moonlight when an intense exaltation took possession of me. It was as though the White Goddess of the moon had thrown some bewitching power into her rays. It seemed to me that our arid satellite was itself a living presence bounding in the sky – I do not myself understand this use of the word 'bounding', but it comes insistently, and I cannot but use it to express some deeply felt vitality. Indeed, the whole night was dancing about me.
>
> It appeared that the moonlight had ceased to be a physical thing and now represented a state of illumination in my own mind. As here in the night landscape the steady white light threw every olive leaf and pebble into sharp relief, so it seemed that my thoughts and feelings had been given an extraordinary clarity and truth. [...] Certainly it grants man a state of mind in which I believe he must come more and more to live: a mood of intensely conscious individuality which serves only to strengthen an intense consciousness of unity with all being. His mind is one infinitesimal node in the mind present throughout all being, just as his body shares in the unity of matter.[170]

She then hears the sound of a caravan of camels approaching. She senses an overpowering feeling of unity and time stops for her:

> I found myself comprehending every physical fact of their passage as though it were a part of my own existence. I knew how the big soft feet of the camels pressed down upon and embraced the rough stones of the path; I knew the warm depth of their fur and the friction upon it of leather harness and the legs of the riders; I knew the blood flowing through

the bodies of men and beasts and thought of it as echoing the life of the anemones which now showed black among the rocks around me. The sound of bells and the chanting seemed rich and glowing as the stuff of the caravan itself.[171]

Ten years later, in 1942 she described this experience in a poem which later appeared in her 1949 book *Symbols and Speculations*. She called this poem *Man in Time*. This was written at least five years before she met Jack Priestley and yet it is clear that her mind was mirroring Jack's ideas on time, consciousness and reality. Is this yet again evidence that in some way Jack and Jacquetta had been "remembering" each other for years before they actually met? I cannot help but note that Jacquetta wrote a poem entitled *Man in Time* in 1942 and just over twenty years later Jack writes a book entitled *Man and Time*. Was this a simple act of honorific imitation by Jack or were there other forces in action, the same forces that pulled the two of them together in the late 1940s?

The new public face of their relationship formalised matters. On 29 July 1952 Jack and Jane were divorced leaving Jacquetta and Jack free to marry as soon as Jacquetta's divorce from her husband Christopher was similarly formalised. On 5 June 1953 the divorce was agreed and on 23 July 1953 the couple were married at London's Caxton Hall. With the stress now in the past Jack was able to focus on his writing with a clear mind.

The period before his divorce was one of huge stress for all involved. In an attempt to distance himself he embarked upon a new project, a series of short stories. With one exception, all the stories were new and initially appeared in *Lilliput* magazine before being published in an anthology entitled *The Other Place* which was published the following year, 1953. According to John Baxendale in his introduction to the 2013 reissue of this collection by Valancourt Books, Jack used the stories as a form of escapism, a way of writing himself out of misery.

Baxendale states that at this time Priestley was rereading the works of Ouspensky and was discovering new avenues of thought with regards to the Russian's philosophy of time and the eternal recurrence. With Jung's work also fresh in his mind after the writing of *The Dragon's Mouth*, it is not at all surprising that all the stories have elements of the uncanny and the strange. Time effects can be seen in many of the stories. The only old story, *Mr. Strenberry's Tale*, first published in 1929, involves a time traveller.

*The Grey Ones* is story of an evil principle that is trying to destroy mankind by eliminating certain states of mind that belong to the positive aspects of human behaviour. The leader of the "Grey Ones" is a creature called Adaragraffa, "Lord of the Creeping Hosts." If this had been written by H.P. Lovecraft it would be considered a classic of its kind. I suspect that he reused this idea in his novel *Saturn Over the Water*. *The Statues* involves a person seeing a future London through the present buildings. This is an application of a Dunnian Observer One perceiving Time Two; and *Night Sequence*, a profoundly Jungian story, has a throwaway reference to the famous Versailles time slip of 1901. What may be less known is that the subsequent book that then described the event, *An Adventure*, in its 1931 edition, had a notes section by none other than J.W. Dunne. The other stories are also constantly good. However, it was two of the stories that stood out for me. One was the title story, *The Other Place*. In this a man is allowed a glimpse of another world that seems to encroach upon this one, but it is happier, more colourful and more real than this one. I would like to suggest that this was yet again evidence of 'future memory' with regards to Priestley's own creativity. This story has elements of an experience he was to have many years later. As we shall discover, the other, *Look After the Strange Girl*, was to reappear many years later in a much-revised and far more satisfactory version.

After his marriage to Jacquetta, Jack was to enter what John

Braine was to call his "Long Indian Summer."[172] This was a period of quiet creativity and reflection. If anything his work became even more philosophical and more preoccupied with time. He knew he was getting old and the prospect of his own "moving over" into Eternity played on his mind. But this was not a morbidity, far from it. His writings reflect a keen mind wanting answers, a mind that was aware that pure truth may only become apparent when personal time runs out.

An example of this was his 1954 fantasy novel, *The Magicians*.

This is a novel that includes some very intriguing approaches to times, consciousness and reality. In this Priestley makes an attempt at having his character glimpse from Dunne's Time One something contained in Time Two.

*The Magicians* is Priestley's short story *The Grey Ones*, referenced above, expanded to novel length. Here the theories of J.W. Dunne are again applied. It involves a new drug called Sepman Eighteen which produces mild euphoria. Central character is Sir Charles Ravenstreet. He witnesses a jet aircraft crash which destroys a pub called *The White Horse*. There are four survivors; a barman named Perkins, and three elderly male guests: Wayland, Perperek and Marot. The three elderly men are invited back to Ravenstreet's home. Here Perperek explains that he and his friends knew in advance about the crash, tried warn people but nobody would listen. Ravenstreet allows Marot to show him his past using a process they call "Time Alive".

He finds himself reliving, in full, an afternoon from September 1926, when he was on holiday with his girlfriend at a cottage on Pelrock Bay. The day is a turning point in his life, as it is the day on which he received a letter calling him back to work early, finally prompting him to break with Philippa to marry the boss' daughter Maureen. Philippa realises what is happening, but Ravenstreet is resolutely dishonest, and his future self finds the experience a torment, particularly as the decision turned out to be a poor one.

Later in the novel Ravenstreet has another past-life experience facilitated by Wayland. This involves reliving the happiest morning of his life back in 1910. This is, yet again, Priestley himself focusing on the period between 1910 and 1913 as being some form of golden age that, for him, still exists in some way. Many years later, in his 1972 autobiographical book *Over the Long High Wall* Priestley suggests that time is an illusion and that in some way past events are still occurring in another form of time, specifically Dunne's Time Two and his own concept of Time Three. We have already encountered a similar 'time slip' in *Bright Day*. For Priestley such 'time slips' are evidence that it is how our 'attention' is drawn to sensory information that opens up another form of time. This idea was to be developed in his 1961 novel *The Thirty-First of June*.

It is clear that Jack had a great deal of fun writing *The Thirty-First of June*. This involves a series of interlocking times taking place in Priestley's favourite time of the year, high summer – a time when his concept of 'the magical' hangs in the air as an ever-present potential of uncanny events. Although this is, in effect, a satire, it still introduces Jack's philosophy of time. In this case the mouthpiece of temporal theories is yet another incarnation of Dr Görtler of *I Have Been Here Before* and the three eponymous magi of *The Magicians*: Malgrim the Enchanter. In the book Malgrim explains that there are six dimensions in our universe. These are the three physical ones of breadth, length and thickness but when consciousness becomes manifest another three must be added: the sphere of attention and material action, the sphere of memory and the sphere of imagination. It is clear that these ideas had been playing on Jack's mind for some time as, a year or so later, he was writing about exactly the same model in his non-fictional work *Man and Time*.

More than a decade later, in 1972, he was to expand upon the philosophy of his Malgrim the Enchanter. In *Over the Long High Wall* Priestley states that his interest in esoteric matters, particularly those relating to time perceptions and anomalies, were based on his own, profound, experiences. For example, in *Over the Long High Wall*, when he speculated about the source of an experience he had had many times in his life, something technically known as "Involuntary Memories":

> There is another and slightly different kind of experience that I have had, though only rarely and even then only in later life. I may have been deceiving myself, but here it is, for what it is worth. Unlike the others, on these occasions I have been recalling a person or a scene as clearly and as sharply as I could, and then there was, so to speak, a little click, a slight change of focus, and for a brief moment I have felt as if the person or scene were not being remembered but were really there still existing, that nobody, nothing, had gone. I can't make this happen: either it happens or it doesn't, and usually it doesn't. And, I repeat, on the very rare occasions when apparently it did happen, I could have been deceiving myself: I am now wide open to the charge. Even so, if you think that what I have related is worth nothing, then I am more fortunate than you are – I live a richer life in a more rewarding universe.[173]

He puts this down to "attention", the very same "attention" discussed by Malgrim in *The Thirty-First of June*. In our modern lives there are so many things that demand our immediate attention. He describes how we have household appliances that cannot be left unattended and how going outside can be fraught with dangers to somebody not attentive to what is going on around him. From this he concludes that we never allow our minds to just drift and open our attention span to a much wider area of apprehension. In this he suggests not just our attention to detail but also our attention to time flow. He argues that for the most part our brain takes out extraneous information and forces us to concentrate our attention on a small area of perception. He likens this attention span to being a "slit" and advises that what we need to do is widen that slit and open ourselves to a much richer perceptual universe.

Although he does later discuss the theories of Henri Bergson in this regard, this is really an aside rather than an explanation. For me this can be linked to the work of Esther Polianowsky Salaman in her book *A Collection of Moments* (1970). In this fascinating work she notes that such powerful memories become more common as we get older. This is exactly the way in which Priestley describes them. With regards to this age relationship Salaman describes how the Russian writer Aksakov was, in old age, to use these involuntary memories to write one of the most evocative books on childhood ever written, *Years of Childhood*. This preoccupation with his own past became stronger and stronger as he got older. He saw a significance in things that in his younger years he had overlooked; on such phenomena was based synchronicity, another great interest of his friend Carl Gustav Jung. He saw these as being manifestations of the guiding force that he sensed in his time in the trenches.

In his biography *Over the Long High Wall* he describes how one day Jacquetta bought three lithographs by Graham Sutherland. One was of a grasshopper. Later that night a grasshopper was found in their bed. This had never happened before nor had grasshoppers ever been seen in the house. JBP added that he had never even seen one in the Garden. Of course this is simply a coincidence rather than a synchronicity but for JBP this was of significance.[174]

John Atkins notes that there are certain themes in these early works, including a preoccupation with time and coincidence. With regards to the latter Jack believed them to be part of a greater plan. Atkins references a later novel, *Saturn Over the Water* (1961); the central character, Tim Bedford, runs into what the narrator describes as being a series of circumstances that "look like ridiculous coincidences, but in fact he doesn't believe them to be *coincidences at all.*" The italics were inserted by JBP himself as part of his role as the invisible narrator.[175]

*Saturn Over the Water* uses the literary device of the discovered manuscript. In this case the manuscript has been written by Tim Bedford, a painter. In the introduction to the manuscript another fictional character, Henry Sulgrove, states that Bedford "combined skepticism of everything with credulity about everything." This is a very clever game that Priestley is playing here. Indeed, if it was written by any of a series of post-modernist authors such as John Fowles, Jorge Borges or Umberto Eco, it would have brought cries of admiration from the critics. Here Priestley (the author) is having a fictional character describe the psychology of another character, the fictional author of the book, by referencing a comment made by a real author (John Cowper Powys) with regards to another real character, Dr Schott.[176] Of course it becomes more labyrinthine in that Jack wrote the original introduction to Powys' autobiography when it was first published in 1934. It is clear that this particular quotation by Powys resonated with Priestley and it is reasonable to conclude that this is because he felt it described his own philosophy of life.

In *Saturn Over the Water* there are two individuals who are precognitives: The Old Man of the Mountain and Mrs Baro. The "water" in the title is consciousness. This is being fought over by the evil Saturninians and the altruistic Uranians.

This novel again is evidence that Priestley was ahead, not behind, the times. *Saturn Over the Water* is a novel about conspiracies and the way in which human consciousness may be manipulated by nefarious beings, both human and non-human. This theme is one he touched upon in his 1952 short story, *The Grey Ones*.

The early 1960s were a period that Priestley was interested in writing adventure stories, *Saturn Over the Water* being an example, and another *The Shapes of Sleep* (1962). These were in the style of a John Buchan or a Graham Greene. The Buchan link is interesting in that here was another author who had been intrigued by the theories of J.W. Dunne and, in 1932, Buchan wrote a novel, *The Gap in the Curtain*, based upon serialism. In this the time theories of a physicist, Professor Moe, are used in an experiment to predict the future. The twist in the tale involves a misreading of a newspaper headline during a precognition session. This mirrors Dunne's misreading of the *Daily Telegraph* headline regarding the Martinique eruption.

## Chapter Ten

# The Man and Time Letters

On the night of the 17th March 1963 Jack Priestley appeared on the hugely popular BBC TV arts programme *Monitor*. The compere was Huw Wheldon. Priestley was keen to discuss his research for his forthcoming book, *Man and Time*. As we have already discovered, Jack was fascinated by time, specifically the idea that in certain circumstances the future can be perceived in dreams.

He shared with the audience one of his own precognitive episodes, one he had written about a few years earlier in his autobiographical work, *Midnight on the Desert*. It involved his first visit to the rim of the Grand Canyon in Arizona.

He described how, while taking in the spectacle, there started in him a feeling that he had seen this all before at some time in his past. Initially he put this down to the fact that the canyon is probably one of the most photographed sights on the planet and that the recognition was stimulated by him seeing a travel poster or something similar. But then, as he became accustomed to the view he realised that the memory was not from a photograph, but from a dream. In *Midnight on the Desert* he described, in detail what he remembered:

> Some years before I had a dream that, unlike nearly all my dreams, had remained in my memory. In this dream I had found my way into an empty theatre, one of those colossal and monstrous dream buildings, like the nightmare prisons that Piranesi drew. This theatre was so high I could not see the roof, and its tiers of balconies were so broad that they came out of the darkness and ran into darkness again. I had climbed up one of the highest of these balconies, and now looked

across the great dark gulf of the building towards the stage. But there was no stage in the ordinary sense, no proscenium, no platform, no curtains. What I saw was a real landscape, and I seem to remember feeling that this was not strange considering the fabulous wealth and influence of the theatre. But the scene itself was quite strange to me, had some of the bright rock-coloring of Egypt and yet it was not Egyptian. Now, looking at the Grand Canyon, I knew what I had seen, years before, in that dream. I had – and I have – no doubt about it. You may say that my dreaming gaze made a prodigious leap through space, catching a glimpse of the Canyon, half the world away. But I prefer to believe, with Dunne, that the self who stood on that theatre balcony had an eye that moved along a time dimension not a spatial one, and went forward years, in a second, to share with my future waking self one of the moments I would spend staring down at the Canyon from the South Rim.[177]

This initiated a lively and stimulating discussion about the nature of time and the power of dreams. As the programme drew to a close Wheldon suggested that viewers may wish to write to Priestley describing their own experiences that would, as he said, "challenge the conventional and common-sense idea of Time."[178]

The response was immediate.

Priestley had expected to receive a few hundred responses at most. Over the next few months he was to receive thousands. He used a handful of these in the final manuscript of the book which appeared in 1964.

Priestley added an additional chapter to *Man and Time* to accommodate a discussion on the letters he had received. In this he describes how he and his secretary placed the letters in five categories labelled alphabetically from "A" to "E". The categories "D" and "E" were of no real interest but the groups "A", "B" and "C" were. Group "A" involved letters that supported Jack's Future Influencing Past (FIP) hypothesis that we discussed earlier. He comments that he wished he had been more specific in what he was looking for when he was on the *Monitor* programme as these were exactly the type of experiences he was looking for. Sadly, this was the smallest group but the responses were constantly fascinating. Group "B" were what Priestley considered to be "trustworthy accounts of precognitive dreams."[179] Finally, he had Group "C" which were "precognitive dreams not clearly stated and not sufficiently trustworthy, of premonitions and queer 'hunches' that came right." I would like to now turn our attention to the letters that impressed Priestley to such an extent that he decided to include them in *Man and Time*.

One that caught my attention, and that of Jack himself, was written by a research officer at the Psychophysical Research Unit at Oxford University. In her dream the researcher found herself in a suburban living room. She was in animated conversation with some people sitting opposite her on a large, white sofa. Up until this point the dream was surprisingly normal. But then a strange thing did then take place. She suddenly lost the contents of her own mind. She found that she could not continue the conversation and found herself falling into silence. This sensation lasted a few seconds then she regained her presence of mind (literally) and began to speak again. She then woke up. As with many dreams she recalled the events for a few seconds then, as her consciousness returned fully, the dream faded away to nothing.

A few days later she was in Cambridge where she was visiting friends in digs. As the conversation picked up tempo the dream images of a few days before invaded her mind. As they did so she realised that her friends were sitting opposite her on a white sofa. This so surprised her that for a few seconds she totally lost her train of thought. With a huge shiver of awareness, she recalled that it was exactly at that point in her dream where she had ceased talking. As with the dream a few seconds passed and she recovered her thoughts sufficiently to pick up the conversation.[180]

The second case is of particular interest because Priestley's respondent was using the techniques suggested by Dunne in *An Experiment with Time*. What is intriguing about this letter is that the correspondent had forgotten the dream and was only reminded of it when the dream scenario began in consensual reality.

The forgotten dream involved a sparrowhawk landing upon the subject's right shoulder. What was vivid from the dream was the feeling of the bird's claws on his flesh. The next day the subject's landlord came down with some things that he had found in his attic. One of these was a stuffed sparrowhawk. The narrator paid little attention to this, as he was absorbed in reading. The narrator's friend, for a prank, detached the bird from its mounting, sneaked up behind him and dug the claws of the bird into the subject's shoulder. He did this with such force that the subject immediately felt the sharpness of the claws. It was at this moment that his dream was recollected. What is particularly important as regards this letter is the comment made by the narrator. He is quite sure that he had lived the moment before rather than he had simply anticipated it.

It is interesting that of all the incidents described in the "*Monitor* letters" there are only a small number that Priestley comments upon in more than one book. One of these involved a child and the tiger toy that Jack discusses in both *Man and Time* and *Over the Long High Wall*. This is how Priestley describes the dream:

My correspondent, the mother of young children, dreamt that "a large savage beast" – a bright orange colour but with a face more like a wolf than a tiger – suddenly leapt up and brought its face close to hers. She was startled of course, but not terrified; this was a dream, not a nightmare. Next day she took her children shopping for a birthday present, and in a toyshop her small daughter cried, "Look Mummy!" and thrust in her face the bright orange wolf-like mask she had seen in her dream. It was actually a kind of glove puppet, made of sponge rubber.[181]

This particular image featured in a very peculiar personal synchronicity that happened to me while researching material for this book. I had met up with Priestley's son, Tom, for lunch in a restaurant near his home in Notting Hill Gate. We had just discussed this particular letter when something caught my eye at the far end of the restaurant. It was a child sitting with its parents. Nothing unusual in this... but the child was waving around a large toy tiger. That this scene should present itself to me a few seconds after I was discussing the "tiger dream" with Priestley's son was, to me anyway, a synchronicity of uncanny power.

Another example of Priestley's previously discussed Future Influencing Past (FIP) model can be found in a letter that on the face of it describes a particularly mundane dream, but when analysed using Jack's FIP model it has greater significance. During World War One the correspondent, at that time a young woman, was out walking in London. She had no particular objective other than a stroll. She found herself outside a hospital. For some unknown reason she burst into tears. She had no association with the hospital and, indeed, was not to encounter it again for many years. But when she did arrive outside of it decades later the reason for the tears became clear. Some years after the First World War ended she shared a house with an older woman. They became good friends and for twenty-five years were close companions. It was then that the friend took seriously ill and died. Her final days were in the very same hospital that had stimulated the mysterious outburst decades before. As Priestley asks, is this not his FIP in action?

If the dreams can be considered as warnings (in which case,

why are the vast majority predicting circumstances of extreme normality?) then Priestley's FIPs can be used to change the circumstances and avoid the outcome depicted in the dream. However, if this is done then the dream was not precognitive and therefore not outside the understanding of modern science. Of course, in actual fact what takes place in these circumstances is that the initial elements of the precognition ARE experienced and it is these that sometimes facilitate the recollection of the original dream and, in doing so, avoiding action can be taken. This cannot be explained by our modern science. But some dreams, or more precisely their outcomes, simply do not allow themselves to be changed. Indeed, some are structured in such a way that the avoiding actions bring about the circumstances. One such case was also featured in *Man and Time*.

In her dream the correspondent found herself on board a bus making her way down the stairs from the upper to lower decks. She was slightly unbalanced as she was also carrying her dog. The dream was so vivid that she could not get it out her mind, particularly as the next day she was due to travel on a bus. As she was coming down the stairs the dream sequence repeated itself in every way. In her letter she underlines the word "identical". As she had been forewarned she was able to grab the handrail before the bus suddenly took off. In this way she was able to counter her fall. Such was the force of the movement that she badly strained her wrist. If she had not done so she would have been badly injured, as would have been her dog. In this case the future was changed and a new injury received. Presumably in her last 'return' she was injured whereas in this one she received a lesser injury of a sprained wrist.

That something happens to consciousness at the point of death is evidenced in probably the saddest of all the letters, written by a lady I will call HW. This letter moved Priestley to such an extent that he also mentions it in his later biographical work *Over the Long High Wall*.[182] I have to agree. On my reading of the letters in Cambridge in 2010 this was the one that evoked for me the strongest emotional reaction.

The first part of the letter describes how, in July 1958, she travelled by train from London back to her home in Macclesfield (not the Midlands as Priestley states in *Over the Long High Wall* but in Cheshire). All the way home she was overcome with sadness and foreboding. When her husband and her nineteen-year-old son met her at the station she immediately knew that the source of her sadness was her son. She was quite right. Three weeks later he was taken ill and died five months later. This was another case of Priestley's Future Influencing Present effect (FIP).

But for me, and for Priestley, it is the second part of the letter that is stunning. HW describes that on the third day of his illness her son started to show short-term precognitive abilities. He seemed to know what was about to happen just before it did. She gives the example of him saying "a dog is going to bark a long way off" and a couple of seconds later a dog is indeed heard barking in the distance. A few seconds later he announced "something is going to be dropped in the kitchen, and the middle door is going to slam." HW writes that after an interval of a few seconds, a pair of scissors crashed down on to the hard kitchen tiles followed by the distinct sound of a door slamming. Later the doctor arrives and HW mentions this ability to see the future. In *Over the Long High Wall* Priestley writes that the doctor stated that this was something he had seen before in other dying patients and that the boy's brain was "working just ahead of time."[183] Can it be that under certain circumstances our perceptions of time can become elastic? That we can stretch our perceptions out into our own future?

In the film *The Matrix* there is an incident where the hero has what is termed a déjà vu. He sees a cat walk past a door and then sees what he takes to be a second cat do exactly the same thing a second later. His companions tell him that it was indeed a replay of the first incident and that all déjà vu experiences are caused by 'reality' being reprogrammed. This is, of course, fiction. This kind of thing does not happen in the real world because if it did it would lead us to doubt what external reality really is. Bear this prejudice in mind as you read the following account taken from one of the letters.

> The only time that time became misplaced for me happened when I was working as a maid in a place called Dunraven Castle in South West Wales. There were three of us in the servery just after Saturday luncheon – Hans, the odd-job boy, Renate, the senior maid and me. The floor of the room was a terra cotta orange colour. I saw Renata pick up a jug, a white jug, of chocolate sauce. As she turned to hand it to Hans she dropped it. It smashed and the pastel-brown sauce formed a very definite pattern on the floor, something like an amoeba as shown in a school biology textbook. As I looked the whole scene melted and, like *a loop of film* (italics mine), started again. It was terrifying! I remember shouting to Renate, as she picked up the jug, not to touch it, and screaming in horror as I watched the sauce make its pre-destined shape on the orange floor. I tried to explain to them how I had watched the scene take place a couple of seconds before it had – and, of course, they said that if I had not shouted the whole thing wouldn't have happened.[184]

This incident suggests that human perception records sensory experiences and presents these recordings to consciousness. How else can we explain such a rewind of time. It is important to realise that this letter was sent in 1963, a time where the concept of rewinding images would have been rarely experienced. These days we regularly rewind video tapes and digital video recordings. But in 1963 few people would have seen such an image. The only form of recorded visual images would be film or television. Neither of these formats would involve rewinding during performances or broadcasts unless there was a fault in the mechanisms.

It will be recalled that Priestley experienced something very similar when he was staying in Florence. It is worth repeating Jack's description as a comparison with the Dunraven Castle incident:

> I had gone up to my wife's room after lunch, to see if she was ready to go out, and found her sleeping. I sat in an arm-chair near the bed to wait, and then began to doze. I saw her open her eyes, smile slowly, rub her eyes, yawn and stretch and then sit up. I stared harder, and the room gave a little quiver, and then I was wide awake and saw that she was still sleeping. Within a minute or so, however, she opened her eyes, smiled slowly, rubbed her eyes, yawned and stretched, and then sat up, just as I had seen her do in my tiny dream a few moments before.[185]

What intrigues me is why he failed to comment upon the similarities in *Man and Time*.

Could it be that the world that is presented to our senses is a recording? If this is the case, then the rewinding at Dunraven Castle is evidence that we are experiencing a facsimile reality that has already been created. Could it be that the future and the past are, in fact, always present? In this regard I am again reminded of T.S. Eliot's poem *Burnt Norton*:

> Time present and time past,
> Are both perhaps present in time future,
> And time future contained in time past.
> If all time is eternally present,
> All time is unredeemable.

But what happened to the rest of the letters? It seems that they were collected together and placed in boxes and were to languish in Priestley's library until his death in 1984. His son, Tom, collected these together and donated them to the Society for Psychical Research archive at Cambridge University Library. And this is where I come in.

In 2009 I had been invited to speak at a Platform Event at the National Theatre in London. The marketing team at the theatre had heard of my work on J.W. Dunne and asked me if I would speak to the audience before a performance of a new production of Priestley's *Time and the Conways*. I was honoured to receive such a request and immediately accepted. A few days later I discovered that Tom Priestley would himself by speaking at a similar event at the Liverpool Playhouse before a production of his father's very popular play *When We Are Married*. I thought this would be a wonderful opportunity to meet Tom and maybe gain some additional information about his father's relationship with Dunne. I contacted the theatre asking if they could contact Tom for me. I received a swift reply that Tom was more than happy to meet for a coffee before his presentation.

The meeting was wonderful. Tom was extremely helpful and was curious about my own writing. On discovering my fascination with precognition and altered states of consciousness Tom told me about the *Monitor* letters and how nobody had actually read them in their entirety since the death of his father. He suggested that maybe I would be interested in doing so, and that he could facilitate access for me. He explained that he had donated them to the Society for Psychical Research (SPR) and the SPR would also have to agree to me having access to them. As a member of the SPR this was music to my ears.

And so it was, in February 2010, I found myself in the Cambridge University Library taking delivery of the first box-load of the letters. As the box was handed to me I had the most overpowering feeling of privilege. As far as I am aware only a handful of individuals had read these letters, and an even smaller number read them in their entirety. Indeed, it is likely that at that time only Jack Priestley and myself had invested the time needed to review them all.

As I opened the box I was stunned to receive a distinct whiff of tobacco smoke. Here was the most amazing link with the man himself. I was immediately reminded of the photograph in *Man and Time* of Jack, with pipe in mouth, looking out over a billiards table strewn with letters.[186]

What I discovered that cold week in February will now be discussed in the final section of this book, and what discoveries they have been. Get ready for an amazing journey back to the early 1960s where we will share with the correspondents how the extraordinary can be found within a lifetime of the ordinary.

Let me remind you again of T.S. Eliot's immortal words:

Footfalls echo in the memory
Down the passage which we did not take
Towards the door we never opened
Into the rose-garden.

We shall now discover that many people do not need to open the door to the rose garden because they are already surrounded by it.

# Chapter Eleven

# The Unpublished Letters

What followed was, to date anyway, the most amazing week of my life. I read literally hundreds of letters and, without exception, each one was fascinating. I made extensive notes and quickly realised that these letters were far more than simply a collection of odd anecdotes about time and precognition; they were a social historian's dream come true. They are a snapshot of Britain in the early 1960s, a time when the austerity of the 1950s was coming to an end and the revolution brought about by four long-haired Liverpudlians had already started. This was a time of optimism and hope. The space age had begun on 12 April 1961 when Yuri Gagarin had flown into space. Only a few months before the *Monitor* broadcast, in October 1962, the USSR and the United Sates had been on the brink of war over the location of nuclear missiles on Cuba, an apocalypse just averted when the Soviets backed down and removed the missiles. America's young President John Kennedy had played brinkmanship and won. But the generation who responded to Priestley's appeal were not, in general, young and 'with it'. Many had fought in the First World War only to see a similar conflagration take place in the 1940s. They had suffered the travails of the Great Depression and seen the breakdown of the old social norms. After World War Two, a war that comes up again and again in the letters, they found themselves in a new world of post-war reconstruction, of 'New Towns' and the National Health Service.

This mid-century maelstrom seems to have created a world in which time had become, most definitely, relative. The theories of Einstein and the revolution that was quantum mechanics had done away with all the old Newtonian certainties.

And it was from this new world that came the letters that were strewn over Jack Priestley's billiards table. And what a tale they had to tell!

In the end I failed in my plan to read all the letters at Cambridge University Library. I managed to note the contents of around two-thirds of them. I plan to return soon to read the remainder. Indeed, I have recently been informed that there are many hundreds more at the J.B. Priestley Archive at Bradford University. I cannot wait to read these communications because I am sure that many will contain priceless examples of the uncanny experienced by the silent majority, a silent majority too scared to share these experiences with their friends and associates for fear of ridicule or worse. We can now give them a voice for the first time.

Below is a selection of the experiences described in the letters. As I have stated above, it is my intention to complete this exercise and I will, hopefully, publish in due course a book that will deal exclusively with the letters. But for now just sit back and read how Priestley's "magical" broke through for a selection of ordinary people.

I have given each letter a heading. They can be read in any order, or simply dipped into in an arbitrary fashion. But may I suggest that when reading about the experiences you keep in mind the works and philosophy of John Boynton Priestley because without him all these experiences will have been long forgotten.

## The Dunne Letter

The most amusing letter was from a correspondent who had known J.W. Dunne quite well and had invited Dunne to give a talk at his home. It seems that Dunne rambled on for far longer than planned, instigating the correspondent's wife to comment that although Dunne may have been an expert on the subject he certainly had no idea how to keep to time.

Priestley states in his 1972 book *Over the Long High Wall* that he received over 1,000 letters in response to his initial British TV appeal and that a few years later the show was shown again in Australia and New Zealand which brought about more letters. The majority of the respondees were women describing weird time-related experiences. Interestingly many had not mentioned these experiences to others for fear of ridicule. JBP calls this "consensus opinion censorship". Another comment made was that many of the dreams described were *vivid*. He suggests that one of the defining factors of precognitive dreams is that they are very real and powerful.[187]

## Future Memory – Trauma

A very disturbing event is never forgotten. It may be sublimated and facilitate psychological problems such as post-traumatic stress disorder. If it is the case that we never forget these incidents, then it is not surprising that some of the letters sent to Priestley describe precognitions of future trauma. In 1963 the Second World War and its events were a recent memory for all British people over 25 years of age and even the First World War was well within living memory; it is therefore surprising that so few of his correspondents describe war-related traumas. One exception was a letter from RJE which is, for me, still a classic of its kind and one that tells us much about the structure of precognitions.

In 1938 RJE was a young man of twenty years of age. One night he woke up with a start. He had heard a huge explosion. Clearly this was the final sequence of a dream, a dream whose contents had been lost. As he sat up in bed he felt a stabbing pain in his left thigh, right forearm, left temple and his left eye. He then had a powerful hypnopompic image of his own reflection directly in front of him. This image reflected the pains he was feeling in that it had a series of bloody wounds including a nasty wound to one of his eyes.

Two years later, on the 29th of May 1940 he was fighting in a rearguard action at Dunkirk in Northern France. He describes in the letter how the British Army positions had been overrun by the Germans and he and his associates were trapped in a small country inn. A hand grenade was thrown into the building by a German soldier and it exploded in front of him. He was wounded in the left thigh, right forearm and a small splinter entered close to his left eye causing the eye to fill up with blood. He was really concerned that he had lost sight in his eye so he rushed to a mirror located behind the bar. The numbness of his leg wound allowed him to move fairly quickly and he was able to reach the mirror with little discomfort. He stood in front of the mirror and wiped the blood from his eye. He immediately realised that the reflection he was seeing in the mirror was exactly what he had seen in his bedroom in 1938.

What can we make of this? This is a precise 'future memory'. The mirror explains fully why he saw the image he did. To argue that this is simply a coincidence, as some sceptics no doubt will, is to show a considerable amount of desperation. This cannot be explained by confirmation bias or attention bias. It is too specific. If RJE is telling the truth (and why would he lie?) then this is yet another classic example of precognition. But, of course, it is simply an anecdote and we know that the plural of anecdote is not proof. In this case I am at a loss as to what would constitute proof.

It is also important to note that Jack experienced a very similar dream that involved him looking into a mirror and seeing himself reflected back. According to his comment in *Man and Time*, he experienced this dream in the late 1930s and this could therefore have influenced the imagery found at the end of *The Long Mirror*. What was strange about the dream was that Jack felt that the reflection was of himself as a much older man. Writing in the early 1960s he describes the mirror image in this way:

My hair, which was dark and plentiful then, was thin and grey on top as it is now, though my face seemed thinner than it is now.[188]

I note from photographs taken in the 1970s that Jack's face did, indeed, become thinner than it had been in the early 1960s. Could this dream have really been a form of flash-forward in time? Priestley certainly seemed to accept this as a possibility.

Another correspondent describes a similar incident from the First World War. When he was seven or eight years old ACJ dreamed about himself being on active service as a soldier. It was in a place with a hot climate and it was located on a small strip of land almost surrounded by water. In front of him was a high wall and behind that were the enemy who were "lobbing cannon balls, black spheres about the size of footballs and glistening in the brilliant sunshine". One of these fell near him but did not explode. Immediately two officers turned up and asked him to point out exactly where the ball had fallen.

At nineteen he was sent to Cape Helles on the Gallipoli Peninsula. On arrival he realised that this was the place of his dream. The water surrounding him was "The Narrows" and the Aegean Sea. In front was the hill called "Achi Baba". His dream scenario was repeated when a shell landed in front of him and, as expected, the artillery officers turned up to ask their questions and do their measurements.

### Earlier-Life Memories Experienced Later

These are incidents that seem to suggest that either we are precognitive or that we have lived this life before and these are memories of the last run through the "eternal return".

As a child, back in 1908, correspondent GB had a particularly vivid dream. She was twelve years old at the time and lived in a small Essex village. She described how the village had a station, church, shops and a few houses then farms and farmland leading out of it on all sides, one road led to two little hamlets. The road was a good cart-road with ditches and fields of corn barley and oats on both sides.

In her 1908 dream she was going towards the village from one of these hamlets and was riding on something high. She could see the village and noticed something strange: all the fields were full of houses and the ditches were pathways. The paths were black and white tiles. On awaking the next morning, she described the strange dream to her father. He told her that the dream was silly as it was impossible to enter the village that way as it was a dead end.

When she grew up she married and moved away from rural Essex to live on the South Coast near Bournemouth. Soon after the end of the Second World War she and her husband decided to take a holiday on the East Coast. While there she excitedly noticed a bus going to her old village and they decided to catch it and see how things had changed over the previous forty years or so. The bus was a double-decker and they decided that they could get a better view from the top deck.

On arrival on the outskirts of the village the bus turned off the main road and approached the village in seemingly the wrong direction. This concerned the woman and her husband and they assumed they had caught the wrong bus. Back in the early years of the century the only way into the village would have been to carry straight on along the main road. After a short while they entered the village from a new direction, the access being what had been, years before, the location of the "dead end" mentioned by her father after her 1908 dream. She suddenly recalled the dream again and remembered the curious high viewpoint and the black and white tiles. The road was full of the new houses she had seen in her dream. She then realised that she was looking down at the houses in exactly the way she was in the dream. In the dream she had been on a double-decker bus going along a road at that time that had no access point. It was then, as the bus turned a corner, she saw the strange black and white "tiles". As part of the wartime black-out precautions the curb stones had been painted black and white.

What is fascinating here is that it was very soon after the end of the war that the black and white patterns on the curb stones were painted over. They had been painted in this way to aid visibility. So, had "GB" and her husband visited the village a year or two later the curb stones would have been back to their regular colour. This suggests that the 1908 dream was precisely related to that specific journey in the late 1940s. As with many of these "future memory" dreams what is striking is the mundane nature of the 'recollection'. Indeed, GB describes a second dream that took place when she was working as a nurse in London just after the First World War.

In the London dream she was shown into a bedroom by a person unknown. Next to the dressing table was a yellow rug that she found particularly repulsive. Averting her gaze, she looked out the window to see outside a much prettier mauve carpet. As is the case with dreams she found it in no way strange that a carpet was outside the house.

A few months later she was asked to attend to a case located in the North of England. On arrival at the house she was shown upstairs to the bedroom of the person she was to look after. She was stunned to see the yellow rug from her dream next to the dressing table. The shock was so profound that she felt quite faint. She gingerly walked round the carpet to look out of the window. What she saw out the window both added to the strangeness of the circumstances, but made her feel a good deal better. Beyond the glass was moorland running to the horizon. The view was magnificent, as was the dense carpet of heather that covered the hills. This was her mauve carpet!

GB finishes her letter to Priestley with a cry for clarification. She asks, "Please can you explain why we can see things before they happen and with so many years in between?" Clearly Priestley had no answer to this question. For me this is powerful evidence that this woman was totally puzzled by what she had experienced and had absolutely no doubt in her mind that she had foreseen in dreams circumstances in her own future. In both cases the precognised items were precise and very unusual. To argue that these are simply 'confirmation bias' is stretching the edge of Occam's Razor to such an extent that it becomes very blunt.

The banal nature of such precognitive dreams also worried FML. In her letter she describes how she had a very vivid dream which featured an ashtray resting on a wooden surface. A few days later she was at a party and to her surprise spotted the dream ashtray on the wooden tabletop. Like GB she asks why such dreams are so mundane.

A similarly mundane, but nevertheless fascinating, dream is described by PM. She was living in rented rooms and she had longed for a house of her own. In her dream she was ironing clothes in a room she described as a "back kitchen." Many years later, in 1960, she was offered a brand new council house on the outskirts of her town. A few days after moving in she was ironing and she realised that she was living her dream; both literally and metaphorically.

The above incident took place on Wirral, Merseyside. An uncannily similar experience in the same geographical area was recorded by AS.

AS was, at the time of her precognitive dream, living in a very old Victorian house that had been converted into flats. In this dream she found herself standing in front of houses and shops that had just been built. She describes how she could almost smell the wet concrete:

No trees, very bare, sunny and windswept, rather cold. Absolutely impersonal the row of low shops on a slight hill with a south-facing aspect. Again windy with deep kerbs. Flats and more flats.

But what particularly caught her attention were the strange lamp-posts. They were not made of metal as they usually were at the time of her dream, but concrete. Years later she was to move to a house located on Prenton Hall Road. As soon as she arrived there she recognised this to be the place of her dream. There was the row of shops on the slight hill and, most noticeably, the concrete lamp-post.

Both the new houses of PM and AS are on the outskirts of Birkenhead, a town I know well. Could it be that the same housing estate features in both dreams? If so, why?

Sometimes the dreams are only remembered when the experience starts to be lived again within consensual reality. In many ways these recollections are identifiable as deja sensations rather than dream precognitions. Of course, according to Deja researcher Dr Arthur Funkhouser, these are still precognitive events in that déjà vu or deja vécu experiences are simply forgotten precognitive dreams in which recognition takes place on a subliminal level. A classic example of such a scenario was described by another correspondent, LM. She was staying in Ireland with her father and stepmother and they had agreed to attend a local point-to-point horse race. She had never been to this course before but on arrival she recognised it straight away. Now what is interesting is that she claims in the letter that she had dreamed the place but "had forgotten the dream". She recognises everything as if "I'd seen it every day of my life". She then turns to her father and implored him to stop her stepmother riding as LM just knew that she would have a terrible fall. She even knew where "at the wall right in front of us". He laughed and ignored her. As predicted her stepmother did, indeed, fall.

## Attempts to Change the Future

A classic FIP dream-warning was described by correspondent DS. In February 1963 he had a vivid dream in which his car went into an amazing skid. He managed to keep control of the car and there was no damage. The dream was crystal-clear to him so when, that morning, on his way into his office in Sutton Coldfield, he skidded on some ice he was totally in control. He knew what to expect and remained calm throughout the incident. He claims that this was because he knew what was going to happen next and felt fully in control of the situation. This was unusual as he considered himself to be a "nervy type".

If he had not had the dream he would have not been forewarned of the skid and as such the accident would have followed through as it did in the dream. Interestingly, the dream did not feature the outcome of the skid, simply the process of skidding. Could this have been because as far as DS was concerned the skid's outcome was loss of consciousness or worse? This begs some fascinating questions. If the future is changed by the dream how can the dream be an accurate prediction of the future? In the dream-amended world of both DS and HR, the future involved no accidents or injuries. So how could that now non-existent future create a dream?

Sometimes the dream directly leads to its own fulfilment, as happened to JGM. She was on holiday during the Second World War. On the night before she and her friend were due to return home she dreamed that she was cycling to the station and en route she was knocked off the bicycle and run over. The dream was so vivid that she knew the exact location that it took place. On the way to the station the next day JGM and her friend were walking along the ditch to the left of the road. She was pointing to the spot where she dreamed the accident took place and then went blank. She had been hit by an army lorry. As she lay in the road she surprised everybody when, in her unconscious state, she kept asking about her bike.

Now did the dream bring about the accident? Had she not been preoccupied by pointing out the location of the accident would she have not been hit? Would they have stopped to discuss it? If so she would have been further down the road when the lorry turned up. In fact, would she have been at the spot in front of her, the spot she had stopped to point out? Had the dream changed the future in a slight way? What about the bike? In some distant run of the 'eternal return' had she been on a bike at the time of the accident?

A very similar incident was described by BEB. Again it seems that the dream was the facilitator by which the subject ended up in the location needed for the dream to be fulfilled. In the case of JGM she would have been travelling along that particular road on her way to the station whether the dream had occurred or not. In the case of BEB it involved him going out of his way to check out the location of his dream and, in doing so, was again nearly killed.

One night in 1937, BEB had a very vivid dream in which he was driving along a road between Hastings in East Sussex and Tenterden in Kent. It can be assumed from the letter that he was aware of the start and finish locations but the road en route was unknown to him. He noticed in the distance a dangerous looking crossroads so he slowed down. As he did so he noticed that there was a large building to his right that may have been a public house. He noted that his road went downhill with high hedges, and there was a fairly sharp right-hand bend. On the left was an entrance drive to a house, and in the mouth of the drive was parked a small dark-coloured van, facing downhill, with the rear doors open. As he was passing the van he saw what he thought to be the body of a man lying in the van with his feet half outside the open doors. He was sure this was a trick of the light but to make quite sure nothing was wrong he stopped a few hundred yards farther on and walked back up hill to the van:

> The van was completely empty and I laughed half-ashamedly to myself for being stupid. Just as I turned away from the van to walk back to my car a big black car (Bentley?) flashed by me downhill and very nearly caught my right elbow.

It was this incident that woke him up.

He was so puzzled by this that the next day he drove his car to the location of his dream. The geography of the scene was exactly as it was in the dream down to the smallest detail, with the exception of the "dead body".

He put the dream to the back of his mind, but he decided that the road was a useful route from his home to Hastings. So when he found he had to travel to Hastings two months later he decided to take the new route. As he drove past the sharp right-hand bend he glanced at the entrance to the house. To his utter surprise he saw, yet again, the van with the body of a man lying with his feet half out. He then followed exactly the same behaviour as he did in the dream stopping a few hundred yards farther down the road and walking back to the drive. There was the van and, again, it was empty with no sign of a body:

> I talked out loud to myself (a thing I am liable to do when I am alone) and said: "Now we want the Bentley to complete the picture." I think I was really more afraid than excited.

He turned and looked up the hill. As he did so he just escaped being hit by the black Bentley coming down the hill at speed. Interestingly he states that from then on his actions were different from the dream in that he sat down on the bank in a state of shock and smoked a cigarette.

Had he not had the dream he would not have discovered the new route and, as such, would not have taken that route on that day, or, indeed any other day. That he ended up in that exact location in order to witness, yet again, the speeding Bentley is uncanny in the extreme. It is logical to conclude that on the previous occasion (the one in which the dream was based) he was similarly missed by the car. So was the dream a future memory? But if it was why was it that without the instigation of the dream BEB would not have been at that location?

One of the most stunning of all the letters was sent in by DP. He describes an incident that took place in early September 1952. He and his wife were planning to drive home early from their holiday in Dorset to watch the Farnborough Air Show on the first public day and then carry on home after the show was over. As they were driving from Dorset his wife told him that she did not want to go to the show. The night before she had experienced a vivid dream that one of the aircraft had exploded during its exhibition and crashed into the crowd. She described the plane as silver with swept-back wings. He convinced her that it was just a dream and that everything would be okay. They had already bought the tickets so she agreed to attend.

About halfway through the show the DH.110 came out piloted by John Derry. This plane took off ready for its display. As it flew past David's wife grabbed his arm and said, "That's the plane I saw in my dream – only it was silver not black." Indeed, this DH.110 was, indeed, black. She was really uneasy throughout the display but when the plane landed safely she was relieved.

They then travelled home to Welwyn Garden City. However, the next day, the 6th of September 1952, the evening papers carried the grim news that the DH.110 piloted by John Derry had crashed into the crowd killing twenty-eight spectators. What was very odd was that the plane that crashed was, as his wife predicted, silver. It was not the machine that they had seen the day before. The black plane had been specially painted for the event but it had developed a fault on the Saturday morning. The first prototype was then used. This had not been painted and was still silver. John Derry had flown back to Hatfield to pick this reserve aircraft up and flew it back to Farnborough for the display.

This is an amazing precognition because it looked as if it was incorrect but then was shown to be uncannily accurate. In turn this dream was reported to somebody other than the dreamer before the accident took place.

## Short Time-Span Dreams

HR describes another dream that also involved only a few hours between the dream experience and the events coming to pass in 'real life'. In her dream she was with her sister-in-law looking out from a window. Everything in front of her was in flames. In the centre of the flames she could see her brother in an airplane. She recalled that in the dream her sister-in-law kept saying, "How will he get down?" She had this dream on a Thursday night. It was so vivid that she decided to visit them the next day (Friday) and warn them. She was sure that her brother was not likely to be in a plane but she sensed that the dream meant danger. When she told them about the dream they laughed at her and asked her what she had had for supper. On the following day her brother and sister-in-law went to Lee-on-the-Solent to do some fishing. I am unsure if Hilda heard of the news the next day or if she is just using this as a description device in her letter, but I suspect from her wording that this is a similar case to Dunne's Martinique dream. She describes it thus:

> In the morning paper on Monday I read "Lee-on-the-Solent pier destroyed by fire" and the following paragraphs described how a 'Mr X' (my brother) was trapped with his small son on the end of the pier, after part had collapsed and had to hold his son and jump 20 feet into sea, to be picked up by a boat. My sister-in-law who was standing on the land side of the pier beyond the gap told me afterwards that she kept saying, "However will they get down."

My research has discovered that the fire took place on 19 June 1932 and destroyed the Golden Hall Pavilion at the end of the pier. This was never rebuilt. Unfortunately, I have not been able to find the original newspaper report but I have found photographs of the event and a website that tells how "a group of fishermen were trapped on the landing stage and had to be rescued by speedboat."[189]

Another correspondent, HD, described how, when visiting Brussels, he had a vivid dream that he suggests was similar to Jack's "Grand Canyon" incident described in the TV programme. HD explained that in his dream he saw a man in a checkered suit pointing at a large building while standing on a stone parapet. The next day he was taken to the Palace of Justice. He immediately recognised it as the building in his dream. And as he did so he noticed a man in a checkered suit standing on the stone parapet pointing in exactly the way he did in the dream. Although clearly not a classic FIP in that the knowledge of the future event did not facilitate a change of behaviour when encountered in normal time, this clearly was an experience that could be explained as a dream-stimulated déjà vu.

## Mundane-Dunnes

As we have already discovered, in his book *An Experiment with Time* J.W. Dunne described how many precognitive dreams relate not to the events depicted in the dream but to the circumstances by which the dreamer encounters the information that creates the dream. The classic example is his own Martinique dream in which his dream was created from information he had read in a future edition of the *Daily Telegraph*.

An example of such a dream is one described by EMD. When she was eighteen EMD had a very vivid dream in which a friend of hers and her son were sitting either side of her but they could not speak to each other. In the dream the son asked Eileen to tell his mother to send on his tie pin which he had left on his dressing table. That was it. The next day, at work, she mentioned this dream to her friend. Three days later the friend came into Eileen's office with a letter that she had received that morning from her son (who was actually away at college). On the final page was written, "Will you please send my tie pin which I left on the dressing table."

For me this is an absolute classic Dunne Dream. It is mundane but curiously precise. Clearly her dream had 'remembered' reading the letter. Possibly due to circumstances building up the few days before when she knew that her friend's son was about to return to college. Could that knowledge have acted as a trigger for the 'future memory' to appear in dream-form?

I semi-jokingly call these "Mundane-Dunnes". It seems that EMD had many of these. In the letter she goes on to describe how she had dreamed of a miniature reel of pink cotton such as one that would be found on a child's sewing machine. The very next day her daughter was playing in the garden and came in to show her mother something she had dug up. It was exactly the object that EMD had dreamed of the night before.

She also dreamed of being in Dartford, a town she had never been to. In the dream she felt very gloomy. Two years later she had to go to Dartford to visit her mother who was in hospital to have her leg amputated. She also had two specific dreams of named factories on fire (one was "Foster Clark's"). Both fires subsequently took place.

However, not all her dreams were Mundane-Dunnes. When she was a youngster she had dreamed that a boy she was engaged to at the time approached her with both his hands on fire. A few years later, in his occupation as an electrician, he was involved in an explosion in which both his hands were severely burned. Had she acted upon this dream she may have been able to warn the young man of the danger and this may have made him extra careful.

Sometimes a Mundane-Dunne involves the perception of something that is outside of the dreamer's normal experience only for them to encounter an identical object in the future. One of my favourites was described in a letter from correspondent JN. In her very vivid dream she found herself in a cottage. She specifically remembered one room and her attention being drawn to an odd electric point in the skirting board. On waking she recalled having asked somebody else in the dream where the cottage was. "Shap," was the reply. When she told her husband his reply was, "Whoever would want a cottage at Shap."

Two years later she and her husband were staying in Penrith and they saw a cottage for sale in an estate agent's window. They decided, on impulse, to view it. On entering the cottage, she immediately recognised the room as being identical to the one in her dream and there on the skirting board was the plug! She then asked the address and she was told "Shap Road". It was about two miles from Shap village. They did, indeed, buy the property.

One of Priestley's correspondents, Mrs AG, describes another classic of this kind.

In the dream, which reoccurred many times, AG found herself standing in a narrow street in front of a curiously built house. After a few moments the dream has her enter the house through the front door. The sparsely furnished living room had white, pastel-coloured walls and two elaborately carved chairs and a chest. Covering the floor was a beautiful "eastern-style" carpet. But what was slightly disturbing was that in the centre of the room stood a little, very fair-haired child. The child acknowledges the presence of AG and holds out her arms as if she wishes to be picked up. AG tries to move towards the child but she finds herself rooted to the spot. At this point the dream fades and she wakes up.

Many months later AG was watching a French film with her husband when she spotted the street and the curious little house as it was in her dream. Much to her frustration the movie showed the actress walk past the house and go into a cafe "on the corner". This really frustrated AG as she clearly hoped that the actress would enter the house and confirm or not her dream. Years later she was reminded of the dream when her own little girl acted in the same fashion as the dream child. This time she was not "rooted to the spot" and was able to pick her up.

It seems as if two future incidents had been cobbled together by AG's subconscious and, in doing so, created a logical narrative.

A classic Dunne Dream involves the subject's subconscious creating a dream out of material that will be encountered at some stage in the future. For example, in Dunne's own dream involving the volcanic eruption on Martinique, the dream was created from information he was to read in a newspaper. In one of the Priestley letters the correspondent describes an example of precognition which is almost a Dunne Dream in reverse. Unfortunately, the writer signs off the letter with an illegible signature so I will call him Tom.

Tom and his friend were regulars at a local public house in Bolton in the North West of England. However, they had not visited it for a few weeks, so it was strange one evening when Tom experienced a very vivid dream involving the pub and its landlord. In the dream Tom finds himself in the bar and in conversation with the landlord. The landlord explained to him that he had found something quite odd in the pub's cellar. Tom is curious and asks if he can be shown the strange object. The landlord agrees and they both go down the steps into the cellar. Tom is amazed as to how many pipes there are in a pub cellar, having never been in one in his non-dream state. In the gloom the landlord points out a curious object in the corner. It is a glass aquarium with a fish in it. Tom then wakes up.

Tom immediately contacted his friend and described the dream to him in great detail. A few days later his friend turns up with a copy of the local evening newspaper. Tom could not believe what he was reading:

There in print ran an article on our landlord who had apparently found a large fish in a glass case, the only thing wrong was that he found it in the attic, not the cellar. He found this the day after the dream.

This stunned both of them. But things got stranger. Four or five weeks later the friends were invited to a party at the pub and decide to go along. The landlord asked them to bring along a tape recorder so they could have some music. On arrival they discover that the party was upstairs and the flex on the recorder was not long enough. Tom asked the landlord for an extension lead; he said he thought that he had one and asked Tom to go with him. "He led me down the cellar and I helped him unconnect the wire." As Tom turned to go back upstairs he saw the fish in the case:

> I asked him why he fetched it down the cellar and he told me he was thinking of putting it up in one of the rooms and was waiting for the fittings. He had put it down there out of the way.

One of Priestley's correspondents (H I-F) opens his letter with the words: "I have waited 25 years for this moment!" He describes how he had been fascinated by the theories of J.W. Dunne since he was a young man. From the age of fifteen he had kept a dream diary as suggested by Dunne. He was keen to share one particular example of how strange precognitions can be. In 1937 he recorded a dream in which he saw what to him was a ridiculous sight:

> Moving across the field from right to left was a line of animals and birds. They appeared to be moving with a purpose like a cordon of men searching the field. I recorded my dream in the morning and said to myself, "There's one dream which is utter nonsense – no precognition here!" I was wrong.

He describes how, three days later, he was looking across the exact field as he saw in his dream and there was the straight line of birds moving across the field from right to left. He excitedly called to his grandfather, who was a naturalist, and asked him what breed the birds were and was what they were doing part of their natural behaviour. His grandfather informed him that the birds were fieldfares but why they were moving collectively and in such a strange way was a mystery to him. The birds soon flew off. H I-F adds that although he has seen large groups of these birds many times over the years this was the only time he observed this peculiar behaviour.

So here again we have a precognition of a specific, and seemingly unique, experience. This clearly was an unusual image and something that a person would remember for many years afterwards. Is this evidence of Ouspensky's "eternal recurrence" in that this image was so unusual that it was remembered from a past life, from when it was last experienced? If this is the case on how many previous occasions had the precognition imbued the whole experience with particular resonance and is that why he remembered it with such clarity? But in this regard one must conclude that at some stage in the past H I-F must have seen this event for the first time; in which case there would be no 'memory' of it happening before and therefore it would not have the uniqueness ascribed to it in later 'recurrences'.

I have managed to research the background to this person and it seems he was a very well respected, and much decorated, high-ranking officer in the British Army and subsequently held senior positions in industry and commerce.

## The Thirty-Three Eggs

One of JBP's respondents was a woman who wrote to him to say that she had a dream that a farmer would arrive at their door with 33 eggs in a bucket. In her dream she was standing on the stairs when another 3 eggs were handed to her. When she wakes she is having breakfast with her family and mentioned the dream. Shortly afterwards a farmer turned up and hands her a bucket containing, he said, three dozen eggs. She put them in a basket and paid the farmer. A few minutes later her husband calls to her whilst she was upstairs. He tells her that her dream was right and that there were only 33 eggs, not 36. As she was counting them out the farmer's wife turned up and as she was standing on the stairs handed her the missing three eggs.

This is an example of how JBP misses the clues. This is a classic Dunne precognition in that the woman dreamed the event as if she had heard the story before she went to sleep. Her mind then garbles up the events and conjures up a dream linked to the information she has. This was not, as JBP believes, a precognition, but a dream linked to what she knew. This was not a precognition but a dream triggered by a memory.

> A woman dreamed that she was on a train. At some point the driver got out to check what was underneath the wheels. The train started again leaving him behind. The train then went on driverless. She recounted this dream to her family that morning. Next day, during the evening, she and her husband were listening to the radio. The announcer said that, "this morning a very curious thing occurred in the South of France"; he then related the events of her dream.

Dunne argued that sometimes precognitive dreams consist of a series of perceptions that are cobbled together in such a way that the dream narrative needs deciphering in order to isolate its meaning. A wonderful example of this was sent to Priestley by JM, a schoolteacher based in Devon.

In her dream JM was taking a class of boys and girls. As she entered the classroom there was a small commotion. Two children had been fighting but as JM entered the room they stopped and sat down in their respective desks. One of them, a little girl, had a badly smashed face. Her head was split in two right down to the bridge of her nose. Concerned, the teacher asked the child what had happened. The child explained that she had been hit by an axe. With this horrible image in her mind JM woke up.

The next day at school, she was asked if she would take a class as someone was ill. She agreed and, as she entered the classroom, she was immediately reminded of her dream from earlier that morning. In front of her was the identical classroom full of boys and girls. But there was no sign of any commotion and, much to her relief, no sweetly smiling little girl with a cleaved head.

When they finished the work she had set them she decided to read them a story from a history book of which they were very fond. She chose a story about Robert the Bruce. At the end of the story there was an account of the battle between Edward II and Robert. This story focused on the fate of an English knight called Henry de Bohun. She read out to the class how de Bohun had charged at Robert the Bruce and in his defence the Scottish king had smashed de Bohun's skull in two with his axe:

> At that moment I looked up from the book and sitting directly in front of me, smiling, was the little girl of my dream. Her name is Bone. I was very glad that she was all in one piece!

Here we have a dream that has all the information taken from a future cognition, but subtly transposed. There is an incident where somebody's skull is split open by an axe and a play on words with regards to the names Bohun and Bone. But it is totally mundane and serves no real purpose. There was no fight and the prior knowledge of the circumstances achieved nothing. Is this simply a 'charged memory' travelling backwards in time?

If this was an isolated incident in life of JM then it could be put down to simple coincidence, an application of the "Law of Large Numbers" and "Confirmation Bias" whereby one set of vaguely coincidental dreams to actuality circumstances are shoe-horned in to create a precognition. But JM describes in her letter other incidents, including a really strange "doppelganger" incident. I would like to quote this in full as I think she describes it so well:

> It was about 9:30 on a very quiet starry night. A beautiful night. I was walking the short distance between the houses. On one side the playing fields, on the other a few cottages. There was no one about but I was aware of someone walking beside me. I didn't feel afraid, which surprised me later. I turned my head to see who it was when I saw myself, quite clearly walking along looking at me. It wasn't really like a mirror reflection for I remember I smiled and the other me didn't smile back! This lasted half a minute I suppose – I don't know – it may have been more – or less. At any rate it has never happened since. Although I often wish it would happen again.

The literal translation from German for the word 'doppelganger' is 'double-walker' and this is exactly what is described here by JM. It is clear from her description that this was a journey she did regularly. Unfortunately, she fails to describe whether her double was wearing identical clothing to herself or not. I suspect from the fact that she doesn't comment about this, and states that the image was not like a mirror reflection, that there were differences. Could the answer here be that it was another form of time slip in which she was encountering a future or, indeed, past, image of herself walking along the same path?

This has curious parallels with an incident described by German writer/philosopher Johann Wolfgang von Goethe in his autobiography *Poetry and Truth, Part 3, Book 11*. In this he describes the following curious event:

> I was riding on the footpath towards Drusenheim, and there one of the strangest presentments occurred to me. I saw myself coming to meet myself on the same road on horseback, but in clothes such as I had never worn. They were light grey

mixed with gold. As soon as I had aroused myself from the daydream the vision disappeared. Strange however, it is that eight years later I found myself on the identical spot, intending to visit Frederika once more, and in the same clothes which I had seen in my vision, and which I now wore, not from choice but by accident.[190]

Let us review this whole event in the light of the information we now have. Goethe sees himself as he will be in eight years' time. For a few seconds Goethe seems to have perceived an event that to him is yet to happen but within the timeless zone of the fifth dimension has concurrent existence.

Of course Priestley had presented exactly this effect in his play *Time and the Conways*. This will be the third time that I have referenced Alan Conway's speech at the end of Act II. We are now in a position to really appreciate the explanatory power of Alan's words:

> ... at this moment, or any moment, we're only a cross-section of our real selves. What we really are is the whole stretch of ourselves, all our time, and when we come to the end of this life, all of those selves, all of our time, will be us – the real you, the real me.[191]

In a similar letter, a male correspondent, RS, describes an event that would have been very at home if it were described by Goethe or, in a fictional capacity, by characters from Priestley's plays *I Have Been Here Before* or *Time and the Conways*.

RS was a student at Cambridge University back in the early 1930s. He states that at that time he had a huge decision to make, one that he knew would change his life. He doesn't tell what this is but he does explain that one option was an easy one and one not so. However, he was also very aware that the decision that he was to make would change not only the path of his own life but also many others. He describes what happened to him that evening as being a "threshold experience".

As soon as he had decided that a decision must be made his mind seemed to take on a life of its own. He was no longer thinking about what would happen, but being shown what would happen. He states that he literally "saw" his future like a film being projected in front of his eyes. It was then that something even stranger happened:

> I felt as if my own centre of consciousness were displaced outside of the time-sequence altogether, and that I was looking down at my whole life, from beginning to end, with complete clarity, intertwined with the lives of others, for all the world as though I were looking at a long, extended map. The past portion of it to the left was all set and crystal-clear. The future portion was more complex, with an added dimension of ambiguities at various points along its length due, presumably, to many minor, but genuine choices which I, and other people, might make. I knew that my choice, then and there, must be along this course – and I saw it all. There is nothing which has happened to me ever since about which I cannot say, "I have already faced this through." I faced it through at that particular timeless moment, swung out of time, and all is well.

Later in the letter he attempts to explain what this experience really was. He felt that he was in some way seeing his life from the viewpoint of another part of him that was subliminal during normal experience:

> It was as though my centre of consciousness were displaced into some deeper, more ground-like level which was always part and parcel of my total self, and yet was transcendent to the plane of time within which the ordinary work-a-day 'I' is constrained.

This suggests that there is a deeper element of our consciousness that exists outside linear time and views everything from a position in the fifth dimension. Dunne called this "Observer 2" and many times Priestley alluded to this timeless part of us. I am reminded here of what is known as the "Tesseract Sequence" from Christopher Nolan's movie *Interstellar*. In this the central character Cooper communicates with his daughter in his own past from a location within the fifth dimension. From here he can see his whole life from outside of space-time. Of course, in a fictional context this is the place that Robert Johnson finds himself in *Johnson Over Jordan* when he is given access to his own past and a potential future involving his wife, Jill.

Usually such perceptions are triggered during periods of high stress or in the liminal states between sleep and wakefulness. One such state is known as the Near-Death Experience, or NDE. One of Priestley's correspondences, JPC, describes what happened to him when he had been driving a car too fast and he skidded off a bridge and the car fell through the air for around forty feet:

> As I fell at the wheel (through trees and branches that smashed through the windscreen and pierced me just above the eye). There were two "Me's" – one hurtling at great speed to crash and utterly wreck the car giving me broken ribs, concussion and chipped teeth, and another 'me' detached and watching this scene high up and in which there was seemingly no time – both these two times – terrific speed and an almost still or photo-static time – were concurrent and the two "me's" fused again as the car and I crashed and hit the ground in the ravine below.

This 'splitting of consciousness' is of profound importance when understanding what is really taking place in these circumstances. Consciousness is not splitting but everyday consciousness suddenly becomes aware of another, higher focus of awareness, that shares our perceptions. Again this may simply be a tuning into Dunne's "Observer 2" or it may be something far more intriguing. Is this the 'shadow self', the 'double-walker' that is always at our shoulder, matching us step by step as we make our way through life? Is it possible that our 'doppelganger' is the part of us that remembers all our lives?

## Simple Precognitions

If the hypothesis is that we have lived our lives many times in the past then sometimes precognitive dreams are simply a memory of the future that is, in a significant way, the past. As such these dreams are not warnings because nothing can be done to change their inevitability as they are beyond human control. One such example was sent to Priestley by AM.

She and her husband had recently moved into a new flat. He was very happy there but she had a continuing bad feeling about it. One night this manifest in a particularly vivid, and very disturbing, dream. In the letter she describes the dream:

> My husband answered a knock on the door and came to me very troubled and said, "There are two men and a woman outside with a coffin and they want to leave it here!" I was horrified and refused saying, "Surely we were not the only ones with a low-door flat!" The quiet voice of the woman persuaded me to let them enter – they set trestles, and after setting the coffin on them departed without saying another word.

She then woke up trembling. Later she mentioned to her husband about her dream. He made a joke of it and even dashed into the room and dashed back, still laughing, to inform her that the room was, indeed, empty. She was so upset by this dream she told many of her friends. One month later those friends were to gather in that very room to pay their respects to her husband who died suddenly of a thrombosis. He was a very healthy man and his passing was a shock to everybody.

This was not the first time this had happened. She claimed that all her life many of her dreams had come true and now, "I am almost afraid to fall asleep in case I dream." She cited an example when she was a child of ten. She dreamed about the new house that the family was moving to. She states that nobody in the family had seen the house as it was over 150 miles away. She was then slapped by her mother for telling her sisters that there were two pear trees in the garden. On arrival at the house there were the two pear trees as she had described.

In her second letter she describes how before World War II she told scores of people about a vivid dream she had had. In this she "saw hundreds of small aircraft, manned by small brown-skinned men, hurling explosives at large battleships in a very peaceful ocean. I saw men swimming around, and one screamed at me, one word only – It was 'repulse'. How my friends laughed at me and said what a shame that even in my dreams the sailors find me 'repulsive'. I really was inclined to blame the cheese I had for supper, but later events made all my friends remember my dream."

I have checked this and can confirm that HMS Repulse was sunk on the 10 December 1941 by the Japanese First Air Force which consisted of 27 bombers and 61 torpedo planes. It was the torpedo planes that did the major damage in that the ship was hit by around twelve torpedoes. This is again a typical Dunne Dream in that her subconscious had created a dream scenario (the man screaming at her in the water, a very similar situation to Dunne's Martinique dream where the French-speaking population describe to him the devastation of St Pierre).

As we have already discussed, recent research has shown that the liminal states between sleep and wakefulness, known as hypnagogia (when dropping off to sleep) and hypnopompia (when waking up), seem to open up the mind to extrasensory awareness. In these states some people report out-of-the-body experiences (OBEs) and other unusual sensations. Others report that they 'see' images that appear unbidden in the mind's eye. I suspect that this may be what was taking place in the life of another of Priestley's correspondences, WTA. In the letter he described how, as a youngster in the 1930s, he used to fall into a semi-sleep state on his mother's lap in the car. As he dozed he would experience, as he terms it, "constantly fleeting glimpses of things".

One of these images was so vivid that it appeared time and time again throughout his teen years. He regularly discussed this with his family and they gently teased him about it. In the image he 'saw' a large "castle-like building close to a tree-lined road. It was built of red brick and had a big impressive wooden door with elaborate iron work. The trees along the road shaded the bottom part of the red cylindrical turrets from the sun."

He was so sure that he would one day find this building that he used to cycle round his locale, sometimes for quite long distances. The original hypnogogic took place when driving through his home area of Pontypridd and the Vale of Glamorgan. Frustratingly he had no success in finding this mystery building in his local area. Later he was to become a teacher of art and had his first interview for a job in Leicester. He arrived at Leicester Station and then took the bus from the station to the location of the school on the outskirts of the town. Much to his amazement the bus went past the building of his "dream" – identical in all respects. The building was Leicester Prison. What is interesting is that he then moved to Leicester and was still living there in 1963. He states that he regularly travels past the building.

Hypnopompic states seem to regularly feature in reported precognitions, and Priestley's *Monitor* letters do seem to support this. In 1951 RH was in hospital recovering from a nervous breakdown. She was awakening from sleep and therefore in a hypnopompic state. As she came to she could hear voices speaking in a broad English dialect. As the images solidified she found herself looking down at her hands using a knife to spread butter on to bread. This was all being seen, as she describes it, "under diffuse evening light". A few days later she suddenly found herself reliving the experience. The voices in dialect were a radio play in the background. Interestingly she recognised what was said "for about a minute whilst I buttered bread exactly as in my dream". She adds that she was delighted to have pinpointed the precognitive state and that it exists "somewhere between waking and sleeping".

One of the oddest incidents was described by PM. In an uncanny real-life reflection of Kay Conway's "future memory" experience in Act II of *Time and the Conways*, this involved a hypnagogic-facilitated time slip element that really plays with our understanding of how time works.

She describes how, late one evening, she was dozing in bed when she was awoken by the sound of a slamming door. She turned to her husband and in her semi-sleep state said, "It was the five boys come in from the pictures." Her husband replied, "Whose boys?" She replied, "They are ours." Her husband was clearly astounded by this and thought that his wife was going crazy. At that time such a situation was absolutely impossible. She had suffered a series of miscarriages and the medical opinion was that she would never be able to carry a baby to full-term. Her words were delivered while her mind was located in what Priestley regularly referred to as the borderland in which the Jungian 'self' can encounter the similarly Jungian 'collective unconscious'. It will be recalled that at the end of Act I of *Time and the Conways* Kay falls into a form of trance, and in this state she perceives all the events depicted in Act II; events that are part of a potential future for her and her family. In the play we never discover if the events as depicted in Act II came to pass as Act III returns us to the day of Kay's 21st birthday. But for PM, time did carry forward and was to prove the medical opinions to be wrong. At the time of writing the letter PM had given birth to five healthy boys, exactly the number she had 'predicted' in her hypnopompic state. If this was all that PM had experienced, it would still be one of the strangest of all the "Priestley Letters". To have five boys in one family is statistically very rare, but to this we have to add the fact that at the time of the precognition the chance of PM having any children was extremely unlikely. But things were stranger still.

She explained that a few weeks before the date of the letter all the boys were out of the house together. They had been to what she calls a "Brooke Bond Tea Film Show". On this particular evening they were late. As they came through the door and slammed it behind them she heard herself say to her husband, "It's only the boys come in from the pictures." Clearly this must have shocked both her and her husband as it was a rerun of the event years before. Could this be evidence that in her liminal state the two times had become muddled and that she had experienced some form of time slip similar to that one fictionally described by Priestley in his play *Time and the Conways*?

It must be stressed here that PM was an ordinary British housewife. It is clear from the tone of the letter that this incident caused her extreme stress and concern. This is not a letter from a person seeking attention or fame from making up or exaggerating an event, but simply an ordinary person who has experienced something extraordinary and seeking answers – answers that modern science simply cannot supply.

It seems that in these liminal states another form of consciousness comes to the fore. In the case of PM something other than her everyday personality vocalized the prediction that "it was the five boys come in from the pictures". This was clearly not PM making this observation, but a source of consciousness that was within her but not her.

DK describes in her letter another hypnagogic precognition. When she was seventeen and working away from home she had an odd "waking dream" that proved to be of profound importance. Back at home her mother was expecting another baby after a break of eleven years. She was, naturally, worried for her mother as she approached term. One day at work she started thinking about her mother and seems to have entered a form of dream state. She ponders about giving her notice in and going home. In this she visualises "walking up the hill to my home". She goes on:

I suddenly came to the top of the hill, looked down the other side to our house. There were two cars parked outside. I knew they were doctors' cars. I hurried in and my father was there telling me my mother was very ill and the baby probably wouldn't live, in fact he thought it would be dead by then.

She then realises where she is and got on with her work. She was so influenced by this liminal image that she does give her notice in and the following Sunday she travelled back home. As she reached the top of the hill and looked down at her mother's house there were the two cars in exactly the location they were in her waking dream. She rushed down to the house and, on entering, discovered her father in a very agitated state.

Absolutely every single thing that she 'dreamed' came to pass in exactly the same order, even to her father's words! The positive side to the story is that her father's fears were not to happen. The doctors managed to save the life of both mother and child. Indeed, in the letter she mentions that her little brother was to "get married next week".

These dream precognitions imply that in such states we can glimpse a section of our own future. Many of these happen in childhood. This is not surprising; as we get older we have less future to experience and therefore less material to precognise. But it does seem that children dream in a far more vivid way than adults and their recall of such dreams seems to be more effective the younger they are. An example of this is the experience of DW. He describes how, when he was eight or nine years old, he experienced a powerfully evocative reoccurring dream that involved multiple sensory inputs:

> I was walking through trees along a path with green-painted hooped railings on either side. There was a sound of falling water close at hand and a sinister little brick building with a concrete roof. I walked through a gate and found that I was standing at about the middle of a long hill. The railings stretched up the road into the distance. A lorry was coming down the hill towards me.

A few months after the dreams ceased he was walking with his mother through Roker and Seaburn Park in Sunderland and found that he was "living my dream". The sound of the water that he heard (but did not see) in the dream was, in fact, an ornamental stream with tiny waterfalls that ran beside the path. The green railings were there as was the little building. It was, in fact, an electricity substation. What is fascinating is that he knew what was going to happen next. This was not a deja type sensation where the information is known as it enfolds. In advance of the events occurring in linear time he knew that in a few seconds a lorry would come down the hill. He ran ahead of his mother to see the dreamed-of lorry do exactly what was expected of it. He claims to have never been to the park before the event. Something that was confirmed by his parents. But even if he had this could not explain the lorry precognition.

As we have already discussed, déjà vu sensations may be a semi-forgotten precognitive dream that is lodged in the subconscious and only vaguely recalled when the precognition circumstances are encountered in real life. If it was the case that the subject remembered the dream, then this would be described as a precognition. A perfect example of this is described by another correspondent, EG. In 1935 he was the Assistant Secretary to the Grand National Archery Society's championship meeting held in Oxford. On the night before his return to Hereford he dreamed that he was in a railway carriage. Sitting opposite was an elderly lady, a stranger to him. She suddenly held out a paper bag towards him and said, "Would you like one of these buns?" He replied, "No, thank you." "Do have one," the old lady insisted. "They are quite fresh."

On the following morning he found himself in an identical situation. The old lady was somebody called "Miss P", a well-known archer at the championships. Now what is interesting is that he had remembered the dream and was therefore in a totally precognitive state. The conversation followed exactly the same course with one, interesting, omission. She actually said, "Do have one, Mr G." It is also important to note that although in real life he clearly recognised Miss P he did not do so in the dream.

## The Time Slip

Earlier, in the published letters, I cited the incident involving the time reversal at Dunraven Castle. You will recall that the correspondent witnessed one of her associates drop a jug of chocolate sauce on the floor only to see the whole event repeat itself seconds later. Can this, in some way, explain the totally odd experience described by BWT. In this letter the correspondent describes what sounds like a time slip. She was not dreaming nor was she in any form of altered state of consciousness. She just seems to have, for a few moments, glimpsed the past.

When she was twelve (23 years before) she often visited her aunt who had a 'modern' flat in the centre of Cardiff. These flats backed on to the cricket ground. While her mother and aunt had tea she would amuse herself by running to the lift (her aunt's flat was on the third floor), going down to the ground floor. Getting out, running through an archway to the back of the building, up the fire escape at the back to the third floor and then repeat the exercise. She had done this four times and was about to run down the front steps and go through the arch again. She stopped dead with a mounting feeling of fear.

> I not only was afraid to step forward but that it was dangerous to step forward because instead of the courtyard there was a harbour with dark, glistening water, old fashioned sailing ships and, in general, a completely different scene. It was uncanny.

She looked at this scene for about thirty seconds then ran back up the front steps to the safety of the lift. She never saw the scene again. However, eighteen years later she opened the evening paper to see an article discussing the site of the Westgate Street Flats and the cricket ground. She found that the site had been built over the old harbour where sailing ships had moored. This was uncannily similar to the scene that she had 'seen' that afternoon many years before.

It is unlikely that a twelve year old would have been aware of how such a scene would have looked in the 19th century. Indeed, such a concept would no doubt be the last thing on her mind as she playfully travelled down the lift and ran up the fire escape. What she did sense was a feeling of danger. What would have happened if she had continued on? The scene was not fleeting; she saw it for around thirty seconds. It did not fade away in that the image ceased solely because she turned her back on it and got back in the lift.

Some of the dreams were totally bizarre, so bizarre in fact that the dreamer himself or herself felt that such events could never be experienced in waking life. One such example involved a man dreaming that he saw a Native American war canoe sailing across the Town Hall Square of his home town. At the time he considered this to be a crazy image. Nine years later he was to relive the dream. He saw it floating past his window. Rushing to find out what was going on he found out that a collection of scenery and props were on their way to a local theatre and had been loaded on a lorry. This was how they were to be seen from a first-floor window. This is again an example of how dreams embroider and elaborate a seemingly illogical future perception to make it more understandable. Of course this suggests that the source of the dream information stopped before the man looked out of the window and confirmed that what he was seeing was understandable and in context. Why did the 'future memory' not contain this crucial piece of additional information?

One letter was from a schoolmaster who had dreamed that he was walking across the playground discussing with the games master the possibility of a certain boy playing in the next match. As they walked through the gateway a small boy ran bang into him. The next day the actual event took place:

> ... and as we approached the gate I suddenly realised that this was the exact repetition of the dream and quite subconsciously I braced myself for the impact of the small boy coming through... and he came.

This is such a mundane event but quite startling in its clarity. It is an example of the sort of precognition that is very similar to déjà vu and indeed does support the theory that déjà vu experiences are, in fact, the instant remembering of a dream a second or two before the actual event takes place in 'reality'.

Some letters contained events that were so strange they almost beggar belief. One such incident was described by a medical photographer, a man who held an extremely responsible position and, as Priestley says, not the kind of person to make up a story. He was in the process of moving into a new building and had ordered some new equipment. All arrived with the exception of two developing tanks. He searches everywhere and as he fails to find them concludes that they have been stolen. One night he dreams that he visits one of the rooms not in use in the new building. In the room he finds some large grey steel cupboards. In the dream he sees that one of the cupboards is labelled as "FJA 39". In the dream he finds a key for this label, opens the cupboard and finds that inside are the two missing tanks.

Later the next day he recalls the dream. He goes to the key box and, to his surprise, finds a key labelled FJA 39. Intrigued he takes the key to the unused room from his dream, finds that the key does open one of the grey cupboards but fails to find anything in it. However, he cannot escape the feeling that the tanks were in there. He went back and, after taking another look, discovers the tanks in the grey cabinet.

This is very interesting in that it involves a prediction of the numbers and letters on the key. If he had not had the dream he would not have picked up that particular key.

## The Green Dress

With regards to this letter it is important to note the long time interval between the dream and the actual event. The lady in question was a schoolgirl just after WWI. She dreamed that she was on a grass covered terrace above a river and there were round rustic tables under the trees. There was, as she said, "a quite extraordinary quality about the feeling of light and happiness in the dream." Also she knew that she was wearing a green frock, something she was never allowed to do because of her mother's superstition.

Ten or eleven years later she was convalescing after a serious illness; she went with her four friends to spend the day in the Forest of St Germain. "The day," she continued:

> ... had a not unpleasant sensation of waiting-for-something about it but I was still enough of an invalid to be quite willing to drift through the hours. Finally, the one French member of the party suggested our going to the river. So we went – and

there was my dream scene – the tables, the trees, my green dress – and above all, the light and slightly floating sensation I had in the dream.

The woman insisted that the two scenes were not "something like" but identical.

I am struck by the similarity between this dream and Priestley's own "Happy Dream" that he describes twelve years after writing *Man and Time*. What is even more surprising is that Priestley himself seems to fail to make a link between the two experiences. In his 1976 short book, *The Happy Dream*, Jack describes how his own dream also has an atmosphere of other-worldliness and expectation.

I feel that a letter that reflected a circumstance similar to Priestley's "Happy Dream" is the perfect ending to this review of the *Monitor* Letters. There are many more that I need to read and, if I can, these will be published soon in a companion volume to this work.

We have now finished our diversion into the world of the "*Monitor* Letters". Although Jack continued to receive correspondence for a few years afterwards he was, as always, a man that quickly moved his attention to his next big project. Although by now far from a young man he was not done yet. He had still a lot more to contribute to British theatre, literature and, dare I say it, philosophy. The sixties may have been a time of great social and cultural change, but Jack had anticipated much of it and was, as usual, so far ahead of his peers that they again confused his forward thinking with conservatism. Also, as usual, they were wrong, but we can only know that now from our position well into the 21st century.

# Chapter Twelve

# The Long Indian Summer

In 1965 there was a very interesting development. BBC Television decided that they would like to do a television adaption of *Johnson Over Jordan* as part of their series *Thursday Theatre*. It was considered fitting by all concerned that Jordan should again be played by Sir Ralph Richardson, who 26 years earlier had played Johnson in the first production of the play back in 1939.

As we have already discovered, the play was not right for the economic and political climate of 1939. Sadly, the 1965 production fared little better. It was anticipated that the heavily expressionistic production values would work well on the small screen, where close-ups of the actors would lend power to the emotional impact of the narrative. The adapted version had new, long monologues by Johnson that allowed the close-ups to be used to best effect. These were of two varieties; his 'deathbed' thoughts which in the TV production were delivered face on and direct to camera. The second type was him trying to make sense of his new environment within the timeless Bardo state.

The cost of casting Richardson in the main role was very expensive. His fee was £1,837. The next most expensive performer was Rachel Gurney who was paid £374. This was a huge percentage of the overall budget of £9,384. At the time of rehearsals Richardson was in Spain filming *Doctor Zhivago*.

Sadly, the play was again not well received. The play was still too experimental and the concepts far too strange for a 1960s British TV audience.

This did not deter the television producers who clearly saw Priestley as a prize to be sought after. In 1968 the BBC was back at Priestley's door requesting a new play. He duly obliged, creating *Anyone for Tennis?* which was broadcast to the nation on

25 September 1968.

In his article in the *Radio Times* Priestley was quite precise in stating that this was another "time play":

> Writing a brief but adequate introduction to this play, *Anyone for Tennis?*, will not be easy, but I will do my best. Let me say at once that it is not a play about ghosts or spiritualism or reincarnation. It is another of my 'Time plays', which were well known to the older generation of playgoers and were in fact produced in many different countries.[192]

The central character, Gary Brendon, is caught in a post-mortem time-loop. Like Robert Johnson in *Johnson Over Jordan*, Brendon is existing within a Priestlian version of the Bardo state. In a reflection of his own guilt involving an embezzlement, he has been reliving the incident over and over again for twenty years of consensual time. An incident occurs whereby one of those present during the act of embezzlement thinks about him, he is released from the time-loop and is given the opportunity to reflect on how his own inability to empathize with others brought about the initial set of circumstances. Here again we have Priestley's preoccupation with how our actions towards others ultimately damage us. In his writings he makes it clear that he believes that at a higher level of consciousness, possibly involved in Dunne's series of 'observers', we eventually become a singular entity and, with this in mind, it becomes clear that actions done unto others are, in the final analysis, actions we do to ourselves. It is only through the development of self-knowledge that we can escape the trap that is the Bardo state.

This idea of 'empathy' was also followed up at the time by the American Science Fiction writer Philip K. Dick. Dick's novel *Do Androids Dream of Electric Sheep*, published the same year that *Anyone for Tennis?* was performed, has as its central premise the idea that to be human is to have empathy for the suffering of others. It is therefore interesting to note that Dick's novel was made into the hugely successful movie *Blade Runner* and Dick is now recognised as being one of the greatest innovative novelists of the late 20$^{th}$ century. Priestley, on the other hand, is dismissed as being old-fashioned and his work to be of no relevance to the modern world. As we have already seen, in a real irony, Dick's greatest supporter, Anthony Boucher, published Priestley's short story *Look After the Strange Girl* in his *Fantasy and Science Fiction* magazine in the January 1954 edition. As an aside, we will discover something really interesting about this story towards the end of this book.

In the original *Listener* review of the play published the following week, 3 October 1968, Priestley is accused of being a "little bit preachy" particularly focusing on the fact that the one of the characters has read J.W. Dunne. This specific trope was used recently in the 2002 movie *Irréversible* by Gaspar Noé and was greeted with really positive reviews. In the 'opening' sequence (which in fact, as the movie runs backwards, is the last sequence) we see a young Italian woman is reading *An Experiment with Time* in a French park. The camera then spins around until it turns into a strobe effect accompanied by a roaring sound. We then dimly perceive an image of the universe and the words "Le Temps Détruit Tout" ("Time destroys everything") appear on screen and the film 'ends' (or begins). This use of Dunne is acceptable but when, back in 1968, Priestley makes a similar reference to *An Experiment with Time* also using a young woman who has read the book, this was considered to be "a bit arch" by the reviewer, Michael Pennington.

In many ways this play is a revisitation by Priestley of the themes he explored in *Johnson Over Jordan*. Just like Johnson, Brendon is existing outside of time. Both characters are, with regards to consensual time, dead, but are clearly still alive within their own perceptual universe.

In *Johnson Over Jordan* "The Figure" takes the role of a guiding spirit for Johnson. Priestley uses a similar process in *Anyone for Tennis?* in that Brendon is helped to overcome his guilt-induced Bardo state by the ministrations and advice of his great-grand-father, Joseph O'Connor. Clearly Joseph is already dead within consensual time so he is literally a 'spirit guide'.

It was in 1971 that Priestley gave evidence again that he may have been experiencing creativity related to unconsciously recalled Dunne Dreams in which elements of the future subtly act as a muse. In 1971, and somewhat out of character, Priestley again decided to write a children's story. *Snoggle* has a group of children encounter two alien creatures. The children call them Snoggle and Snaggle. The three children and their two alien friends have a series of adventures avoiding the police and army who have been instructed to catch the creatures and shoot them. A very similar plot was to appear in Steven Spielberg's hugely successful movie *E.T. the Extra-Terrestrial*. This may be a classic example of how Priestley was ahead, not behind, public tastes or else evidence that he was in some subliminal way able to scan the contents of his own future and incorporate some of the imagery in his own works of fiction. Sadly, this book was virtually ignored by the public whereas, in 1982, only eleven years later, the public could not get enough of cuddly aliens and plucky children taking on the authorities.

The concepts of Jung seemed to resonate more and more with Priestley the older he became. In the 1970s he became particularly interested in the Jungian concept of *individuation*. As we have already discussed in relation to Priestley's play *Johnson Over Jordan*, this was a process whereby the ego transforms into the *Self*. This tended to happen after a long life and at a time when death was on the horizon. But for Priestley this seemed pointless. As he wrote in *Man and Time*, "Why struggle for a goal overshadowed by a grave? Why at last understand how to live just when you are about to stop living?"[193]

Jack's solution to this mystery was a simple one; we don't die;

we just move out of this time into another one. Of course, this is exactly what Priestley has his character Alan describe in *Time and the Conways* and such a scenario is suggested in *Music at Night* and *Johnson Over Jordan*.

It was in the early 1970s that Priestley attempted a return to his great fascination, time. He felt that he still had one more play in him; a play that would pull together all of his ideas in one, satisfactory, swansong. And this is where his little-known short story, *Look After the Strange Girl*, from his 1953 anthology *The Other Place*, was to make a surprising and quite amazing contribution to Priestley's legacy.

This classic and quite mind-bending story was good enough to subsequently be selected to appear in the American magazine, *Fantasy and Science Fiction*, in its January 1954 edition. The work of few British writers appeared in this magazine. Jack never discusses this in any of his autobiographical writings and as none of his biographers mention this fact, it is impossible to know whether he saw this as of any significance or, indeed, even knew about it.

But what is of significance within modern culture is that the editor of *Fantasy and Science Fiction* was Anthony Boucher, the editor and anthologist who initially nurtured the career of Philip K. Dick, an author who shared many of Jack's interests. Many years later, *Look After the Strange Girl* was to appear in an anthology entitled *The Other Side of the Clock* published in 1969 by Van Nostrand Reinhold. This to me is evidence that Priestley, had he tried his hand at it, could have been a very successful science fiction writer.

We will probably never know why, of all his stories, it was this one that Priestley selected to be the source of his last play. The story is an interesting one. One evening in the high summer of 1952 a college lecturer by the name of Mark Denbow had decided to go for an early evening swim in a lake in the grounds of the old mansion that had been converted into his place of work. On diving into the lake he strikes his head and is knocked out. On regaining consciousness, he finds that he has been dragged out of the water by a young man dressed in curiously dated formal clothing. His new friend introduces himself as Ronald Buller. To his horror Mark recognises the name from an inscription on the War Memorial in the grounds of the future college, that Ronald Buller was to die at Neuve Chapelle in 1915. He then realises why Ronald is dressed so strangely. His accident has caused a time slip and he is back in 1902 and that he has become a 'gatecrasher' at an upper-class summer evening garden party. The old house is no longer a place of further education, but as it was in the early Edwardian period, the private home of Lord Broxwood and his family.

He becomes a focus of interest, with his strange way of speaking and his odd manners. One young woman, Dorothy Buller, seems to remind him of an elderly aristocrat, Lady Purzley, that he had met with that afternoon at the college. He quickly realises that this is more than a resemblance. Twenty-year-old Dorothy is, indeed, the 1902 version of the formidable Lady Purzley. Using his future knowledge regarding the life of Lady Purzley he offers to tell her fortune. He describes exactly what will happen to her, who she will marry and how many children she shall have and that she will end up being a formidable old lady. Of course, the young woman considers such a future to be ridiculous.

He then discovers that there is another person who has similarly appeared as if out of thin air and has caused quite a stir, a young woman who is also somewhat confused. He subsequently discovers that this "strange girl", Ann, is also a time traveller from the future. Her time slip seems to have been facilitated by a thunderstorm, something that is later implicated in some way with Mark's own temporal journey.

There are interesting parallels between the storyline of *Look After the Strange Girl* and that of *Time and the Conways*. Mark, like

Kay Conway does in Act II of the play, has moved into another timeline. Both characters acquire knowledge of a potential future; Kay from moving forward along her own 'serial time' to a place in her own future, and Mark by taking knowledge from the future into an earlier time. However, whereas Kay's future perceptions can be explained using Dunne's model of Serial Time, Mark encounters a past that he can never have experienced as he had not been born. Indeed, later in the story there is another similar theme to *Time and the Conways*. We discover that Ann's time slip has been facilitated by her entering a "day-dream" state while being shown round the grounds of the college in 1952. It is a day-dream state that similarly catapults Kay Conway into her own future.

In another very close parallel to *Time and the Conways*, there is scene where Mark dances with Maud, one of the daughters of Lord Broxwood. He knows from his knowledge of the family memorial in the chapel of the house, in 1952 a college of further education, that Maud died in 1923 after a long illness. A similar knowledge is carried back from the future by Kay Conway with regards to her doomed younger sister, Carol.

The story concludes with Mark slowly moving back into his own time whereas Ann has always been in 1952 with her experiences of 1902 having been facilitated by her hypnopompic reverie. We find that Ann is, in fact, the granddaughter of Lady Purzley. In a final twist we discover that she too had experienced a hypnopompic reverie:

> I dreamt I was back here as a girl, before I was even engaged to Geoffrey Purzley, and somebody told me I would marry him. But whether that really happened once or I merely dreamt it, I cannot remember.[194]

We will probably never know exactly what stimulated Priestley to take this obscure short story and to turn it into what may become his greatest-ever play. As I have already mentioned the storyline of *Look After the Strange Girl* is very clever but it is nowhere near as brilliant as the twists and turns and the cultural references of the play that Jack was to eventually call *Time Was, Time Is*. It is a magical exercise in precise writing and careful stagecraft. But why did Jack change the plot to such an extent that the two works may stand alone with just the basic premise being shared? I would like to believe that the most intriguing theme may have had as its inspiration one of the '*Monitor* Letters' from ten years earlier.

As I have already suggested, Priestley was fascinated by the "magical", particularly the other-worldly feeling of high summer evenings; a time when other dimensions of space and time seem to be just a gossamer thread away from being perceived by our senses. Priestley symbolised this gateway as being a "rose garden". I have already suggested that this may have been an echo of T.S. Eliot's use of a rose garden to symbolise timelessness in his poem *Burnt Norton*. But as with all artists, inspiration can come from many sources. I suspect that although Eliot may have been a literary source of this wonderful analogy, there may have been another, far more prosaic influence.

One of the original *Monitor* Letters was sent to Priestley by a junior member of a West London drama group. The young woman describes how one day she had been informed by the director that the next play the drama group would perform would be a production of a play by the Italian playwright Luigi Pirandello. That night she experienced a very vivid dream in which she found herself in Italy, a country she had never been to. This is how Priestley describes the dream:

> She was in a long narrow room with arches along one side leading into a rose garden. There was a long table with people in medieval costumes eating and drinking. As she passed through the arch a bat flew in from the garden and she

reached up and caught it in her hand. The dream was so vivid that she told two or three people about it the next morning. Later that day she went to the local public library and looked at a book on Pirandello's collected plays. She said, "The very first play I started to read has as its setting the exact room of my dream complete with a rose garden seen through arches. More amazing still, later in the action there is the most improbable stage direction I have ever met – 'a bat flies in'."[195]

Here we have a dream precognition, something we know that fascinated Priestley, and integral to the dream is a bat flying from a rose garden, the very place that contains much offstage mystery in *Time Was, Time Is*. This is yet another intriguing link to this fascinating play. Now, at long last, I would like to take the opportunity to discuss this 'new' work by J.B. Priestley.

## Chapter Thirteen

# The Unknown Play – Time Was, Time Is

In spring of 2016 I met Priestley's son, Tom, for lunch near his home in Notting Hill Gate. The discussion turned, inevitably, to the "Time Plays". I was stunned when Tom informed me that there was a time play written by his father that had never been performed. Indeed, had never been published and was virtually unknown outside of a very small group of individuals. He told me that this play, entitled *Time Was, Time Is*, was written by JBP sometime in 1974. He knew very little about it other than his father's literary agents, United Agents, had a typed-up copy and that he would have them send it to me. Tom then explained that the original version was sent by his father to theatre director Braham Murray as soon as it had been completed. Murray had recently been involved in a very successful adaption of *Time and the Conways* at the Manchester Cotton Exchange and Priestley had spoken after one of the performances. Evidently the young director had impressed Jack and he was keen to have Murray produce this new work.

This intrigued me. What had happened to this play? While waiting for the manuscript to be sent to me I decided to investigate it in greater detail. To my surprise the play is virtually unknown. Of the writers who have discussed Priestley only Holger Klein mentions the play and this is simply to acknowledge that it was written and was "unperformed and unpublished in any shape."[196]

I contacted Braham Murray and arranged to have a Skype conversation with him and, a few days later, the manuscript arrived from the agency. I was surprised to discover that the play may not have been formally published but it had been typeset and an introduction to the play had been written by Gareth

Lloyd-Evans. The typesetting looked very professional, suggesting that Priestley had invested in having this done.

As we have already discovered, *Time Was, Time Is* is based upon the short story *Look After the Strange Girl* which was published in Priestley's 1953 short-story anthology, *The Other Place*. In the original story the time slip has two characters from 1952 appearing in 1902. In the play Jack uses a similar 50-year gap but updates it to be 1974 and 1914. This simple change makes the cultural dynamics far more effective. For example, as Lloyd-Evans points out in his introduction, Priestley cleverly uses language to highlight the differing cultures of 1914 and 1974. For example, there is an amusing exchange between "Ann", who is from 1974, and Sir Charles Cheviot, a career diplomat from 1914:

**Ann:** I've some vague recollection of a psychiatrist and taking lots of tranquillisers –

**Sir Charles:** Now you're talking either above or below my head.

This would not have worked as well had the years been 1902 and 1952. British culture went through one of its most dramatic changes between the early 1950s and the early 1970s. The sixties had swept away many of the social norms and attitudes that 1952 had, in many ways, shared with 1902. In *Look After the Strange Girl* there are passing references to the odd way that Ann and Mark react to certain sets of circumstances but these are simply matters of etiquette rather than behaviours. The way people spoke, particularly the upper and middle classes, had not really changed from the start to the middle of the twentieth century. All had changed by 1974. Working class and regional accents were heard on television and the radio and "Received English" was considered to be quaint and very dated. Priestley was a proud Yorkshireman who had kept his regional accent and his north-country values. Indeed, this was one of the reasons that he was never fully accepted by the self-proclaimed intelligentsia of the pre-war years. As a wordsmith he revelled in using these linguistic changes to illustrate the differences between the stuffy formality of those living in 1914, and the free and easy language of the 1970s. Indeed, he even drops in a swear word or two.

The play has many of these amusing exchanges. Sadly, it was Priestley's inability to really reflect the linguistic patterns of 1974 that made Murray, a man very much of the early 1970s and somebody very aware of the speech patterns of the time, decide to not produce the play.

But now we are nearly as far away in time from 1974 as 1974 was from 1914. Any piece using the social context of the early 1970s is a "period piece" in its own right. It was this time gap that had Murray revisit the play and, on doing so, he concluded that now is the time to produce it.

Priestley opens the play with a similar atmosphere to that of *Time and the Conways*. Although the audience does not know it, it is the evening of 28 June 1914, the evening before the storm that became the First World War. The atmosphere is imbued with Edwardian gentility and optimism. The party involves individuals from early twenties to early seventies and takes place at the country home of Lord George Braxwood.

The 1914 sequences take place in a corridor between a smoke room which is off stage on the left and an entrance to a conservatory on the right. All the action takes place here. A place that is mentioned many times, but is never seen, is "the Rose Garden". This seems to be a magical location where love and other emotions become manifest. It is of possible significance, over and above the historical importance, that Priestley places the play in late June. Again, in much of his writing at that time he was fascinated by "the magical" and felt that long midsummer evenings have a special liminal quality. He had used this device in his 1950 play *A Summer's Day Dream*.

As we have already discovered, in *Margin Released*, Priestley describes in great detail his own feelings in June 1914. This was a special, almost "magical" time for him where he lived life to the full. I have suggested that this throwing himself into life was because, in some subliminal way – possibly through his vivid dreams – he had precognised that war was to break out within a few short weeks. This idea of knowing that the Great War will happen and how awful it was to be is a subtle but central theme in *Time Was, Time Is*.

In his to-date unpublished introduction to the play, Gareth Lloyd-Evans makes the following observation:

> The rose-garden, although we never see it in the play, is real enough for some of the characters who use it largely with affectionate familiarity. Yet there is something beyond the palpable about it – just as there is about the white harebells "white and fragile and perfect at the edge of the great dark moor" in *I Have Been Here Before*. The garden seems to be emblematic of yet another fugitive time area, which some catch glimpses of, can even enter for a short while, but which perhaps is the destiny of all of us.[197]

We know that Priestley was fascinated by "the magical" and considered the long evenings of high summer to be imbued with this otherworldliness, something that other writers, such as Shakespeare in his *Midsummer Night's Dream*, used to great effect. Indeed, Priestley himself, in his little-performed 1950 play, *Summer Day's Dream*, mirrored the title of Shakespeare's ethereal work. The historical fact that World War One began at this time of year must have allowed Priestley the opportunity to imbue *Time Was, Time Is* with a similar magical quality. But he needed more; his creation of an offstage location reflecting the liminality zone, the place that dreams and reality border each other, was a work of subtle genius. Why a Rose Garden? Why not a maze which would have been a feature of some large country houses at that time and would have conveyed, albeit not very subtly, the magical confusion of dreams overlaying reality? We will return to this mystery later.

Another theme that Priestley applies within the play is that only certain members of the 1914 group can perceive the time travellers. For example, the manservant Cumber repeatedly is confused when he is asked to serve Ann and Mark drinks. In a direct, but unacknowledged reference to Peter Ouspensky's concept of "byt people", Mark explains to Ann that "people sunk in routine – butlers, policemen, postmen, don't come into this." In his book *A New Model of the Universe*, which we know was a huge influence on Priestley, Ouspensky describes what he means by "byt" people:

These are, first of all, people of byt, of deeply-rooted, petrified, routine life. Their lives succeed one another with the monotony of the hand of the clock moving on the dial. There can be in their lives nothing unexpected, nothing accidental, no adventures. They are born and die in the same house where their fathers and grandfathers were born and died and where their children and grandchildren will be born and will die. National calamities, wars, earthquakes, plagues, sometimes wipe out hundreds of thousands of them from the face of the Earth at one stroke. But apart from such events, their whole life is strictly ordered and organized on a plan... There can be no new events in the lives of such people.[198]

Clearly the words Priestley has Mark utter in this respect are very close to Ouspensky's description of these people trapped in a "deeply-rooted, petrified, routine life."

Later in the play Priestley uses a reoccurring musical theme to point out how time seems to be running in parallel streams. He used a similar device in *Johnson Over Jordan* when a particular refrain occasionally appears. Written by Benjamin Britten, this is heard by Johnson and the audience. An inner voice that is the part of Johnson attuned to the Jungian collective unconscious comments, "That music does not belong to this place. But then neither do I."[199] But in *Time Was, Time Is*, the tune is a mid-1970s pop tune, a leaking through from one of Dunne's "Serial Times" to another. As we have already discovered with regards to his play *Music at Night*, Jack felt that music could facilitate altered states of consciousness and open up the mind to a much broader reality. I cannot help but wonder if Jack had a particular pop record in mind and, if so, what song was it?

How Priestley uses this pop song to suggest something very strange is, for me, an inspired piece of stage-writing. A police sergeant is announced by one of the 1914 characters. As the uniformed police officer appears on stage he seems to be ignored by all the characters with the exception of Mark (then simply known as "the intruder"). Mark asks the policeman what the problem is. Before the sergeant can explain, Mark asks, "My youngsters making too much noise again?" It is at this point we hear the pop tune playing off stage and the policeman not only reacts to it, but nods his head in tune with the music. This is a very odd thing for a "Bobby" of 1914 to do. We then realise why it is that nobody else reacts to him. He is, like Ann and Mark, a person from 1974 who has moved from one Serial Time to another. The policeman then explains how the police station had received an odd telephone call and he decided to call round to the house to check that everything was okay.

Here we have an echo of *An Inspector Calls* in that we have a police officer who is a transposition from another time or place. If the sergeant had interacted with any of the 1914 characters he would have been seemingly precognitive as he would have known about the outbreak of the First World War as a historical fact.

Mark, after assuring him that things are all okay, suggests to the policeman that he leave the house "through the rose garden."

The policeman replies that there has not been a rose garden at Braxwood Place for years and that it was something he heard talked about when he was a youngster. This is again a clue to the fact that the policeman is also a time traveller.

Yet again Priestley uses the rose garden as a link between parallel times. The policeman returns to 1974 by leaving "through the rose garden." I suspect that Jack's use of the Rose Garden as a symbol of the borderland between the mystic and the mundane, between linear and serial time and between Jung's "self" and the "individuated mind", was also influenced by the poet T.S. Eliot. In his book *J.B. Priestley – The Dramatist* Gareth Lloyd-Evans, the author of the unpublished introduction to *Time Was, Time Is*, draws parallels between the plays of Priestley and the time-related poems of T.S. Eliot:

> Priestley, like Eliot, is concerned with realities which lie behind the apparent actualities of the common world. For Eliot, those realities are spiritual and religious. For Priestley they are magical. Eliot's concern is to show how these realities are at work, if we could but surrender to them within the fabric of our so-called everyday world. Priestley's concerns are very similar – to convince that the magic and the mystery that swirls about us, that to be aware of it is to be aware of the oneness of humanity.[200]

In 1939 Priestley's production company, the London Mask Theatre, produced Eliot's play *The Family Reunion*. This was an attempt by Eliot to place poetic dialogue in a dramatic setting. Jack believed that such an approach was "opera without the orchestra" but he did feel that Eliot had come very close to solving this problem.[201] We know that in 1936 a poem entitled *Burnt Norton* had appeared in Eliot's anthology *Collected Poems, 1909–1935*. This meditation on time and eternity was to subsequently appear as the first of a cycle of four poems published in

1943 under the title *Four Quartets*. It is therefore reasonable to conclude that Priestley would have been very aware of *Burnt Norton*. The poems in *Four Quartets* have a series of themes, one of which is that, under certain circumstances, human consciousness can escape or transcend time to achieve a sense of eternity or timelessness. In *Burnt Norton*, Eliot calls this the "still point of the turning world." I cannot therefore wonder whether these subsequent lines, again from *Burnt Norton*, were the source of the mysterious rose garden in *Time Was, Time Is*:

Footfalls echo in the memory
Down the passage which we did not take
Towards the door we never opened
Into the rose-garden.[202]

In its extremely clever, one may even say incredible, ending, *Time Was, Time Is* echoes Eliot's wonderful description of life-paths not taken but existing in potentiality and all ending in the mysterious "rose garden" of eternity.

As the play develops there is a curious section where it is suggested that once out of their own time characters have to be in the thoughts or sensory location of the two time travellers, Mark and Ann. As soon as Mark ceases to pay attention to the existence of a character, for example, when Tim Braxwood finds himself fading away in Act II – "I know I am not a ghost, but I am starting to feel like one" – Mark realises what is happening. By willing himself and those around him forward in time he is pulling Tim away from his real existence. This is intriguing in that in one of Priestley's earliest fictional works, *Albert Goes Through*, we have a "real" character bringing into existence, by an act of observation, fictional people. In *Albert Goes Through* it is a movie screen character. A few years later, in 1939, Priestley discusses this idea in greater detail in *Johnson Over Jordan*. Here the fictional character Don Quixote explains to Johnson how his very continued existence depends upon people imagining him when they read Cervantes' novel:

> Your great poet once said that the best of our kind are bit shadows, though I think he knew that your kind too – who appear so solid to yourselves for a little time – are also only shadows. And perhaps you do take life from the mind that beholds you and your little tale, so you live as we must do, in another greater being's imagination, memory and affection.[203]

I will leave this play at this point because I do not wish to ruin it for future audiences. In a curious twist of time that J.W. Dunne would have delighted in, you, as my readers, will already know if my friend Braham Murray did manage to get a production of *Time Was, Time Is* on stage and whether it was as successful as I believe it should be from my restricted viewpoint this dark afternoon in late November 2016.

By now Jack Priestley was an elderly man, a much respected man of letters and respected, in some quarters at least, as being, as John Atkins called him in his 1981 book, *The Last of the Sages*. He spent his final years looking back over his long life and writing a series of deeply philosophical books and essays. As his days became numbered Jack was still asking the Big Questions. We will now review the final days of his Long Indian Summer.

## Chapter Fourteen

# Crossing The Long High Wall

It is to John Atkins' excellent book that we first turn our attention. In his 1981 biography of Priestley, Atkins cites a fascinating quotation from Jack which appeared in *The Times* Diary for 12 September 1973. The article was reporting on a dinner to celebrate Priestley's 79th birthday and the publication of his new book *The English*. For me this is evidence that as he became older Priestley's timeline was evoking memories of his past as if they were part of his "present". This is a known aspect of old-age but with regards to Priestley, with his preoccupation with Ouspensky and the circularity of time, this takes on a far more intriguing sheen. He states what it is like to grow old:

> It is as though walking down Shaftesbury Avenue as a fairly young man, he was suddenly kidnapped, rushed into a theatre and made to don the grey hair, the wrinkles and the attributes of age, then wheeled on stage. Behind the appearance of age, he was the same person, with the same thoughts, as he was when younger.[204]

This has echoes of the speech made by Alan Conway in Act III of *Time and the Conways*; that in some way we are all our lives and that it is time that cuts us into segments. The real person is the whole life. Is it reasonable to suppose that for the 79-year-old Priestley the past was becoming more real than the present? In my book *Opening the Doors of Perception* I suggest that Alzheimer's facilitates this timeless awareness. There is absolutely no evidence that JBP suffered in any way from this illness but I would argue that Alzheimer's simply exaggerates the sensations that all elderly people have as they approach their 'moving on' into the fifth dimension.

TV again came calling in 1975. This time it was not the BBC but its opposition, the Independent Television Network. One of the ITN subsidiaries, Thames Television, was working on a series of supernatural short plays under the collective title of *Shadows*. This time Jack and Jacquetta worked on the teleplay together. Indeed, in most references it is Jacquetta who is given major writer acknowledgements. The short play, *The Other Window*, was broadcast on 15 October 1975. In the story a professional scientist brings home a transparent thermoplastic disc to show his three children. He places the adhesive disc on to one of the windows overlooking the garden. He explains to the children that the disc, using a process of refraction first discovered by French physicist Augustin-Jean Fresnel, gives a distorted image of the garden outside. Later, the youngest daughter looks through the disc at the garden and sees a scene from history. The other children do not believe her but later they, too, have their own experiences of seeing events from the past through the lens. Playing the role of the typical scientist, the father tries to rationalize what his children have seen. He argues that it is simply "autosuggestion". Later the children's grandmother arrives and she too sees something. The elder daughter suggests that these glimpses of the past are like a TV signal but on a huge scale and that somewhere out there the Norman Conquests are still happening. The term "Fifth Dimension" is dropped in as if from nowhere and with no explanation, a clear reference for those viewers aware of Priestley's writings. The father then sees something and demands that the images disappear. For some altogether unknown reason the disc melts away and everything returns to normal. Later the wise old grandmother says that "maybe one day you scientists will understand what time is really about." Clearly this is not the greatest story Priestley ever wrote, but he only had 25 minutes to get across some fairly deep ideas. In this he and Jacquetta had a success of a fashion.

The idea of past-time being somehow being present now was clearly playing on Priestley's mind as he entered his twilight years. In his 1975 essay *Particular Pleasures*,[205] he wonders why it is that he has a great attraction for Smetana's *Piano Trio in G Minor*. He asks is he, in some way, linked to someone who knew Smetana in 1855 or does this piece of music come from an association in his own future. Suggesting that this may be linked to his own last moments of life… "so that fatal heart attack will arrive in the middle of the third movement?" This is a curious comment and, yet again, suggests that Priestley was of the opinion that in some way he knew elements of his own future.

In my opinion, one of his best pieces of writing is a short book he wrote in 1976 entitled *The Happy Dream*. In this beautiful little book Priestley discusses a particularly vivid dream he had in his early 80s and subsequently attempts to suggest a series of alternative explanations. He then moves on to discuss dreaming in general, particularly powerful dreams that suggest significance. It is interesting to note that he states that he never experiences reoccurring dreams. Indeed, he finds such dreams rather sinister as they suggest a form of warning regarding a future event, like "repeated SOS signals."[206] This fear of such dreams did not stop him writing themes addressing recurrence or the circularity of time in his plays and philosophical writings.

He goes on to write that for him there are two types of dream – precognitive and "unsatisfactorily, ordinary dreams". The vast majority of dreams are the latter but, sometimes, we experience the significant ones. These are of a different order of vividness and power.

By this time JBP had been rereading the writings of Jung and applied them to his own dream theories. In this series of essays, he observes that dreams:

> … seem to me to be definite creations just as a produced play or a film is a definite creation… it might be described as the

unconscious cornering consciousness.[207]

He mentions again the dream of the angry favourite uncle and how, years later on leave from the army, he saw the uncle look angrily at him from across a crowded bar. He acknowledges that he has referenced this dream many times. Sadly, since his writing of *Man and Time* in the early 1960s, he has experienced no precognitive dreams. He adds that the time of his "Big Dreams" as he calls them was when he was in his 30s and 40s and wonders if this is because as we get over the hump of life and start our descent from the summit and, perhaps, "seeing far below an ancient village with its church and graveyard"[208] beckoning the traveller to the certainty of death. With this knowledge our future becomes less interesting and not a place we wish to know about in advance. beckoning the traveller to the certainty of death. With this knowledge our future becomes less interesting and not a place we wish to know about in advance.

One historical dream that played on his mind in his later years was what he called his Dream of the Birds. He comments upon this in *The Happy Dream* but does not elaborate. He gave a detailed description of the dream in his 1947 autobiographical essay *Rain Upon Godshill*. This startling series of images, more like an LSD or DMT sequence than an ordinary dream, clearly affected him. I feel that it is important to quote his description of this dream in full:

I dreamt I was standing at the top of a very high tower, alone, looking down on millions of birds all flying in one direction; every kind of bird was there, all the birds in the world. It was a noble sight, this vast aerial river of birds. But now in some mysterious fashion the gear was changed and time speeded up, so that I saw generations of birds, and watched them break their shells, flutter into life, mate, weaken, falter and die. Wings grew only to crumble; bodies were sleek and then, in a flash, bled and shrivelled. And death struck everywhere at every second. What was the use of all this blind struggle towards life, this eager trying of wings, this hurried mating, this flight and surge, all this gigantic meaningless biological effort?[209]

In his later years these "Big Dreams" seem to have ceased. That is, until one night in 1976 when Jack experienced a dream so powerfully vivid that he was to immediately write about it in great detail. His description of this experience was the central theme of his short book *The Happy Dream*.

I am reminded here of the visions of the great religious mystics such as Jacob Boehme, Ezekiel and John Bunyan. If quoted in isolation I am sure that most people would identify the source as being either Dante's *Inferno* or John Milton's *Paradise Lost*. It is not at all surprising that Priestley believed this dream to be far more than a simple brain-created fantasy. Indeed, it was a similar, if less disturbing, "big memorable dream" that inspired him to write *The Happy Dream*. Again, such was the vividness of this new dream, experienced only a few weeks before, that Jack began to question the true nature of these nocturnal experiences.

In the dream he found himself transposed to a breezy May day in what felt like a newly made world. He feels that he is, as he describes it, "wearing a new body." He is not an old man but a young man in his early twenties. The dream was so vivid that he found he could move with a grace and speed that he had long lost as the years took their toll. He discovers that his mental state also reflects his youthful body. But behind the youthful body and spirit was his older self, the observer watching events unfold... but not in a detached way. It was at this point that he was overwhelmed with a sensation of happiness more powerful than anything he had experienced before in waking life or in dreams. He refers to the "sudden ecstasy" he experienced at the end of his birds dream and states that this "belonged to a different order of feeling."

He argues that such dreams are important not because anything fantastical or salutary takes place in them, but they are:

> As I suggested in the previous section, an important dream of this kind, important because whatever is central in it persistently haunts the memory, is a definite creation. It is the opposite of the hotchpotch. It is designed, shaped, coloured, to make a certain impression. It might be described as the unconscious cornering consciousness. A point has to be driven home.[210]

In the dream there were no striking events, just a glorious atmosphere imbued with happiness. It is this feeling that is carried through into waking life and buries itself into memory. "What this Happy Dream celebrated so richly was the defeat of Time."[211]

He knew that the dream location was Cambridge, even though there were no visual clues that this was the case. He points out that in dreams one just knows such things. This is interesting because in his waking life he had no fond memories of his time in Cambridge in 1921–2. He suggests that the dream had mixed up his own time in that in 1947–8 he had very positive memories of the city as he associated with his frequent contact with his to be future wife Jacquetta Hawkes, "A Cambridge girl if ever there was one."[212]

After an encounter with a curious group of musicians practising in a large hanger-like shed the location suddenly changes and he finds himself in the Isle of Wight. Again there are no clues to this change of location. Just an inner knowledge. He and his happy group of friends are walking along a broad path to a castle. Immediately in front of him is a young woman. He never sees her face. He believes this girl to be a symbol of all women, of womanhood and femininity.

The group never arrive at the castle... located, as he describes, "on some isle of Wight in an unknown dimension." He then wakes up.

In section Three of the book he tries to understand what the dream meant. He creates a hypothetical discussion with a representative of rationalist materialist-reductionist academic world that he calls "Dr. Consensus". The good doctor suggests to Priestley that his dream was simply an absurd and childish wish-fulfilment. Consensus points out that it is impossible to be young and old at these times and to accept this is to be very foolish. But Priestley cannot accept this argument. He points out that we live in a cosmos that is imbued with mystery and the magical. In this he cites the then recent discovery of black holes as an example of a universe that is far more mysterious than modern science would like to believe. For me this is also an example of how well read Jack was and how he was willing and able to take on board the new science.

In his attempt to explain his "Happy Dream" Jack then turns his attention to the work of his old friend Carl Gustav Jung. He specifically focuses in on Jung's theory of the Collective Unconscious and from this suggests that humanity is part of a much broader perceptual field that goes back 800, 8,000, 80,000, or 800,000 years whereas the individual ego carries, with regards to its perceptual world, 80 years. With such a greater amount of temporal experience, the unconscious can tell the ego a thing or two about how the universe really works. In many ways this mirrors his comment to his son Tom in his 1982 interview cited above.

Priestley ends *The Happy Dream* with the following reiteration of a similar question he had his character Mrs Tenbury ask in his 1940 play *The Long Mirror*, and subsequently asked himself in his 1949 book of essays, *Delight*:

How can we still say "only a dream"? This one brief dream

towered above and outshone all the recent events of my old age. It has been the greatest gift that has lately come my way.[213]

The actual book has an interesting history. It was first published in April 1976 in a limited edition of 400 copies, handset in Caslon type and printed on mould-made paper. I was fortunate to have had one of these original prints sent to me by West Sussex Libraries. I therefore used this as my source. However, I was surprised to subsequently discover that a slightly amended version can be found as the second to last section of Priestley's very last published work, *Instead of the Trees*. Bearing this in mind one can reasonably state that omitting the section entitled "Some Afterthoughts" in *Instead of the Trees*, this comment regarding his dream was, literally, one of his last published pieces of writing.

It is to *Instead of the Trees* we now turn our attention. Published in 1977 it contains a snapshot of the issues going through the mind of a man that knew death was just around the corner. In this he revisits many of the philosophical musings found in his earlier works. He again discusses the mystery of the "other self" that takes over in times of great danger and stress. He writes:

There is this sense of being suddenly taken over by somebody or something quite different, with mild curiosity taking the place of terror. Unless we are victims of dissociation – meat and drink for alienists – we have only one ego, not two. And clearly one ego can't take over itself so dramatically. So we have to look outside the ego.[214]

As we have discovered, all through his writing career Jack Priestley was intrigued by the act of creation, or, more specifi-cally, the source of artistic inspiration. As a writer he knew that sometimes the words that appeared on his paper were not his; they had a source that was, in some way, outside of him. It is therefore not surprising that he postulates the existence of something else beyond the ego. He calls this entity the *Immortal Observer*. He dismisses the idea that this being is a saint or an angel. Furthermore, he argues from his knowledge of Jung that this is the Self taking over the Ego.

He again reiterates that it was Jung's *Collective Unconscious* that was the source of his own inspiration and the real identity of the mysterious Immortal Observer:

> His unconscious is as much part of ourselves as our consciousness; and indeed to a creative writer at times a far more important part of ourselves. For what happens when we are working at our highest pitch? A play or a novel seems to be arriving magically, without any conscious effort. It is coming, as dreams come, from the unconscious [...] It supplies the genie of the magic lamp and ring.[215]

Earlier we discussed how Priestley believed that the script for his play *Time and the Conways* seemed to download from elsewhere, the author being simply a cipher. Here, in his twilight days he reviews this with the wisdom of old age.

Priestley argues that the Jungian Self moves itself away from the ego and positions itself closer to the boundary between consciousness and the Collective Unconscious. It is here that the Self can attune in to the vast knowledge stored within the collective mind. This is why he stresses the idea of the Immortal Observer in that the knowledge available to this entity covers all ages and all times. This information exists outside of time and space, located in what he calls the Sixth Dimension. From our viewpoint such a position or viewpoint seems to take in all eternity.

He acknowledges that this belief is based upon his readings of Ouspensky and George Gurdjieff. Although Priestley never met either Gurdjieff or Ouspensky he did spend time in the company of many of their followers such as A.R. Orage, J.G. Bennett, and Kenneth Walker. In the final chapter of *Man and Time* Priestley discusses in great detail the teachings of this group.

Priestley was intrigued by the process of "Self-Remembering" as advocated by Gurdjieff's teachings, collectively known as *The Work*. This is a technique whereby focusing inwardly on one's own subjective existence can open up a wider perception field. This is achieved by attempting to switch off all the objective information and focusing on the inner self. In this way the ego can be lost and the Self becomes the centre of self-reflective consciousness. As we have already discovered, Priestley believed that the Self, released from the mundane ego-driven reactions to objective existence as presented by the senses, moves closer to the liminal areas between everyday consciousness and collective unconscious.

In his book *J.B. Priestley, The Last of the Sages*, John Atkins describes how Jack was fascinated by "borderlands" as Atkins terms them. These can include the contrasts between real life and the illusion created by the theatre and the border areas between the city and the countryside.[216] This was part of Priestley's interest in the magical. This borderland is the place where everyday consciousness perceives another form of reality. In *Man and Time* Priestley suggested that we fully cross the border at death:

I believe that consciousness does not entirely exist within passing time and that death does not bring complete oblivion.[217]

A consistent theme in his 1977 collection of essays, *Instead of the Trees*, a book with a telling subtitle of *A Final Chapter of Autobiography*, is a looking back to his teenage years that he had not done in any great extent in his earlier autobiographies. The years 1910, 1911 and 1912 reoccur throughout the book. Is this to do with the fact that he was about to return to those days and that the memories of his teens were welling up from his subconscious, tinged with information from his collective unconscious? Had his Self, as his impending death loomed, moved itself right up to the border between consciousness and the collective unconscious? This is a reported psychological state so this is a distinct possibility. Priestley draws his own conclusion:

> I was about to declare that there seemed to me no reason for doing this, but further reflection gave me one. At my age now everything is closing in; little that is new can be attempted; the shining lands of opportunity and golden promise have vanished; your friends are leaving you for the grave; you are living, not without bewilderment, in a repetitious Farewell.[218]

This may be the case, but later in the book we find Priestley going even further back, in exactly the way it is expected; the closer to death the closer the spontaneous memories move towards birth. These are not recalled memories because they were never 'remembered' by the ego in the first place. These memories are drawn up from the subconscious, the subliminal and the collective unconscious. Here Priestley describes a memory that is, as he puts it, "nearer the time of *David Copperfield* than it is to myself here":

> I am being held up among a mystery company of large adults in Blackpool, though how I realised, at such an age, we were in Blackpool, I can't imagine. I am sitting on my grandfather's knee in a horse-bus and I am fascinated by the straw on the floor, it being winter.[219]

This is a classic "charged memory" as described by Esther Salaman and discussed earlier. The focusing in on specific elements is particularly standard. In a particularly moving section he describes how he recollects lying on a small, grassy mound at around five years of age. His infant self felt that somewhere in the mound was buried treasure. He then found himself, seventy-five years later, reliving or, more accurately, re-sensing that feeling of wonderment.

Clearly his approaching death was playing on his mind. The book has a whole section on death and its mysteries. He has no time for those "experts" who know with absolute certainty that death is the end. He jokingly gives them a singular identity, that of somebody called Dr. Knowall. This person is clearly related to Dr. Consensus in his previous book *The Happy Dream*. He reiterates his observation that we never identify with our own body. We state that we "have a body" but not that we are a body. It is something that belongs to us but is not us in the same way that our clothing is not us.

His reasoning that death is not the end was based upon personal experiences rather than simple belief. He describes how his friend, "Edward D.", had died three or four years before and that Edward had subsequently appeared in one of the vivid dreams that he described in his earlier work, *The Happy Dream*. This was, in fact, his old friend Edward Davison.

Priestley met Davison during his post-graduate year at Cambridge. Like Jack, Davison attended Cambridge on an ex-serviceman's grant but unlike Jack, he really enjoyed his time there receiving a first-class honours degree in English and history. They met when, as editor of the *Cambridge Review*, Davison agreed to publish one of Jack's essays. He was so impressed that he ended up publishing a whole series of essays by the developing writer. Indeed, Judith Cook, in her 1997 biography *Priestley*, suggests that it may have been Davison who suggested to Jack that he seek out a publisher for the essays.[220] And it was soon after that Bowes and Sons bought the rights to both *Brief Diversions* and *Papers from Lilliput*. Priestley and Davison remained friends until Davison's death.

In this dream Davison appears in a slightly awkward and self-conscious way. Priestley was particularly interested in how he could vividly recall the rough tweed of Edward's jacket when he placed a comforting hand on his deceased friend's shoulder.

Is it this dream that stimulated Priestley to include an additional section to *Instead of the Trees* consisting of the limited-edition essay *The Happy Dream* published in April of the previous year together with an additional section entitled "Some Afterthoughts"?

Jack Priestley died on the 13 August 1984. He had been ill with pneumonia and slipped away surrounded by his family. In an odd coincidence, his good friend Gareth Lloyd-Evans, himself dying of leukaemia, was on holiday in Majorca. On the afternoon of the 14th of August he was sitting on a headland looking out to sea when his wife Barbara rhetorically asked how Jack was. Gareth replied, "Oh, Jack's gone." "Gone where?" Barbara replied, assuming that Gareth was suggesting that his friend had gone on one of his travels. Gareth replied that, "He's gone. Dead." She was confused as he assured her that he had not read any newspapers in the local town. (In those days English newspapers arrived in such isolated places at least one day late, more likely two or three and this was the following afternoon after Jack's death.) The description that owls were hooting immediately after Jack died suggests that he died in the evening of the 13th so the chance of a newspaper carrying a report of the death being published later that evening and then being available in a newsstand in Majorca the next day is highly unlikely. Barbara rang the Priestley home when they got back to the hotel and Jack's death was confirmed.[221] Is this yet another example of the workings of the Collective Unconscious? Or is it simply that the Jungian "Selves" of close friends seem to become "entangled" in the same way that subatomic particles do, a spiritual version of Einstein's "spooky action at a distance"?

And so it was that Jack Priestley passed over. I would like to believe that he was quickly given answers to all the questions that he asked during his long, productive life. His ideas regarding post-mortem survival were sophisticated and elegant. Not for him the simplistic answers proposed by organized religion or materialist reductionist science.

For many Priestley's lasting legacy is not his plays or novels but his 1964 tabletop book *Man and Time*. This was a work of profound intelligence and one that summed up his "five decades of wondering, reading, brooding about time" as Susan Cooper so succinctly put it in her 1970 biography *J.B. Priestley: Portrait of an Author*.[222] In his final analysis Priestley concluded that there was "something else" within life that we can never properly grasp using our everyday logic. We receive brief glimpses of it during times of heightened awareness, in those quiet moments of reflection, times when true reality can be sensed, if only for a split second. This was reflected in a poem by Priestley's favourite poet, William Wordsworth:

And I have felt
A presence that disturbs me with the joy
Of elevated thoughts; a sense sublime
Of something far more deeply interfused,
Whose dwelling is the light of setting suns,
And the round ocean and the living air,
And the blue sky, and in the mind of man;
A motion and a spirit, that impels
All thinking things, all objects of all thought,
And rolls through all things.[223]

This "something far more deeply interfused" is what Priestley called "something else" in his book *Man and Time*:

This something else is impossible to prove and hard to capture in words. It can come at high moments of love and, though rarely, at meetings of friends; it can transform some sudden glimpse of a landscape into an irradiated sign; it haunts some music for us; its light and its strange shadows fall on certain scenes in drama and fiction. Always it adds depth to life, suggests an ampler Time, opens up a new dimension.[224]

John Boynton Priestley left us a huge legacy. His novels, plays and works of non-fiction show one of the greatest minds of the twentieth century at work. Contrary to the received wisdom of the self-ordained intelligentsia, Priestley was not an old-fashioned, Edwardian-fixated middle-brow writer but probably one of Britain's most perceptive writers. Only now are we in a position to really appreciate just how far ahead of his time he was.

It is my hope that Braham Murray's production of *Time Was, Time Is* will bring about a re-evaluation of the amazing contribution this great writer made to both the worlds of literature and philosophy, and will introduce his work to a whole new generation of readers and theatregoers. The world may now have caught up with him. We now live in a world of quantum mechanics, virtual reality and altered states of consciousness. We can appreciate as never before the powerful ideas of the man that John Atkins, quite rightly, described as being "The Last of the Sages."

Priestley ends *The Happy Dream* with the following reiteration of a similar question he had his character Mrs Tenbury ask in his 1940 play *The Long Mirror*, and subsequently asked himself in his 1949 book of essays, *Delight*:

How can we still say "only a dream"? This one brief dream towered above and outshone all the recent events of my old age. It has been the greatest gift that has lately come my way.[225]

I think that this is the perfect question to end this book.

Thank you for purchasing *Time and the Rose Garden*. My sincere hope is that you derived as much from reading this book as I have in creating it. If you have a few moments, please feel free to add your review of the book at your favourite online site for feedback. Also, if you would like to connect with other books I have written and new titles that I have coming in the near future, please visit my website for news on upcoming works, recent blog posts and to sign up for my newsletter: www.anthonypeake.com

I am also very active on Facebook and I am keen to have reader-feedback there. My FB page is:

https://www.facebook.com/anthony.peake

# References

## Introduction

1. Priestley, JB. *Monitor* TV Programme, BBC, 17<sup>th</sup> March (1963)
2. Priestley, JB. *Man and Time*, Aldus Books, p. 244 (1964)
3. Lyttelton, E. *Some Cases of Prediction*, G. Bell & Sons Ltd. (1937)
4. Gurney, E.; Myers, FWH & Podmore, MA. *Phantasms of the Living*, SPR Books (1886)
5. Saltmarsh, H. *Foreknowledge*, G. Bell & Sons Ltd., pp. 9–11 (1934)
6. Saltmarsh, H. *Foreknowledge*, G. Bell & Sons Ltd., p. 11 (1934)
7. Priestley, JB. *Man and Time*, Aldus Books, p. 244 (1964)
8. Priestley, JB. *Monitor* TV Programme, BBC, 17<sup>th</sup> March (1963)
9. Priestley, JB. *Priestley MS 17/8, University of Bradford Special Collections*
10. Priestley, JB. *Man and Time*, Aldus Books, p. 297 (1964)

## Chapter One: Priestley The Boy, The Soldier and The Student

11. Priestley, JB. *Man and Time*, Aldus Books, p. 171 (1964)
12. Hanson, Neil. *Priestley's Wars*, Great Northern Books, p. 13 (2008)
13. Cooper, Susan. *J.B. Priestley: Portrait of an Author*, Heinemann, p. 17 (1970)
14. Cook, Judith. *Priestley*, Bloomsbury, p. 33 (1997)
15. Priestley, JB. *Margin Released*, Harper & Row, p. 80 (1962)
16. Priestley, JB. *Man and Time*, Aldus Books, p. 285 (1964)
17. Priestley, JB. *Margin Released*, Harper & Row, p. 109 (1962)
18. Priestley, JB. *Man and Time*, Aldus Books, p. 285 (1964)

19. Priestley, JB. *Man and Time*, Aldus Books, p. 287 (1964)
20. Priestley, JB. *Margin Released*, Harper & Row, p. 125 (1962)
21. Priestley, JB. *Instead of the Trees: A Final Chapter of Autobiography*, Heinemann, p. 46 (1977)
22. McTaggart, JE. "The Unreality of Time", *Mind: A Quarterly Review of Psychology and Philosophy*, 17, pp. 456–473 (1908)
23. Jaszczolt, KM. *Representing Time*, Oxford University Press, p. 1 (2009)
24. Priestley, JB. *Man and Time*, Aldus Books, p. 71 (1964)
25. Cook, Judith. *Priestley*, Bloomsbury, p. 57 (1997)
26. Atkins, John. *J.B. Priestley: The Last of the Sages*, John Calder, p. 31 (1981)
27. Cook, Judith. *Priestley*, Bloomsbury, p. 69 (1997)
28. Priestley, JB. *Man and Time*, Aldus Books, p. 286 (1964)
29. Baxendale, John. *Priestley's England: J.B. Priestley and English Culture*, Manchester University Press, p. 60 (2007)
30. Priestley, JB. *Margin Released*, Harper & Row, p. 181 (1962)
31. Priestley, JB. *Margin Released*, Harper & Row, p. 181 (1962)
32. Atkins, John. *J.B. Priestley: The Last of the Sages*, John Calder, p. 55 (1981)
33. Priestley, JB. *Thoughts in the Wilderness*, Heinemann, p. 41 (1957)

## Chapter Two: The 1920s: John William Dunne and the question of time

34. Dunne, JW. *An Experiment with Time*, Faber & Faber, p. 136 (1950)
35. Rotondi, Armando. "James Whale's *The Old Dark House*: Classic Gothic Cinema as the Origin of *The Rocky Horror Show*", in Eoghain Hamilton (ed.) *The Gothic – Probing The Boundaries*, Inter-Disciplinary Press (2011)
36. Braine, John. *J.B. Priestley*, Weidenfeld & Nicolson, p. 57 (1978)
37. Priestley, JB. *Angel Pavement*, Great Northern Books, p. 47

(2012)

38. Priestley, JB. *The Art of the Dramatist*, Heinemann Educational, pp. 84–5 (1957)

## Chapter Three: Before The Time Plays – 1930–1937

39. Braine, John. *J.B. Priestley*, Weidenfeld & Nicolson, p. 39 (1978)

40. Innes, Christopher. *Modern British Drama: The Twentieth Century*, Cambridge University Press, p. 23 (2002)

41. Priestley, JB. *Margin Released*, Harper & Row, p. 198 (1962)

42. Atkins, John. *J.B. Priestley: The Last of the Sages*, John Calder, p. 62 (1981)

43. Atkins, John. *J.B. Priestley: The Last of the Sages*, John Calder, p. 62 (1981)

44. Priestley, JB. *The Plays of J.B. Priestley: Volume 1*, Heinemann, p. viii (1948)

45. Cousin, Geraldine. *Playing for Time*, Manchester University Press, p. 12 (2007)

46. Koenig, Rhoda. Review of *Dangerous Corner*, the *Independent*, 24 September (2001)

47. Priestley, JB. *Faraway*, Heinemann, p. 109 (1950)

48. Heller, Joseph. *Catch-22*, Simon & Schuster, p. 194 (1999)

49. Atkins, John. *J.B. Priestley: The Last of the Sages*, John Calder, p. 165 (1981)

50. Atkins, John. *J.B. Priestley: The Last of the Sages*, John Calder, p. 165 (1981)

51. Ouspensky, PD. *Tertium Organum*, Alfred Knopf, p. 258 (1981)

52. Priestley, JB. *Albert Goes Through*, Heinemann, p. 63 (1933)

53. Braine, John. *J.B. Priestley*, Weidenfeld & Nicolson, p. 66 (1978)

54. Priestley, JB. *Eden End*, Oberon Books, p. 96 (2001)

55. Priestley, JB. *Eden End*, Oberon Books, p. 107 (2001)

56. Braine, John. *J.B. Priestley*, Weidenfeld & Nicolson, p. 68

(1978)

57.  Priestley, JB. *Midnight on the Desert*, Heinemann, p. 243 (1937)

58.  Priestley, JB. *Over the Long High Wall*, Heinemann, p. 127 (1972)

59.  Priestley, JB. *Over the Long High Wall*, Heinemann, p. 127 (1972)

60.  Priestley, JB. *Over the Long High Wall*, Heinemann, p. 127 (1972)

61.  Priestley, JB. *Over the Long High Wall*, Heinemann, p. 128 (1972)

62.  Priestley, JB. *Over the Long High Wall*, Heinemann, p. 128 (1972)

63.  Priestley, JB. *Over the Long High Wall*, Heinemann, p. 130 (1972)

64.  Priestley, JB. *Midnight on the Desert*, Heinemann, p. 88 (1937)

65.  Priestley, JB. *Man and Time*, Aldus Books, p. 229 (1964)

66.  Priestley, JB. *Rain Upon Godshill*, Heinemann, p. 303 (1947)

67.  Priestley, JB. *Rain Upon Godshill*, Heinemann, p. 303 (1947)

68.  Brome, V. *J.B. Priestley*, Hamish Hamilton, p. 189 (1998)

69.  Priestley, JB. *Rain Upon Godshill*, Heinemann, p. 309 (1947)

70.  Priestley, JB. *Midnight on the Desert*, Heinemann, p. 246 (1937)

71.  Priestley, JB. *Midnight on the Desert*, Heinemann, p. 246 (1937)

72.  Priestley, JB. *Midnight on the Desert*, Heinemann, p. 227 (1937)

73.  Webb, B. *The Diary of Beatrice Webb, Volume 4*, "Entry 27/10/37"

74.  Priestley, JB. *An Inspector Calls and Other Plays*, Penguin, p. 138 (2000)

75.  Priestley, JB. *An Inspector Calls and Other Plays*, Penguin, p. 152 (2000)

76.  Priestley, JB. *An Inspector Calls and Other Plays*, Penguin, p.

128 (2000)

77. Priestley, JB. *An Inspector Calls and Other Plays*, Penguin, p. 152 (2000)

78. Priestley, JB. *An Inspector Calls and Other Plays*, Penguin, p. 152 (2000)

79. Priestley, JB. *An Inspector Calls and Other Plays*, Penguin, p. 148 (2000)

## Chapter Four: Time and The Conways (1937)

80. Priestley, JB. *Rain Upon Godshill*, Heinemann, p. 39 (1939)

81. Priestley, JB. *Rain Upon Godshill*, Heinemann, p. 39 (1939)

82. Matz, Jesse. "J.B. Priestley in the Theater of Time", *Modernism/modernity*. Vol. 19, No. 2, p. 341 (Footnote) (2012)

83. Brome, Vincent. *J.B. Priestley*, Hamish Hamilton, p. 195 (1988)

84. Braine, John. *J.B. Priestley*, Weidenfeld & Nicolson, p. 81 (1978)

85. Priestley, JB. *Man and Time*, Aldus Books, p. 71 (1964)

86. Priestley, JB. *An Inspector Calls and Other Plays*, Penguin, p. 60 (2000)

87. Priestley, JB. *An Inspector Calls and Other Plays*, Penguin, p. 61 (2000)

88. Dunne, JW. *The New Immortality*, Faber & Faber, p. 78 (1938)

## Chapter Five: Johnson Over Jordan

89. Jung, CG. *The Archetypes and the Collective Unconscious*, Routledge, p. 43 (1991)

90. Evans-Wentz, WY. *The Tibetan Book of the Dead*, Oxford University Press, p. 66 (1975)

91. Priestley, JB. *Johnson Over Jordan and All About It*, Heinemann, pp. 119 & 123 (1939)

92. Cook, Judith. *Priestley*, Bloomsbury, p. 163 (1998)

93. Priestley, JB. *Johnson Over Jordan and All About It*, Heinemann, pp. 124–25 (1939)

94. Priestley, JB. *Johnson Over Jordan and All About It,* Heinemann, p. 125 (1939)

95. Priestley, JB. *An Inspector Calls and Other Plays,* Penguin, p. 61 (2000)

96. Priestley, JB. *Johnson Over Jordan and All About It,* Heinemann, p. 125 (1939)

97. Priestley, JB. *The Plays of J.B. Priestley: Volume 1,* Heinemann, p. 276 (1962)

98. Wolff, HG & Curran, D. "Nature of Delirium and Allied States: The Dysergastic Reaction". *Archives of Neurology and Psychiatry,* 33, 1175–1215 (1935)

99. Hanson, Lee. "Johnson over Jordan: J.B. Priestley's Masterpiece of the Theatre". *JBP Journal* (Vol. 15) p. 35 (2014) (from *C.G. Jung, Collected Works,* Vol 7, in Anthony Storr, ed., *The Essential Jung,* p. 94)

100. Hanson, Lee. "Johnson over Jordan: J.B. Priestley's Masterpiece of the Theatre". *JBP Journal* (Vol. 15) p. 33 (2014)

101. Priestley, JB. *The Plays of J.B. Priestley: Volume 1,* Heinemann, p. 290 (1962)

102. Priestley, JB. *The Plays of J.B. Priestley: Volume 1,* Heinemann, p. 286 (1962)

103. Priestley, JB. *The Plays of J.B. Priestley: Volume 1,* Heinemann, p. 300 (1962)

104. Priestley, JB. *The Plays of J.B. Priestley: Volume 1,* Heinemann, p. 300 (1962)

105. Priestley, JB. *The Plays of J.B. Priestley: Volume 1,* Heinemann, p. 313 (1962)

106. Priestley, JB. *The Plays of J.B. Priestley: Volume 1,* Heinemann, pp. 300–301 (1962)

107. Priestley, JB. *The Plays of J.B. Priestley: Volume 1,* Heinemann, p. 306 (1962)

108. Priestley, JB. *The Plays of J.B. Priestley: Volume 1,* Heinemann, p. 305 (1962)

109. Priestley, JB. *The Plays of J.B. Priestley: Volume 1*, Heinemann, p. 322 (1962)

110. Priestley, JB. *The Plays of J.B. Priestley: Volume 1*, Heinemann, p. 286 (1962)

111. Priestley, JB. *Man and Time*, Aldus Books, pp. 93–99 (1964)

## Chapter Six: The War Years – 1939–1946

112. Priestley, JB. *Margin Released*, Harper & Row, pp. 78–79 (1962)

113. Priestley, JB. *Margin Released*, Harper & Row, p. 79 (1962)

114. Cook, Judith. *Priestley*, Bloomsbury, p. 175 (1998)

115. Hanson, Neil. *Priestley's Wars*, Great Northern Books, p. 191 (2008)

116. Priestley, JB. *Let the People Sing*, p. 418 (1939)

117. Priestley, JB. *Let the People Sing*, p. 353 (1939)

118. Priestley, JB. *Margin Released*, Harper & Row, p. 46 (1962)

119. Priestley, JB. *Margin Released*, Harper & Row, p. 46 (1962)

120. Innes, Christopher. *Modern British Drama: The Twentieth Century*, Cambridge University Press, p. 452 (2002)

121. Priestley, JB. *The Art of the Dramatist*, Heinemann Educational, p. 52 (1973)

122. Priestley, JB. *Three Plays*, Heinemann, p. 76 (1943)

123. Priestley, JB. *Three Plays*, Heinemann, p. 78 (1943)

124. Priestley, JB. *Three Plays*, Heinemann, p. 78 (1943)

125. Priestley, JB. *Three Plays*, Heinemann, pp. 118–119 (1943)

126. Shuttleworth, Ian. "The Long Mirror" (Theatr Clwyd), Review, the *Financial Times* (1996)

127. Bentley, Eric. *The Playwright as Thinker: A Study of Drama in Modern Times* (1946)

128. Priestley, JB. *Four Plays (2nd Edition)*, Harper & Bros., p. vii (1944)

129. Priestley, JB. *Four Plays (2nd Edition)*, Harper & Bros., p. 246 (1944)

130. Priestley, JB. *Four Plays (2nd Edition)*, Harper & Bros., p. 254

(1944)

131. Klein, Holger. *J.B. Priestley's Plays*, Macmillan Press, p. 109 (1988)

132. Lloyd-Evans, Gareth. *J.B. Priestley – The Dramatist*, Heinemann, p. 36 (1964)

133. Klein, Holger. *J.B. Priestley's Plays*, Macmillan Press, p. 108 (1988)

134. Priestley, JB. *Margin Released*, Harper & Row, p. 195 (1962)

135. Priestley, JB. *Bright Day*, Great Northern Books, p. 41 (2006)

136. Priestley, JB. *Bright Day*, Great Northern Books, p. 120 (2006)

137. Priestley, JB. *Bright Day*, Great Northern Books, p. 122 (2006)

138. Priestley, JB. *Over the Long High Wall*, Heinemann, p. 60 (1972)

139. Braine, John. *J.B. Priestley*, Weidenfeld & Nicolson, p. 123 (1978)

140. Braine, John. *J.B. Priestley*, Weidenfeld & Nicolson, p. 139 (1978)

141. Wilson, Colin. "Reflections and speculations on life, death and time", *New Scientist*, 21 September (1972)

142. Priestley, JB. "Thoughts on the Outsider", *New Statesman*, 7 July (1956)

## Chapter Seven: The Post-War Years

143. Priestley, JB. *An Inspector Calls and Other Plays*, Penguin, p. 207 (2000)

144. Priestley, JB. *An Inspector Calls and Other Plays*, Penguin, p. 220 (2000)

145. Priestley, JB. *Man and Time*, Aldus Books, p. 171 (1964)

146. Lloyd-Evans, Gareth. *J.B. Priestley – The Dramatist*, Heinemann, p. 184 (1964)

147. Cousin, Geraldine. *Playing for Time*, Manchester University Press, p. 1 (2007)

148. North, Dan (ed.). *Sights Unseen: Unfinished British Films*, Cambridge Scholars Publishing (2009)

149. Wisdom, Norman. *My Turn: An Autobiography*, Random House, pp. 291/2 (2003)

## Chapter Eight: After the War – Dunne & Jacquetta

150. Priestley, JB. Article on *Anyone for Tennis?*, *Radio Times*, 19 September (1968)

151. Priestley, JB. *Rain Upon Godshill*, Heinemann, p. 290 (1947)

152. Priestley, JB. *Three Plays*, Heinemann, p. 322 (1943)

153. Priestley, JB. *Three Plays*, Heinemann, p. 144 (1943)

154. Priestley, JB. *Man and Time*, Aldus Books, p. 201 (1964)

155. Priestley, JB. *Over the Long High Wall*, Heinemann, p. 87 (1972)

156. Priestley, JB. *Over the Long High Wall*, Heinemann, p. 88 (1972)

157. Cook, Judith. *Priestley*, Bloomsbury, p. 211 (1998)

158. Schoenl, William. "BBC Broadcasters' unpublished views on Jung: Priestley and Freeman". *International Journal of Jungian Studies*, Vol. 1, No. 2, September, p. 159 (2009)

159. Jung, CG. *C.G. Jung: Letters, Volume 2: 1951–1961*, Routledge, p. 192 (2015)

160. Priestley, JB. *Rain Upon Godshill*, Heinemann, p. 300 (1947)

161. Priestley, JB. *Four Plays*, Heinemann, p. vi (1944)

162. Priestley, JB. *Three Plays*, Heinemann, p. 66 (1943)

163. Priestley, JB. *Three Plays*, Heinemann, p. 67 (1943)

164. Hicks, Bill. *Love All the People*, Constable, p. 26 (2005)

165. Priestley, JB. *Margin Released*, Harper & Row, p. 207 (1962)

166. Priestley, JB. *Delight*, Heinemann (1949)

## Chapter Nine: The Post-War Period – 1950–1960

167. Cook, Judith. *Priestley*, Bloomsbury, p. 232 (1998)

168. Hawkes, Jacquetta. *Man On Earth*, Random House, p. 7 (1955)

169. Hawkes, Jacquetta. *Man On Earth*, Random House, p. 7 (1955)

170. Hawkes, Jacquetta. *Man On Earth*, Random House, pp. 9–11 (1955)

171. Hawkes, Jacquetta. *Man On Earth*, Random House, pp. 9–11 (1955)

172. Braine, John. *J.B. Priestley*, Weidenfeld & Nicolson, p. 132 (1978)

173. Priestley, JB. *Over the Long High Wall*, Heinemann, p. 60 (1972)

174. Priestley, JB. *Over the Long High Wall*, Heinemann, p. 86 (1972)

175. Atkins, John. *J.B. Priestley: The Last of the Sages*, John Calder, p. 26 (1981)

176. Powys, JC. *Autobiography*, Faber & Faber (2013)

## Chapter Ten: The Man and Time Letters

177. Priestley, JB. *Midnight on the Desert*, Heinemann, p. 289 (1937)

178. Priestley, JB. *Man and Time*, Aldus Books, p. 187 (1964)

179. Priestley, JB. *Man and Time*, Aldus Books, p. 192 (1964)

180. Priestley, JB. *Man and Time*, Aldus Books, p. 192 (1964)

181. Priestley, JB. *Over the Long High Wall*, Heinemann, p. 80 (1972)

182. Priestley, JB. *Over the Long High Wall*, Heinemann, pp. 88–89 (1972)

183. Priestley, JB. *Man and Time*, Aldus Books, p. 203 (1964)

184. Priestley, JB. *Man and Time*, Aldus Books, p. 207 (1964)

185. Priestley, JB. *Rain Upon Godshill*, Heinemann, p. 309 (1947)

186. Priestley, JB. *Man and Time*, Aldus Books, p. 191 (1964)

## Chapter Eleven: The Unpublished Letters

187. Priestley, JB. *Over the Long High Wall*, Heinemann, p. 81 (1972)

188. Priestley, JB. *Man and Time*, Aldus Books, p. 216 (1964)

189. http://www.portsmouth.co.uk/heritage/fishermen-rescued-in-this-dramatic-end-of-pier-show-1-5223408

190. Davies, R. *Doubles: The Enigma of the Second Self*, Robert Hale, p. 121 (1998)

191. Priestley, JB. *An Inspector Calls and Other Plays*, Penguin, p. 61 (2000)

## Chapter Twelve: The Long Indian Summer

192. Priestley, JB. Article on *Anyone for Tennis?*, *Radio Times*, 19 September (1968)

193. Priestley, JB. *Man and Time*, Aldus Books, p. 307 (1964)

194. Priestley, JB. *The Other Place*, Valancourt Books, p. 73 (2013)

195. Priestley, JB. *Man and Time*, Aldus Books, p. 227 (1964)

## Chapter Thirteen: The Unknown Play – Time Was, Time Is

196. Klein, Holger. *J.B. Priestley's Plays*, Macmillan Press, p. 3 (1988)

197. Unpublished manuscript supplied to the author by Tom Priestley, p. x

198. Ouspensky, Peter. *A New Model of the Universe*, Kessinger, p. 481 (2010)

199. Priestley, JB. *The Plays of J.B. Priestley: Volume 1*, Heinemann, p. 286 (1962)

200. Lloyd-Evans, Gareth. *J.B. Priestley – The Dramatist*, Heinemann, p. 147 (1964)

201. Gale, Maggie B. *J.B. Priestley*, Routledge, p. 20 (2008)

202. Eliot, TS. *Four Quartets*, Faber & Faber, p. 3 (2001)

203. Priestley, JB. *The Plays of J.B. Priestley: Volume 1*, Heinemann, p. 322 (1962)

## Chapter Fourteen: Crossing The Long High Wall

204. Atkins, John. *J.B. Priestley: The Last of the Sages*, John Calder,

p. 55 (1981)

205. Priestley, JB. *Particular Pleasures*, Heinemann (1975)

206. Priestley, JB. *The Happy Dream*, The Whittington Press, p. 5 (1976)

207. Priestley, JB. *The Happy Dream*, The Whittington Press, p. 3 (1976)

208. Priestley, JB. *The Happy Dream*, The Whittington Press, p. 8 (1976)

209. Priestley, JB. *Rain Upon Godshill*, Heinemann, pp. 304–06 (1947)

210. Priestley, JB. *The Happy Dream*, The Whittington Press, p. 31 (1976)

211. Priestley, JB. *The Happy Dream*, The Whittington Press, p. 15 (1976)

212. Priestley, JB. *The Happy Dream*, The Whittington Press, p. 22 (1976)

213. Priestley, JB. *The Happy Dream*, The Whittington Press, p. 22 (1976)

214. Priestley, JB. *Instead of the Trees*, Heinemann, p. 49 (1977)

215. Priestley, JB. *Instead of the Trees*, Heinemann, p. 49 (1977)

216. Atkins, John. *J.B. Priestley: The Last of the Sages*, John Calder, p. 53 (1981)

217. Priestley, JB. *Man and Time*, Aldus Books, p. 281 (1964)

218. Priestley, JB. *Instead of the Trees*, Heinemann, p. 72 (1977)

219. Priestley, JB. *Instead of the Trees*, Heinemann, p. 85 (1977)

220. Cook, Judith. *Priestley*, Bloomsbury, p. 55 (1998)

221. Cook, Judith. *Priestley*, Bloomsbury, p. 295 (1998)

222. Cooper, Susan. *J.B. Priestley: Portrait of an Author*, Heinemann, p. 219 (1970)

223. Wordsworth, William. "Lines Composed a Few Miles above Tintern Abbey" (1798)

224. Priestley, JB. *Man and Time*, Aldus Books, p. 306 (1964)

225. Priestley, JB. *The Happy Dream*, The Whittington Press, p. 31 (1976)

BOOKS

# O-BOOKS

# SPIRITUALITY

O is a symbol of the world, of oneness and unity; this eye represents knowledge and insight. We publish titles on general spirituality and living a spiritual life. We aim to inform and help you on your own journey in this life.
If you have enjoyed this book, why not tell other readers by posting a review on your preferred book site?

# Recent bestsellers from O-Books are

### Heart of Tantric Sex
Diana Richardson
Revealing Eastern secrets of deep love and intimacy to Western couples.
Paperback: 978-1-90381-637-0 ebook: 978-1-84694-637-0

### Crystal Prescriptions
The A-Z guide to over 1,200 symptoms and their healing crystals
Judy Hall
The first in the popular series of five books, this handy little guide is packed as tight as a pill-bottle with crystal remedies for ailments.
Paperback: 978-1-90504-740-6 ebook: 978-1-84694-629-5

### Take Me To Truth
Undoing the Ego
Nouk Sanchez, Tomas Vieira
The best-selling step-by-step book on shedding the Ego, using the teachings of *A Course In Miracles*.
Paperback: 978-1-84694-050-7 ebook: 978-1-84694-654-7

### The 7 Myths about Love...Actually!
The journey from your HEAD to the HEART of your SOUL
Mike George
Smashes all the myths about LOVE.
Paperback: 978-1-84694-288-4 ebook: 978-1-84694-682-0

**The Holy Spirit's Interpretation of the New Testament**
A course in Understanding and Acceptance
Regina Dawn Akers
Following on from the strength of *A Course In Miracles*, NTI
teaches us how to experience the love and oneness of God.
Paperback: 978-1-84694-085-9 ebook: 978-1-78099-083-5

**The Message of A Course In Miracles**
A translation of the text in plain language
Elizabeth A. Cronkhite
A translation of *A Course In Miracles* into plain, everyday
language for anyone seeking inner peace. The companion
volume, *Practicing A Course In Miracles*, offers practical lessons
and mentoring.
Paperback: 978-1-84694-319-5 ebook: 978-1-84694-642-4

**Rising in Love**
My Wild and Crazy Ride to Here and Now, with Amma, the
Hugging Saint
Ram Das Batchelder
*Rising in Love* conveys an author's extraordinary journey of
spiritual awakening with the Guru, Amma.
Paperback: 978-1-78279-687-9 ebook: 978-1-78279-686-2

**Thinker's Guide to God**
Peter Vardy
An introduction to key issues in the philosophy of religion.
Paperback: 978-1-90381-622-6

**Your Simple Path**
Find happiness in every step
Ian Tucker
A guide to helping us reconnect with what is really important in
our lives.
Paperback: 978-1-78279-349-6 ebook: 978-1-78279-348-9


**365 Days of Wisdom**
Daily Messages To Inspire You Through The Year
Dadi Janki
Daily messages which cool the mind, warm the heart and guide
you along your journey.
Paperback: 978-1-84694-863-3 ebook: 978-1-84694-864-0


**Body of Wisdom**
Women's Spiritual Power and How it Serves
Hilary Hart
Bringing together the dreams and experiences of women across
the world with today's most visionary spiritual teachers.
Paperback: 978-1-78099-696-7 ebook: 978-1-78099-695-0


**Dying to Be Free**
From Enforced Secrecy to Near Death to True Transformation
Hannah Robinson
After an unexpected accident and near-death experience,
Hannah Robinson found herself radically transforming her life,
while a remarkable new insight altered her relationship with
her father; a practising Catholic priest.
Paperback: 978-1-78535-254-6 ebook: 978-1-78535-255-3

### Quantum Bliss
The Quantum Mechanics of Happiness, Abundance, and Health
George S. Mentz
*Quantum Bliss* is the breakthrough summary of success and
spirituality secrets that customers have been waiting for.
Paperback: 978-1-78535-203-4 ebook: 978-1-78535-204-1


### The Upside Down Mountain
Mags MacKean
A must-read for anyone weary of chasing success and happiness
– one woman's inspirational journey swapping the uphill slog
for the downhill slope.
Paperback: 978-1-78535-171-6 ebook: 978-1-78535-172-3


### Your Personal Tuning Fork
The Endocrine System
Deborah Bates
Discover your body's health secret, the endocrine system, and
'twang' your way to sustainable health!
Paperback: 978-1-84694-503-8 ebook: 978-1-78099-697-4

Readers of ebooks can buy or view any of these bestsellers by clicking on the live link in the title. Most titles are published in paperback and as an ebook. Paperbacks are available in traditional bookshops. Both print and ebook formats are available online.

Find more titles and sign up to our readers' newsletter at http://www.johnhuntpublishing.com/mind-body-spirit

Follow us on Facebook at
https://www.facebook.com/OBooks/
and Twitter at https://twitter.com/obooks